A GRAMMAR OF THE ENGLISH LANGUAGE

A GRAMMAR OF THE ENGLISH LANGUAGE

WILLIAM COBBETT

WITH AN INTRODUCTION BY
ROBERT BURCHFIELD

Oxford   New York

OXFORD UNIVERSITY PRESS

1984

Oxford University Press, Walton Street, Oxford OX2 6DP

London New York Toronto
Delhi Bombay Calcutta Madras Karachi
Kuala Lumpur Singapore Hong Kong Tokyo
Nairobi Dar es Salaam Cape Town
Melbourne Auckland

and associated companies in
Beirut Berlin Ibadan Mexico City Nicosia

Oxford is a trade mark of Oxford University Press

Introduction © Robert Burchfield 1984

First published 1819
This edition first published 1823
First issued as an Oxford University Press paperback 1984 with
an introduction by Robert Burchfield

British Library Cataloguing in Publication Data

Cobbett, William
A grammar of the English language.—(Oxford paperbacks)
1. English language—Grammar
I. Title
428.2   PE1112
ISBN 0-19-281474-5

Set by Herts Typesetting Services, Hertford
Printed in Great Britain by
Richard Clay (The Chaucer Press) Ltd.
Bungay, Suffolk

INTRODUCTION

ROBERT BURCHFIELD

William Cobbett is the noblest English example of the noble
calling of an agitator.

G. K. Chesterton[1]

It was the rare full sense of "putting people first" which founded
his social position. It was what set him against the old order of a
few to be served, of the many serving, and against the newer
orders in which it was made to appear rational that people had to
be repressed . . . in the name of some greater good.

Raymond Williams[2]

COBBETT was born on 9 March 1763 in a small public house called
The Jolly Farmer in Farnham, Surrey, and looked likely to become
a farm labourer. From 1785 to 1791 he served in a British
regiment of foot in New Brunswick, Canada, and then left the army
when he failed in an attempt to bring some officers of his regiment
to trial at a court martial. After a period in revolutionary France he
moved to America and there became a proselytizing journalist, for
the most part using the pseudonym Peter Porcupine. He returned
to England in 1799 and went on with his polemical writing,
especially in his *Political Register* (1802–13). In 1810 he was
imprisoned for two years in Newgate, an episode described with
some force in his Grammar (p. 145). In 1817 he returned to the
United States and it was while he was there that his Grammar was
published in 1818. He returned to England the following year and
remained a thorn in the flesh of the authorities for the rest of his
life. But his acrimony was tempered by a series of works on
agrarian and other matters—it was the period of his *Cottage Economy*
(1821–2), *Rural Rides* (1825–30), *The English Gardener* (1829), and

---

[1] In the preface to his edition of Cobbett's *Cottage Economy* (1916).
[2] *Cobbett* (1983), p. 77.

Advice to Young Men (1830). And his linguistic activities extended
to another language, *A Grammar of the French Language*, which was
published in 1824. He became an MP (representing Oldham) in
1832 in the first Reform Parliament, and he died in 1835.

*

In his standard work *English Grammatical Categories and the Tradition
to 1800* (1970), Ian Michael identified over 270 separate English
grammars written before 1800. Some of these were attached to
dictionaries, for example to Dr Johnson's in 1755, and others to
spelling books, for example Daniel Fenning's *The Universal
Spelling-Book* (1756). About thirty of them formed parts of works
of a more general kind, for example *The Lady's Polite Secretary*
(1771) by Dorothea Du Bois.

The earliest known English grammar, William Bullokar's
Pamphlet for Grammar (1586), is a very slight work. The best
known ones before 1818 were (in chronological order):

> Ben Jonson, *The English Grammar* (written in the early 1630s, first
> published in 1640)
> John Wallis, *Grammatica Linguae Anglicanae* (1653)
> Samuel Johnson, (in the prefatory matter of) *A Dictionary of the English
> Language* (1755)
> Joseph Priestley, *The Rudiments of English Grammar* (1761)
> Robert Lowth, *A Short Introduction to English Grammar* (1762)
> Lindley Murray, *English Grammar* (1795).

Of these Cobbett refers only to Priestley, Lowth, and Murray, and
it must be assumed that it was to these three he turned as his main
sources.

Cobbett had set himself at an early age to compile a grammar of
the English language. In a letter of 1817 he declared:

> I am, you will perceive, getting ready a *Grammar of the English Language*.
> This, which is a work which I have always desired to perform, I have put
> into the shape of a series of letters addressed to my beloved son
> James ... In this work, which I have all my life, since I was nineteen, had
> in my contemplation, I have assembled together the fruits of all my

observations on the construction of the English language; and I have given them the form of a book, not merely with a view to profit, but with a view to fair fame, and with the still more agreeable view of instructing, in this foundation of all literary knowledge, the great body of my ill-treated and unjustly condemned countrymen.[3]

In the book itself he addresses his son, James Paul Cobbett, directly:

You have now arrived at the age of fourteen years without ever having been bidden, or even advised, to look into a book; and all you know of reading or of writing you owe to your own unbiassed taste and choice. (p. 1)

Young James had learnt to read and write from his "elders", just as he had learnt "to ride and hunt and shoot, to dig the beds in the garden, to trim the flowers and to prune the trees". These activities had provided him with "a sound mind in a sound body", but these were attributes "possessed by millions". The next step was to acquire "knowledge connected with books":

In the immense field of this kind of knowledge, innumerable are the paths, and GRAMMAR is the gate of entrance to them all. (p. 4)

Grammar was the prize to be won because it provided the possessor with power. "The long-imprisoned, the heavily-fined, the banished WILLIAM PRYNNE," says Cobbett, "returning to liberty, borne by the people from Southampton to London, over a road strewed with flowers" (pp. 4–5), could never have performed any of his acts against tyranny and injustice without a knowledge of grammar. Such knowledge was an indispensable prerequisite for anyone struggling against tyranny and misgovernment. It was also a discipline to be used to diminish the authority of men of letters like Dr Johnson, the lexicographer, Dr Isaac Watts, the logician, and Fellows of English Colleges, "who live by the sweat of other people's brows".

*

The Grammar's Table of Contents shows how Cobbett approached

[3] Cited from Daniel Green, *Great Cobbett* (1983), p. 418.

his subject.   First, like the good non-commissioned officer that he
had been, came "the naming of parts":

> Before the serjeant begins to teach young soldiers their *exercise* of the
> musket, he explains to them the different parts of it; the butt, the stock,
> the barrel, the loops, the swivels, and so on; because, unless they know
> these by their names, they cannot know how to obey his instructions in
> the handling of the musket. (p. 11)

And so the parts of speech were dealt with one by one.   Syntax
followed—the syntax of articles, nouns, pronouns, and so on, dealt
with in an orderly manner in strict sequence.   That done, in Letter
XXI, Cobbett quotes examples of "false grammar", especially from
the works of Samuel Johnson and Isaac Watts.   He believed
profoundly that "a knowledge of the Latin and Greek Languages
does not prevent men from writing bad English":

> Those Languages are, by impostors and their dupes, called, "the *learned*
> languages;" . . . These appellations are false, and, of course, they lead to
> false conclusions. (p. 117)

Neatly, clinically, and with self-assurance he launched himself into
a fault-finding exercise of remarkable severity, and no one was
spared.   Judge Blackstone was "careless in the use of personal
pronouns" (p. 73).   Milton, "who has committed many hundreds,
if not thousands, of grammatical errors" (p. 82), is attacked for a
contextual use of *than whom*.   After opposing some pronominal
"misuses" in the work of Blair and Addison he adds:

> My dear James, let chamber-maids and members of the House of
> Commons, and learned Doctors, write thus: be you content with plain
> words which convey your meaning. (pp. 85–6)

He excuses himself from treating the formation of words like *to
outlive*, *to undervalue*, *thankful*, *thankless*, and so on, as matters of
"mere curiosity":

> It is for monks, and for Fellows of English Colleges, who live by the
> sweat of other people's brows, to spend their time in this manner, and to
> call the result of their studies *learning*. (p. 55)

Again and again he returns to the theme of plain English, the English of the ordinary people, as against the prolixities of men of letters and of politicians. Unlike Latin, English, he believed, was in the end a simple language:

> those who have written English Grammars, have been taught Latin; and, either unable to divest themselves of their Latin rules, or unwilling to treat with simplicity that, which, if made somewhat of a mystery, would make them appear more *learned* than the mass of the people, they have endeavoured to make our simple language turn and twist itself so as to become as complex in its principles as the Latin language is. (p. 104)

The Six Lessons at the end of the Grammar indignantly and impertinently attack the language of politicians. They are offered as a warning to the statesmen of his day. He selects sentences which "are conveyed in the language of the sedentary and circumspect keeper of a huckster's stand, or the more sturdy perambulating bearer of a miscellaneous pack" (p. 161). The phrase "follow up a principle", he says, "is low as the dirt" (p. 162). Other constructions and phrases are dismissed as "intolerable fustian" (p. 163), "thorough-paced vulgarity" (p. 165), or in "the counting-house style" (p. 166). Perhaps his most venomous remarks are reserved for Castlereagh:

> What do you say, what can you say, of such a man, but that nature might have made him for a valet, for a strolling player, and possibly for an auctioneer; but never for a Secretary of State. (p. 163)

His arrows often reach the target. But inevitably he overstates the case and occasionally breaks his own rules, as, for example, when he uses *throwed* as a past participle (p. 7) as against the paradigmatic form *thrown* (p. 46). And he repeats some customary misconceptions of his time, for example (p. 54) that the *a* in "I am *a* hunting" is a shortening of *at*, whereas it is now known to be a reduced form of *on*.

*

No one could quarrel with the main aim of the book:

> Grammar . . . teaches us *how to make use of words*; that is to say, it teaches us how to make use of them in a proper manner, as I used to teach you how to sow and plant the beds in the garden; for you could have throwed about seeds and stuck in plants of some sort or other, in some way or other, without any teaching of mine; and so can any body, without rules or instructions, put masses of words upon paper; but to be able to choose the words which ought to be employed, and to place them where they ought to be placed, we must become acquainted with certain principles and rules; and these principles and rules constitute what is called Grammar. (p. 7)

Nor could anyone oppose his acceptance of usage as the ultimate test:

> *Thou* is here given as the *second person singular*; but, common custom has set aside the rules of Grammar in this case; and though we, in particular cases, still make use of *Thou* and *Thee*, we generally make use of *You* instead of either of them. According to ancient rule and custom this is not correct; but, what a whole people adopts and universally practices, must, in such cases, be deemed correct, and to be a superseding of ancient rule and custom. (p. 26)

In many specific matters his views are those of an unbiased and unopposable authority as, for example, his treatment of the "nouns of numbers, or multitude, such as *Mob, Parliament, Rabble, House of Commons, Regiment, Court of King's Bench, Den of Thieves*, and the like". These, he correctly says, "may have pronouns agreeing with them either in the singular or in the plural number" (p. 74). Moreover, he did not fall prey to the preposterous reductive rules of Horne Tooke, the author of *The Diversions of Purley* (2nd edn., 1798–1805), whose techniques, including that of "subaudition", led him to regard English as consisting only of nouns and verbs. For Tooke, the words *bond, band*, and *bound* were "still one and the same word" and "merely the past participle of the verb *to bind*" (vol. II, ch. iv, p. 121). But for all his polemicism, and despite his careful analysis of the English language of the early nineteenth century, Cobbett was a prisoner of the main grammatical doctrines of his time—doctrines ultimately derived from an examination of Greek and Latin and based on the assumption that because English had hardly any inflexions it was therefore a simple language to master if only one said what one meant to say. His mode of dissent was to attribute solecism and carelessness to men of letters and to politicians because "he who writes badly thinks badly" (p. 146). One feels that if necessary he would have gone to prison, had the need arisen, for his passionate views on linguistic correctness as well as for his views on the flogging of German soldiers by English militiamen. Fortunately, then as now, grammarians, however bound down they may be by preconceived ideas and by the legacies of former ages, may speak without fear of suffering anything worse than the derision of other grammarians. Despite its shortcomings and its occasional shrillness, this most colourful of all grammars deserves to be widely studied as a period piece in the tradition that later produced, in other areas of dissent, George Orwell and Alexander Solzhenitsyn.

NOTE ON THE TEXT

COBBETT's Grammar was first published in 1818 in New York and was reprinted in unaltered form, but with a different typeface, in London the following year. This edition contained Letters I to XXIII. In the 1823 edition, the version reprinted here, Cobbett retained the original text but added "six lessons, intended to prevent Statesmen from using false grammar, and from writing in an awkward manner". In these he attacked the grammar of speeches made by Lord Castlereagh, the Duke of Wellington, and others, "as a warning to the Statesmen of the present day". For example, he did not like the construction "I should have liked to have been informed":

> A phraseology like this can be becoming only in those Houses, where it was proposed to relieve the distresses of the nation by setting the labourers to dig holes one day and fill them up the next. (p. 106)

Cobbett's *Grammar of the English Language* has not been available in any version for many years. The most recent reprint, *Cobbett's Easy Grammar*, with a Preface by The Rt. Hon. J. R. Clynes MP, was a poor "improved" version. It was published in 1923 and was revised in 1940 in Foulsham's Cloth-Bound Pocket Library.

The text of the 1823 edition was chosen because it contained the Six Lessons as well as the original text of 1818. The 1823 version, printed for John M. Cobbett, Fleet Street, London, by B. Bensley, Bolt Court, Fleet Street, London, ran to 230 pages: Letters I to XXIII, the grammar proper, occupied the first 184 pages, and the Six Lessons the rest. In 1866 Cobbett's son James Paul Cobbett (the "My Dear James" of the 1818, 1819, and 1823 versions) added a chapter "Pronunciation: Certain Common Errors pointed out and Corrected". As this chapter had no observable merits it did not seem worth reprinting here.

The text of the 1823 original has been reset here with all its main conventions retained. Departures from the original are restricted to three minor matters: the correction of broken or turned letters, a clarification of the running heads from the beginning of the Six Lessons, and the abandonment of the double inverted commas which were regularly given at the beginning of each line of quoted matter in books of that date. The typographical distinctions of the original—italic, bold-face, capital and lower case letters, and so on—have been retained. The punctuation, with what now seems like an over-use of the comma, and, by modern standards, occasional strange uses of colons and semicolons, has been retained too. A few obvious errors in the italicizing of words, or the absence of italicization, have been corrected. For all practical purposes, the text reproduced here is that of the 1823 edition, and follows the spelling and layout of the original.

ACKNOWLEDGEMENTS

I AM indebted above all to Dr Henry Hardy, who noticed an advertisement printed on the last page of Cobbett's *The Woodlands* (1825) claiming that the *Grammar of the English Language* had been "published to the amount of fifty-five thousand copies, without ever having been mentioned by the old shuffling bribed sots, called Reviewers", and immediately wanted to publish it in Oxford Paperbacks; and to Marilyn Butler who pointed out to me that Cobbett "thought the right of our betters to dictate [linguistic] correctness was an insidious part of their hold on power". Mr D. J. Edmonds assisted me with the reading of the proofs; and Ms K. H. Emms, Mrs H. Feldman, Miss E. A. Knight, Mrs M. Y. Offord, and Mrs Oliver H. Orr, Jr. gave me practical help with various aspects of the Introduction.

A

GRAMMAR

OF THE

ENGLISH LANGUAGE,

IN A SERIES OF LETTERS.

Intended for the Use of Schools and of Young Persons in general ; but more especially for the Use of Soldiers, Sailors, Apprentices, and Plough-boys.

BY WILLIAM COBBETT.

TO WHICH ARE ADDED,

Six Lessons, intended to prevent Statesmen from using false grammar, and from writing in an awkward manner.

LONDON:

PRINTED FOR JOHN M. COBBETT, FLEET STREET.

1823.

The 1823 edition was printed by B. Bensley, Bolt Court, Fleet Street, London. A facsimile of its title-page appears overleaf.

DEDICATION.

TO HER MOST GRACIOUS MAJESTY,

QUEEN CAROLINE.

MAY IT PLEASE YOUR MAJESTY,

A work, having for its objects, to lay the solid foundation of literary knowledge amongst the Labouring Classes of the community, to give practical effect to the natural genius found in the Soldier, the Sailor, the Apprentice, and the Plough-boy, and to make that genius a perennial source of wealth, strength, and safety to the kingdom; such a work naturally seeks the approbation of your Majesty, who, amongst all the Royal Personages of the present age, is the only one that appears to have justly estimated the value of The People.

The Nobles and the Hierarchy have long had the arrogance to style themselves, the Pillars that support the Throne. But, as your Majesty has now clearly ascertained, Royalty has, in the hour of need, no efficient supporters but The People.

During your Majesty's long, arduous, magnanimous, and gallant struggle against matchless fraud and boundless power, it must have inspired you with great confidence to perceive the wonderful intelligence and talent of your millions of friends; while your Majesty cannot have failed to observe, that the haughty and insolent few who have been your enemies, have, upon all occasions, exhibited an absence of knowledge, a poverty of genius, a feebleness of intellect, which nothing but a constant association with malevolence and perfidy could prevent from being ascribed to dotage or idiocy.

That, to Her, whose great example is so well calculated to inspire us with a love of useful knowledge and to stimulate us to perseverance in its pursuit; that, to Her, the records of whose magnanimity and courage will make mean spite and cowardice hide their heads to the end of time; that, to Her, who, while in foreign lands, did honour to Britain's Throne, and to Britain herself, by opening the Debtor's prison, and by setting the Captive Christian free; that, to Her, who has so long had to endure all the sufferings that malice could invent and tyranny execute; that, to Her, God may grant, to know no more of sorrow, but long to live in health, prosperity, and glory, surrounded and supported by a grateful and admiring People, is the humble prayer of

Your Majesty's

Most dutiful

And Most devoted Servant,

WM. COBBETT.

London, Nov. 25, 1820.

TABLE OF CONTENTS.

Mr. JAMES PAUL COBBETT.

LETTER I.

INTRODUCTION.

North Hempstead, Long Island, Dec. 6, 1817.

My Dear Little James,

YOU have now arrived at the age of fourteen years without ever having been bidden, or even advised, to look into a book; and all you know of reading or of writing you owe to your own unbiassed taste and choice. But while you have lived unpersecuted by such importunities, you have had the very great advantage of being bred up under a roof, beneath which no cards, no dice, no gaming, no senseless pastime of any description, ever found a place. In the absence of these, books naturally became your companions during some part of your time: you have read and have written because you saw your elders read and write, just as you have learned to ride and hunt and shoot, to dig the beds in the garden, to trim the flowers and to prune the trees. The healthful exercise, and the pleasures, unmixed with fear, which you have derived from these sources, have given you " a sound mind in a sound body," and this, says an English writer, whose works you will by-and-by read, " is the greatest blessing that God can give to man."

It is true, that this is a very great blessing; but, mere soundness of mind, without any mental acquirements, is possessed by millions; it is an ordinary possession; and it gives a man no fair pretensions to merit, because he owes it to accident, and not to any thing done by himself. But knowledge, in any art or science, being always the fruit of observation, study, or practice, gives, in proportion to its extent and usefulness, the possessor a just claim to respect. We do, indeed, often see, all the outward marks of respect bestowed upon persons merely because they are rich or powerful; but these, while they are bestowed with pain, are received without pleasure. They drop from the tongue or beam from the features, but have no communication with the heart. They are not the voluntary offerings of admiration, or of gratitude; but are extorted from the hopes, the fears, the anxieties, of poverty, of meanness, or of guilt. Nor is respect due to honesty, fidelity, or any such qualities; because, dishonesty and perfidy are crimes. To entitle a man to respect there must be something of his own doing, beyond the bounds of his well known duties and obligations.

Therefore, being extremely desirous to see you, my dear James, an object of respect, I now call upon you to apply your mind to the acquiring of that kind of knowledge which is inseparable from an acquaintance with books: for, though knowledge, in every art and science, is, if properly applied, worthy of praise in proportion to its extent and usefulness, there are some kinds of knowledge which are justly considered as of a superior order, not only because the possession of them is a proof of more than ordinary industry and talent, but because the application of them has naturally a more powerful influence in the affairs and on the condition of our friends, acquaintances, neighbours, and country. BLAKE, the Titchfield thatcher, who broke his leg into splinters in falling from a wheat-rick, was, on account of the knowledge, which he possessed beyond that of labourers in general, an object of respect; but, in its degree, and in the feelings from which it arose, how different was that respect from the respect due to our excellent neighbour Mr. BLUNDELL, who restored the leg to perfect use, after six garrison and army surgeons had declared that it was impossible to preserve it, and that, if the leg were not cut off, the man must die within twenty-four hours. It is probable, that the time of Mr. Blundell was not, on this occasion, occupied more, altogether, than four days and four nights; yet, the effect was, a great benefit to be enjoyed by Blake for probably thirty or forty years to come: and while we must see, that this benefit would necessarily extend itself to the whole of his numerous family, we must not overlook those feelings of pleasure, which the cure would naturally produce amongst friends, acquaintances, and neighbours.

The respect due to the profession of the Surgeon or Physician is, however, of an order inferior to that which is due to the profession of the Law; for, whether in the character of Counsellor or of Judge, here are required, not only uncommon industry, labour, and talent, in the acquirement of knowledge, but, the application of this knowledge, in defending the property of the feeble or incautious against the attacks of the strong and the wiles of the crafty, in affording protection to innocence and securing punishment to guilt, has, in the affairs of men and on their condition in life, a much more extensive and more powerful influence than can possibly arise from the application of Surgical or Medical knowledge.

To the functions of Statesmen and Legislators is due the highest respect which can be shown by man to any thing human; for, not only are the industry, labour, and talent, requisite in the acquirement of knowledge, still greater and far greater here, than in the profession of the Law; but, of the application of this knowledge the effects are so transcendant in point of magnitude as to place them beyond all the bounds of comparison. Here it is not individual persons with their families, friends, and neighbours, that are affected; but whole countries and communities. Here the matters to be discussed and decided on, are peace or war, and the liberty or slavery, happiness or misery, of nations. Here a single instance of neglect, a single oversight, a single error, may load with calamity millions of men, and entail that calamity on a long series of future generations.

But, my dear James, you will always bear in mind, that, as the degree and quality of our respect rise in proportion to the influence, which the different branches of knowledge naturally have in the affairs and on the condition of men; so, in cases of an imperfection in knowledge, or of neglect of its application, or of its perversion to bad purposes, all the feelings which are opposite to that of respect, rise in the same proportion. To ignorant pretenders to Surgery and Medicine we award our contempt and scorn: on time-serving or treacherous Counsellors, and on cruel, or partial Judges, we inflict our detestation and abhorrence; while, on rapacious, corrupt, perfidious, or tyrannical Statesmen and Legislators, the voice of human nature cries aloud for execration and vengeance.

The particular path of knowledge, to be pursued by you, will be of your own choosing; but, as to knowledge connected with books, there is a step to be taken before you can fairly enter upon any path. In the immense field of this kind of knowledge, innumerable are the paths, and GRAMMAR is the gate of entrance to them all. And, if grammar is so useful in the attaining of knowledge, it is absolutely necessary in order to enable the possessor to communicate, by writing, that knowledge to others, without which communication the possession must be comparatively useless to himself in many cases, and, in almost all cases, to the rest of mankind.

The actions of men proceed from their *thoughts*. In order to obtain the co-operation, the concurrence, or the consent, of others, we must communicate our thoughts to them. The means of this communication are *words*; and grammar teaches us *how to make use of words*. Therefore, in all the ranks, degrees, and situations of life, a knowledge of the principles and rules of grammar must be useful; in some situations it must be necessary to the avoiding of really injurious errors; and in no situation, which calls on a man to place his thoughts upon paper, can the possession of it fail to be a source of self-gratulation, or the want of it a cause of mortification and sorrow.

But, to the acquiring of this branch of knowledge, my dear son, there is one motive, which, though it ought, at all times, to be strongly felt, ought, at the present time, to be so felt in an extraordinary degree: I mean, that desire, which every man, and especially every young man, should entertain to be able to assert with effect the rights and liberties of his country. When you come to read the history of those Laws of England, by which the freedom of the people has been secured, and by which the happiness and power and glory of our famed and beloved country have been so greatly promoted; when you come to read the history of the struggles of our forefathers, by which these sacred Laws have, from time to time, been defended against despotic ambition; by which they have been restored to vigour when on the eve of perishing; by which their violators have never failed, in the end, to be made to feel the just vengeance of the People; when you come to read the history of these struggles in the cause of freedom, you will find, that tyranny has no enemy so formidable as the pen. And, while you will see with exultation the long-imprisoned, the heavily-fined, the

banished WILLIAM PRYNNE, returning to liberty, borne by the
people from Southampton to London, over a road strewed with
flowers; then accusing, bringing to trial and to the block, the
tyrants, from whose hands he and his country had unjustly and
cruelly suffered; while your heart and the heart of every young man
in the kingdom will bound with joy at the spectacle, you ought all to
bear in mind, that, without a knowledge of *grammar*, Mr. PRYNNE
could never have performed any of those acts, by which his name
has been thus preserved, and which have caused his memory to be
held in honour.

Though I have now said what, I am sure, will be more than
sufficient to make you entertain a strong desire to take this first step
in the road to literary knowledge, I cannot conclude this introduc-
tory letter, without observing, that you ought to proceed in your
study, not only with diligence, but with *patience*; that, if you meet
with difficulties, you should bear in mind, that, to enjoy the noble
prospect from Port's-Down Hill, you had first to climb slowly to the
top; and that, if those difficulties gather about you and impede your
way, you have only to call to your recollection any one of the many
days that you have toiled through briers and brambles and bogs,
cheered and urged on by the hope of at last finding and killing your
game.

I have put my work into the form of Letters, in order that I might
be continually reminded, that I was addressing myself to persons,
who needed to be spoken to with great clearness. I have *numbered*
the Letters themselves, and also the *paragraphs*, in order that I
might be able, in some parts of the work, to *refer* you to, or *tell you
where to look at*, other parts of the work. And here I will just add,
that a *sentence*, used as a term in grammar, means one of those
portions of words, which are divided from the rest by a *single dot*,
which is called a *period*, or full point; and that a *paragraph* means,
one of those collections, or blocks, of *sentences*, which are divided
from the rest of the work by beginning *a new line* a little *further in*
than the lines in general; and, of course, all this part, which I have
just now written, beginning with " *I have put my work into the form*,"
is a *paragraph*.

In a confident reliance on your attentiveness, industry, and patience, I have a hope not less confident of seeing you a man of real learning, employing your time and talents in aiding the cause of truth and justice, in affording protection to defenceless innocence, and in drawing down vengeance on lawless oppression; and, in that hope, I am your happy as well as affectionate father,

WILLIAM COBBETT

LETTER II.

DEFINITION OF GRAMMAR AND OF ITS DIFFERENT BRANCHES OR PARTS.

My Dear James,

1. In the foregoing Letter I have laid before you some of the inducements to the study of Grammar. In this, I will define or describe, the thing called *Grammar*; and also its different *Branches* or *Parts*.

2. Grammar, as I observed to you before, teaches us *how to make use of words*; that is to say, it teaches us how to make use of them in a proper manner, as I used to teach you how to sow and plant the beds in the garden; for you could have throwed about seeds and stuck in plants of some sort or other, in some way or other, without any teaching of mine; and so can any body, without rules or instructions, put masses of words upon paper; but to be able to choose the words which ought to be employed, and to place them where they ought to be placed, we must become acquainted with certain principles and rules; and these principles and rules constitute what is called Grammar.

3. Nor must you suppose, by-and-by, when you come to read about *Nouns* and *Verbs* and *Pronouns*, that all this tends to nothing but mere ornamental learning, that it is not altogether necessary, and that people may write to be understood very well without it. This is not the case; for without a pretty perfect knowledge relative to these same Nouns and Verbs, those who write are never sure that they put upon paper what they mean to put upon paper. I will, before the close of these letters, show you, that even very learned men have frequently written and caused to be published, not only what they did not mean, but the very contrary of what they meant; and if errors, such as are here spoken of, are sometimes committed by learned men, into what endless errors must those fall, who have no knowledge of any principles or rules, by the observance of which the like may be avoided? Grammar, perfectly understood, enables us, not only to express our meaning fully and clearly, but so to

express it as to enable us to defy the ingenuity of man to give to our words any other meaning than that which we ourselves intend them to express. This, therefore, is a science of substantial utility.

4. As to the different *Branches* or *Parts* of Grammar, they are *four*; and they are thus named: *Orthography*, *Prosody*, *Etymology*, and *Syntax*.

5. There are two of these branches, on which we have very little to say, and the names of which have been *kept* in use from an unwillingness to give up the practice of former times; but, as it is usual to give them a place, in books of this kind, I will explain to you the nature of all the four Branches.

6. ORTHOGRAPHY is a word made up of two Greek words, which mean *spelling*. The use of foreign words, in this manner, was introduced at the time when the English Language was in a very barbarous state; and, though this use has been continued, it ought to be a rule with you, always, when you either write or speak, to avoid the use of any foreign or uncommon word, if you can express your meaning as fully and clearly by an English word in common use. However, *Orthography* means neither more nor less than the very humble business of putting *Letters* together properly, so that they shall form *Words*. This is so very childish a concern, that I will not appear to suppose it necessary for me to dwell upon it; but, as you will, by-and-by, meet with some directions, under the head of Etymology, in which directions *Vowels* and *Consonants* will be spoken of, I will here, for form's sake, just observe, that the letters A, E, I, O, and U, are *Vowels*. Y, in certain cases, is also a *Vowel*. All the rest of the letters of the alphabet are *Consonants*.

7. PROSODY is a word taken from the Greek Language, and it means not so much as is expressed by the more common word PRONUNCIATION; that is to say, the business of using the proper *sound* and employing the due *length of time*, in the uttering of syllables and words. This is a matter, however, which ought not to occupy much of your attention; because *pronunciation* is learnt as birds learn to chirp and sing. In some counties of England many words are pronounced in a manner different from that in which they are pronounced in other counties; and, between the pronunciation of Scotland and that of Hampshire the difference is very great

indeed. But, while all inquiries into the causes of these differences are useless, and all attempts to remove them are vain, the differences are of very little real consequence. For instance, though the Scotch say *coorn*, the Londoners *cawn*, and the Hampshire folks *carn*, we know that they all *mean* to say *corn*. Children will pronounce as their fathers and mothers pronounce; and if, in common conversation, or in speeches, the matter be good and judiciously arranged, the facts clearly stated, the arguments conclusive, the words well chosen and properly placed, hearers, whose approbation is worth having, will pay very little attention to the accent. In short, it is sense, and not sound, which is the object of your pursuit; and, therefore, I have said enough about *Prosody*.

8. ETYMOLOGY is a very different matter; and, under this head, you will enter on your study. This is a word, which has been formed out of two Greek words; and it means, the *pedigree*, or *relationship of words*, or, the manner in which one word grows out of, or comes from, another word. For instance, the word *walk* expresses an action, or movement, of our legs; but, in some cases we say *walks*, in others *walked*, in others *walking*. These three latter words are all different from each other, and they all differ from the original word, *walk*; but, the action, or movement, expressed by each of the four, is precisely the same sort of action, or movement, and the three latter words grow out of, or come from, the first. The words here mentioned differ from each other with regard to the letters of which they are composed. This difference is made in order to express differences as to the *Persons* who walk, as to the *Number* of persons, as to the *Time* of walking. You will come, by-and-by, to the principles and rules, according to which the varying of the spelling of words is made to correspond with these and other differences; and these principles and rules constitute what is called *Etymology*.

9. SYNTAX is a word, which comes from the Greek. It means, in that language, the *joining of several things together*; and, as used by grammarians, it means those principles and rules, which teach us how to put words together so as to form *sentences*. It means, in short, *sentence-making*. Having been taught by the rules of *Etymology*, what are the relationships of words, how words grow out of each other,

how they are varied in their letters in order to correspond with the variation in the circumstances to which they apply, *Syntax* will teach you how to give to all your words their *proper* situations, or places, when you come to put them together into sentences. And here you will have to do with *points* as well as with words. The *points* are four in number, the *Comma*, the *Semi-Colon*, the *Colon*, and the *Period*. Besides these Points, there are certain *marks*, such as the *mark of interrogation*, for instance; and, to use these points and marks properly is, as you will by-and-by find, a matter of very great importance.

10. I have now given you a description of Grammar and of its separate Branches, or Parts. I have shown you, that the two first of these Branches may be dismissed without any further notice; but, very different indeed is the case with regard to the two latter. Each of these will require several Letters; and those Letters will contain matter, which it will be impossible to understand without the greatest attention. You must read soberly and slowly, and you must think as you read. You must not hurry on from one Letter to another, as if you were reading a history; but you must have patience to get, if possible, at a clear comprehension of one part of the subject before you proceed to another part. When I was studying the French language, the manner, in which I proceeded, was this: when I had attentively read over, three times, a lesson, or other division of my Grammar, I wrote the lesson down upon a loose sheet of paper. I then read it again several times in my own hand writing. Then I copied it, in a very plain hand, and without a blot, into a book, which I had made for the purpose. But, if, in writing my lesson down on a loose sheet of paper, I committed one single error, however trifling, I used to tear the paper, and write the whole down again; and, frequently, this occurred three or four times in the writing down of one lesson. I, at first, found this labour very irksome; but, having imposed it on myself as a duty, I faithfully discharged that duty; and long before I had proceeded half the way through my grammar, I experienced all the benefits of my industry and perseverance.

LETTER III.

ETYMOLOGY.

The different Parts of Speech, or, Sorts of Words.

MY DEAR JAMES,

11. IN the second Letter I have given you a description of *Etymology*, and shown you, that it treats of the *pedigree*, or *relationship*, of words, of the nature of which relationship I have given you a specimen in the word *walk*. The next thing is to teach you the *principles* and *rules*, according to which the spelling and employing of words are varied in order to express the various circumstances attending this relationship. But, before I enter on this part of my instructions, I must inform you, that there are several *distinct sorts* of words, or, as they are usually called, *Parts of Speech*; and, it will be necessary for you to be able, before you proceed further, to distinguish the words, belonging to each of these Parts of Speech, from those, belonging to the other Parts. There are *Nine* Parts of Speech, and they are named thus :

ARTICLES,
NOUNS,
PRONOUNS,
ADJECTIVES,
VERBS,
ADVERBS,
PREPOSITIONS,
CONJUNCTIONS,
INTERJECTIONS.

12. Before the serjeant begins to teach young soldiers their *exercise* of the musket, he explains to them the different parts of it; the butt, the stock, the barrel, the loops, the swivels, and so on; because, unless they know these by their names, they cannot know how to obey his instructions in the handling of the musket. Sailors, for the same reason, are told which is the tiller, which are the yards, which the shrouds, which the tacks, which the sheets, which the booms, and which each and every part of the ship. Apprentices are

taught the names of all the tools used in their trade; and Plough-boys the names of the various implements of husbandry. This species of preliminary knowledge is absolutely necessary in all these callings of life; but not more necessary than it is for you to learn, before you go any further, how *to know the sorts of words one from another*. To teach you this, therefore, is the object of the present Letter.

13. ARTICLES. There are but *three* in our language; and these are, *the*, *an*, and *a*. Indeed, there are but two, because *an* and *a* are the same word, the latter being only an abbreviation, or a shortening of the former. I shall, by-and-by, give you rules for the using of these Articles; but, my business in this place is only to teach you how to know one sort of words from another sort of words.

14. NOUNS. The word *Noun* means *name*, and nothing more; and *Nouns* are the *names of persons and things*. As far as persons and other animals and things that we can *see* go, it is very easy to distinguish *Nouns*; but, there are many *Nouns*, which express what we can neither see, nor hear, nor touch. For example: *Conscience*, *Vanity*, *Vice*, *Sobriety*, *Steadiness*, *Valour*; and a great number of others. Grammarians, anxious to give some easy rule, by which the scholar might distinguish *nouns* from other words, have directed him to put the words, *the good*, before any word: and have told him, that, if the three words make *sense*, the last word is a *noun*. This is frequently the case; as, the good *house*, the good *dog*; but the good *sobriety* would not appear to be very *good sense*. In fact, there is no rule of this kind that will answer the purpose. You must employ your *mind* in order to arrive at the knowledge here desired.

15. Every word which stands for a person or any animal, or for any thing of *substance*, dead or alive, is a *Noun*. So far the matter is very easy. Thus, *man*, *cat*, *tree*, *log*, are Nouns. But, when we come to the words which are the names of things, and which things are *not substances*, the matter is not so easy; and it requires a little sober thought. This word, *thought*, for example, is a *Noun*.

16. The only sure rule is this: that a word, which stands for any thing that has *an existence*, is a Noun. For example, *Pride*, *Folly*, *Thought*, *Misery*, *Truth*, *Falsehood*, *Opinion*, *Sentiment*. None of these have any *substance*. You cannot see them, or touch them; but, they

all have an *existence*. They all *exist* in the world; and, therefore, the words which represent them, or stand for them, are called Nouns. If you be still a little puzzled here, you must not be impatient. You will find the difficulty disappear in a short time, if you exert your powers of thinking. Ask yourself what *existence* means. You will find that the words, *very*, *for*, *think*, *but*, *pretty*, do not express anything which has an *existence*, or a *being*; but, that the words, *motive*, *zeal*, *pity*, *kindness*, do express things which have a *being*, or *existence*.

17. PRONOUNS. Words of this sort *stand in the place of Nouns*. Their name is from the Latin, and it means *For-nouns*, or *For-names*; that is to say, these words, called Pronouns, are used *for*, or *instead of*, Nouns. *He*, *She*, *Her*, *Him*, *Who*, for example, are pronouns. The use of them is to prevent the repetition of Nouns, and to make speaking and writing more rapid and less encumbered with words. An example will make this clear to you in a minute. Thus:

18. A woman went to a man, and told *him*, that *he* was in great danger of being murdered by a gang of robbers, *who* had made preparations for attacking *him*. *He* thanked *her* for *her* kindness, and, as *he* was unable to defend himself, *he* left his house and went to a neighbour's.

19. Now, if there were no pronouns, this sentence must be written as follows:—A woman went to a man, and told *the man*, that *the man* was in great danger of being murdered by a gang of robbers; as *a gang of robbers* had made preparations for attacking *the man*. *The man* thanked *the woman* for *the woman's* kindness; and, as *the man* was unable to defend *the man's self*, *the man* left *the man's* house, and went to a neighbour's.

20. There are several different classes of Pronouns; but, of this, and of the manner of using Pronouns, you will be informed by-and-by. All that I aim at here is, to enable you to form a clear idea with regard to the difference in the sorts of words, or Parts of Speech.

21. ADJECTIVES. The word *Adjective*, in its full literal sense, means, *something added to something else*. Therefore this term is used in grammar as the name of that Part of Speech, which consists of

words, which are added, or put, to Nouns, in order to express something relating to the Nouns, which something could not be expressed without the help of *Adjectives*. For instance, there are several Turkeys in the yard, some black, some white, some speckled; and, then, there are large ones and small ones of all the colours. I want you to go and catch a *turkey*; but I also want you to catch a *white* turkey, and not only a white turkey, but a *large* turkey. Therefore, I add, or *put to* the Noun, the words *white* and *large*, which, therefore, are called *Adjectives*.

22. Adjectives sometimes express the *qualities* of the Nouns to which they are put; and this being very frequently their use, some grammarians have thrown aside the word Adjective, and have called words of this sort, *Qualities*. But, this name is not sufficiently comprehensive; for there are many words which are Adjectives, which have nothing to do with the *quality* of the Nouns to which they are put. *Good* and *bad* express qualities, but *long* and *short* merely express dimension, or duration, without giving any intimation as to the quality of the things expressed by the Nouns to which they are put; and yet, *long* and *short* are Adjectives. You must read very attentively here, and consider soberly. You must keep in mind the above explanation of the *meaning* of the word Adjective: and, if you also bear in mind, that words of this sort always express some quality, some property, some appearance, or some distinctive circumstance, belonging to the Nouns to which they are put, you will very easily, and in a very short space of time, be able to distinguish an Adjective from words belonging to any other Part of Speech.

23. VERBS. Grammarians appear to have been at a loss to discover a suitable appellation for this important sort of words, or Part of Speech; for, the word, *Verb*, means nothing more than *Word*. In the Latin it is *verbum*, in the French it is *verbe*; and the French in their Bible, say *Le Verbe*, where we say *The Word*. The truth is, that there are so many properties and circumstances, so many and such different powers and functions belonging to this Part of Speech, that the mind of man is unable to bring the whole of them into any short and precise description. The first grammar that I ever looked into told me, that "a *Verb* is a word which signifies, to *do*, to *be*,

or to *suffer*." What was I to understand from this laconic account?

24. Verbs express all the different *actions* and *movements* of all creatures and of all things, whether alive or dead. As, for instance, to *speak*, to *bark*, to *grow*, to *moulder*, to *crack*, to *crumble*, and the like. In all these cases there is *movement* clearly understood. But, in the cases of, to *think*, to *reflect*, to *remember*, to *like*, to *detest*, and in an infinite number of cases, the *movement* is not so easily perceived. Yet these are all *verbs*, and they do indeed express *movements* which we attribute to the *mind* or the *heart*. But what shall we say in the cases of to *sit*, to *sleep*, to *rot*, and the like? Still these are all *verbs*.

25. Verbs are, then, a sort of words, the use of which is to express the *actions*, the *movements*, and *the state or manner of being*, of all creatures and things, whether animate or inanimate. In speaking with reference to a man, to *fight* is an action; to *reflect* is a movement; to *sit* is a state of being.

26. Of the manner of using verbs you will hear a great deal by-and-by; but, what I have here said will, if you read attentively, and take time to consider, be sufficient to enable you to distinguish Verbs from the words which belong to the other Parts of Speech.

27. ADVERBS are so called because the words which belong to this part of Speech are *added* to *verbs*. But this is an inadequate description; for, as you will presently see, they are sometimes otherwise employed. You have seen, that Verbs express *actions*, *movements*, and *states of being*; and it is very frequently the use of adverbs to express *the manner* of actions, movements, and states of being. Thus: the man fights *bravely*; he reflects *profoundly*; he sits *quietly*. In these instances the adverbs perform an office, and are placed in a situation which fully justify the name that has been given to this sort of words. But there are many adverbs, which do not express the manner of actions, movements, or states of being, and which are not added to Verbs. For instance: " *When* you sow small seeds, make the earth *very* fine, and if it have, *of late*, been dry weather, take care to press the earth *extremely* hard upon the seeds." Here are four adverbs, but only the last of the four expresses any thing connected with a verb. This shows, that the name of this class of words does not fully convey to our minds a description of their use.

28. However, with this name you must be content; but, you must bear in mind, that there are adverbs of *time*, of *place*, and of *degree*, as well as of manner; and that their business is to express, or describe, some circumstances in addition to all that is expressed by the Nouns, Adjectives, and Verbs. In the above sentence, for example, the words *when*, *very*, *of late*, and *extremely*, add greatly to the precept, which, without them, would lose much of its force.

29. PREPOSITIONS. The prepositions are *in*, *to*, *for*, *from*, *of*, *by*, *with*, *into*, *against*, *at*, and several others. They are called *Prepositions*, from two Latin words, meaning *before* and *place*; and this name is given them because they are in most cases *placed before* Nouns and Pronouns: as, " Indian Corn is sown *in* May. *In* June and the three following months, it is carefully cultivated. When ripe, *in* October, it is gathered *in* the field, *by* men who go *from* hill *to* hill *with* baskets, *into* which they put the ears. The leaves and stalks are then collected *for* winter-use; and, they not only serve as food *for* cattle and sheep, but are excellent *in* the making of sheds to protect animals against the inclemency *of* the weather."

30. Prepositions are not very numerous, and, though you will be taught to be very careful in using them, the above sentence will be quite sufficient to enable you to know the words belonging to this Part of Speech from the words belonging to any other Part of Speech.

31. CONJUNCTIONS are so called, because they *conjoin* or *join together*, words, or parts of sentences: as, " Peas *and* Beans may be severed from the ground before they be quite dry; *but* they must not be put into stacks or barns until perfectly dry; *for*, if they be, they will mould." The word *and* joins together the words Peas and Beans, and, by the means of this *junction*, makes all the remaining part of the sentence apply to both. The word *but* connects the first with the second member of the sentence. The word *for*, which is sometimes a conjunction, performs, in this case, the same office as the word *but*: it continues the connexion; and thus does every part of the sentence apply to each of the two nouns which are the subject of it.

32. INTERJECTIONS. This name comes from two Latin words: *inter*, which means *between*, and *jection*, which means

something thrown. So that, the full literal meaning of the word is, *something thrown between.* The Interjections are *Ah! Oh! Alas!* and such like, which, indeed, are not *words*, because they have no definite meaning. They are mere *sounds*, and they have been mentioned by me, merely because other grammarians have considered them as being a Part of Speech. But, this one notice of them will be quite sufficient.

33. Thus, then, you are now able to distinguish, in many cases, at least, to what Part of Speech belongs each of the several words which may come under your observation. I shall now proceed to the Etymology of each of these Parts of Speech. As we have done with the *Interjections*, there will remain only *eight* Parts to treat of, and this I shall do in eight Letters, allotting one Letter to each Part of Speech.

LETTER IV.

ETYMOLOGY OF ARTICLES.

My Dear James,

34. In Letter III, paragraph 13, you have seen what sort of words Articles are; that is to say, you have there learnt how to distinguish the words belonging to this Part of Speech from words belonging to other Parts of Speech. You must now turn to Letter II, paragraph 8. Having read you find there under the head of *Etymology*, you will see at once, that my business, in this present Letter, is, to teach you those principles and rules, according to which articles are varied in order to make them suit the different circumstances which they are used to express.

35. You have seen, that there are but *three* articles; namely, A or AN, and THE. The two former are, in fact, the *same word*, but, of this, I shall say more presently. They are called *indefinite* Articles, because they do *not define*, or *determine*, what particular object is spoken of. The Nouns, to which they are prefixed, only serve to point out the *sort* of person or thing spoken of, without defining

what person or *what* thing; as, *a tree is blowed down*. From this we learn that *some* tree is blown down, but not *what* tree. But, the definite Article, THE, determines the particular object of which we speak; as, *the tree, which stood close beside the barn, is blowed down*. In this last instance, we are not only informed that a tree is blowed down, but the sentence also informs us what particular tree it is. This article is used before nouns in the plural as well as before nouns in the singular number. It is sometimes used before words, expressive of degrees of comparison: as, *the best, the worst, the highest, the lowest*. When we use a noun in the singular number to express a whole species, or sort, we use the definite article: thus, we say, *the oak* is a fine tree, when we mean, that oaks are fine trees.

36. The Article A becomes AN when this article comes immediately before *any* word which begins with a *vowel*. This is for the sake of the *sound*; as, *an adder, an elephant, an inch, an oily seed, an ugly hat*. The word *an* is also used before words which begin with an *h* which is *mute*, that is to say, which, though used in writing, is *not sounded* in speaking; as, *an hour*. This little variation in the article is, as I said before, for the sake of the *sound*; for, it would be very disagreeable to say, *a adder, a elephant, a inch, a oily seed, a ugly hat, a hour*, and the like. But, *a* is used, in the usual way, before words which begin with an *h* which is sounded in speaking; as, *a horse, a hair*, and the like. The indefinite article can be used before nouns in the *singular number only*. There is a seeming exception to this rule in cases where the words *few* and *many* come before the noun; as, *a few* horses; *a great many* horses; but, in reality, this is not an exception, because the words *few* and *many*, mean *number*; thus: a *small number* of horses; a *great number* of horses; and the indefinite article agrees with this word *number*, which is understood, and which is in the *singular*.

———

LETTER V.

ETYMOLOGY OF NOUNS.

37. THIS, my Dear James, is a Letter of great importance, and,

therefore, it will require great attention from you. Before you proceed further, you will again look well at Letter II, paragraph 8, and then at Letter III, paragraphs 14, 15, and 16, and there read carefully every thing under the head of *Nouns*.

38. Now, then, as Letter III has taught you how to distinguish Nouns from the words which belong to the other Parts of Speech, the business here is to teach you the principles and rules, according to which Nouns are to be varied in the letters of which they are composed, according to which they are to be used, and according to which they are to be considered in their bearings upon other words in the sentences in which they are used.

39. In a Noun there are to be considered, the *branches*, the *numbers*, the *genders*, and the *cases*; and all these must be attended to very carefully.

40. THE BRANCHES. There are two; for Nouns are some of them PROPER and some COMMON. A Noun is called *proper*, when it is used to distinguish one particular individual from the rest of the individuals of the same species, or kind; as, *James, Botley, Hampshire.* The Noun is called *common*, when it applies to all the individuals of a kind; as *Man, Village, County. Botley* is a proper Noun, because all villages have not this name; but *Village* is a common Noun, because all villages are called by that name: the name is *common* to them all. Several persons have the name of *James*, to be sure, and there is a *Hampshire* in America as well as in England; but, still, these are proper names, because the former is not common to *all* men, nor the latter to *all* counties. Proper nouns take no articles before them, because the extent of their meaning is clearly pointed out in the word itself. In *figurative* language, of which you will know more by-and-by, we sometimes, however, use the article; as, " Goldsmith is a very pretty poet, but not to be compared to *the* Popes, *the* Drydens, or *the* Otways." And again; " I wish I had the wit of *a* Swift." We also use the definite article before proper nouns when a common noun is understood to be left out; as, *The Delaware*, meaning the *River* Delaware. Also when we speak of more than one person of the same name; as, "*the Henries, the Edwards.*"

41. THE NUMBERS. These are the *Singular* and the *Plural*.

The Singular is the original word; and, in general, the Plural is formed by adding an *s* to the singular; as *dog*, *dogs*. But, though the greater part of our Nouns form their plurals from the singular in this simple manner, there are many which do not; while there are some Nouns which have no plural number at all, and some which have no singular. Therefore, considering the above to be the FIRST RULE, I shall add other rules with regard to the Nouns which do not follow that rule.—The SECOND RULE. Nouns, the singular numbers of which end in *ch*, *sh*, *s*, or *x*, require *es* to be added in order to form their plural number; as *church*, *churches*; *brush*, *brushes*; *lass*, *lasses*; *fox*, *foxes*.—The THIRD RULE is, that Nouns, which end in *y*, when the *y* has a consonant coming immediately before it, change the *y* into *ies* in forming their plurals; as *quantity*, *quantities*. But, you must mind, that, if the *y* be not immediately preceded by a consonant, the words follow the *First Rule*, and take only an *s* in addition to their singular; as *day*, *days*. I am the more anxious to guard you against error as to this matter, because it is very common to see men of high rank and profession writing, *vallies*, *vollies*, *attornies*, *correspondencies*, *conveniencies*, and the like, and yet all these are erroneous. *Correspondence* and *convenience* should have simply an *s*; for they end in *e*, and not in *y*. The FOURTH RULE is, that Nouns which end in a single *f*, or in *fe*, form their plurals by changing the *f*, or *fe*, into *ves*; as, *loaf*, *loaves*; *wife*, *wives*. But, this rule has exceptions in the following words, which follow the *First Rule*: *Dwarf*, *mischief*, *handkerchief*, *chief*, *relief*, *grief*. The two last are seldom used in the plural number; but, as they sometimes are, I have included them.—The FIFTH RULE is, that the following Nouns have their plural in *en*: *man*, *men*; *woman*, *women*; *ox*, *oxen*; *child*, *children*. And *brethren* is used sometimes as the plural of *brother*.—The SIXTH RULE is, that all which nature, or art, or habit has made plural has no singular; as *ashes*, *annals*, *bellows*, *bowels*, *thanks*, *breeches*, *entrails*, *lungs*, *scissors*, *snuffers*, *tongs*, *wages*, and some others. There are also some nouns which have no plural, such as those which express the qualities or propensities or feelings of the mind or heart; as, *honesty*, *meekness*, *compassion*. There are, further, several names of herbs, metals, minerals, liquids, and of fleshy substances, which have no plurals; to which may be added the names of almost all sorts of grain. There are exceptions here; for, while *Wheat* has no plural, *Oats* have seldom any singular. But all these words, and others which are irregular in a similar way, are of such very common use, that you will hardly ever make a mistake in applying them; for I will not suppose it possible for my dear James to fall into either the company or the language of those persons, who talk, and even write, about *Barleys*, *Wheats*, *Clovers*, *Flours*, *Grasses*, and *Malts*. There remain to be noticed, however, some words, which are too irregular in the forming of their plurals to be brought under any distinct head even of irregularity. I will, therefore, insert these as they are used in both numbers.

SINGULAR.	PLURAL.	SINGULAR.	PLURAL.
Die,	Dice.	Goose,	Geese.
Mouse,	Mice.	Penny,	Pence.
Louse,	Lice.	Tooth,	Teeth.
Deer,	Deer.	Foot,	Feet.

42. THE GENDERS. In the French language, and many other languages, every noun is of the masculine or of the feminine gender. *Hand*, for instance, is of the feminine and *arm* of the masculine, *pen* of the feminine and *paper* of the masculine. This is not the case with our language, which, in this respect, has followed the order of nature. The names of all *males* are of the masculine gender; the names of all *females* are of the feminine gender; and all other nouns are of the *neuter gender*. And, you must observe, that, even in speaking of living creatures, of which we do not know the gender, we consider them to be of the *neuter*. In strictness of language, we could not, perhaps, apply the term *gender* to things destitute of all sexual properties; but, as it is applied with perfect propriety in the case of males and females, and, as the application in the case of inanimate or vegetable matter can lead to no grammatical error, I have thought it best to follow, in this respect, the example of other grammarians. It may be said, that the rule, which I have here laid down, as being without any exception, has many exceptions; for, that, in speaking of a *ship*, we say *she* and *her*. And, you know, that our country folks in Hampshire call almost every thing *he* or *she*. Sailors have, for ages, called their vessels *shes*, and it

has been found easier to adopt, than to eradicate, the vulgarism, which is not only tolerated but cherished by that just admiration, in which our country holds the species of skill and of valour, to which it owes much of its greatness and renown. It is curious to observe, that country labourers give the feminine appellations to those things only which are more closely identified with themselves, and by the qualities and condition of which their own efforts and their character as workmen are affected. The mower calls his scythe a *she*; the ploughman calls his plough a *she*; but a prong, or a shovel, or a harrow, which passes promiscuously from hand to hand, and which is appropriated to no particular labourer, is called a *he*. It was, doubtless, from this sort of habitual attachment that our famous maritime solecism arose. The deeds of labourers in the fields and of artisans in their shops are not of public interest sufficiently commanding to enable them to break in upon the principles of language; if they were, we should soon have as many *hes* and *shes* as the French, or any other nation in the world.

43. While, however, I lay down this rule as required by strict grammatical correctness, I must not omit to observe, that the licence allowed to figurative language enables us to give the masculine or feminine gender to inanimate objects. This has been justly regarded as a great advantage in our language. We can, whenever our subject will justify it, transform into masculine, or into feminine, nouns which are, strictly speaking, neuter; and, thus, by giving the functions of life to inanimate objects, enliven and elevate our style, and give to our expressions great additional dignity and force.

44. THE CASES OF NOUNS. The word *case*, as applied to the concerns of life, has a variety of meanings, or of different shades of meaning; but, its general meaning is, *state of things*, or *state of something*. Thus we say, " in *that case*, I agree with you." Meaning, " that being *the state of things*, or that being *the state of the matter*, I agree with you." Lawyers are said, " to make out *their case*; or not to make out *their case*:" meaning the *state of the matter*, which they have undertaken to prove. So, when we say, that a horse is *in good case*, we mean that he is in a *good state*. Nouns may be in different *states*, or *situations*, as to other nouns, or other words. For instance, a

noun may be the name of a person who *strikes* a horse, or of a person who *possesses* a horse, or of a person whom a horse *kicks*. And these different situations, or states, are, therefore, called *cases*.

45. You will not quite fully comprehend the use of these distinctions till you come to the Letter on *Verbs*; but, it is necessary to explain here the nature of these *cases*, in order that you may be prepared well for the use of the terms, when I come to speak of the Verbs. In the Latin language each noun has several *different endings*, in order to denote the different Cases in which it may be. In our language there is but one of the Cases of nouns which is expressed or denoted by a change in the ending of the noun; and of this change I will speak presently.

46. There are three Cases; the *Nominative*, the *Possessive*, and the *Objective*. A noun is in the *Nominative* case, when it denotes a person, or thing, which *does* something or *is* something; as, *Richard strikes*; *Richard is good*.

47. A noun is in the *Possessive* case, when it names a person or thing that *possesses* some other person or thing, or when there is one of the persons or things *belonging to* the other; as *Richard's hat*; the *mountain's top*; the *nation's fleet*. Here *Richard*, *mountain*, and *nation*, are in the *possessive case*, because they denote persons or things which *possess* other persons or things, or have other persons or things *belonging to* them. And here is that change in the ending of the noun, of which I spoke above. You see that *Richard*, *mountain*, *nation*, has, each of them, an *s* added to it, and a mark of *elision* over; that is to say, a *comma*, placed above the line, between the last letter of the word and the *s*. This is done for the purpose of distinguishing this case from the plural number; or, at least, it answers this purpose in all cases where the plural of the noun would end in an *s*; though there are different opinions as to the origin of its use. In nouns, which do not end their plurals in *s*, the mark of elision would not appear to be absolutely necessary. We might write *mans* mind, *womans* heart; but it is best to use the mark of elision. When plural nouns end with *s*, you must not add an *s* to form the possessive case, but put the elision mark only after the *s*, which ends the noun; as, *mountains'* tops; *nations'* fleets; *lasses'* charms. Observe, however, that, in *every* instance, the possessive case may be

expressed by a turn of the words; as, *the hat of Richard*; *the top of the mountain*; *the fleet of the nation*; *the mind of man*; and so on. The nouns, notwithstanding this turn of the words, are still in the possessive case; and, as to when one mode of expression is best, and when the other, it is a matter which must be left to taste.

48. A noun is in the *objective* case, when the person or thing that it names or denotes is the *object*, or *end*, of some act or of some movement, of some kind or other; Richard *strikes Peter*; Richard gave a blow *to Peter*; Richard goes *after Peter*; Richard *hates Peter*; Richard *wants arms*; Richard seeks *after fame*; falsehood leads *to mischief*; oppression *produces resistance*. Here you see, that all these nouns in the objective case, are the *object*, the *end*, or the *effect*, of something *done* or *felt* by some person or thing, and which other person, or thing, is in the nominative case.

LETTER VI.

ETYMOLOGY OF PRONOUNS.

My Dear James,

49. You will now refer to paragraphs 17, 18, and 19, in Letter III; which paragraphs will refresh your memory as to the general nature and use of *Pronouns*. Then, in proceeding to become well acquainted with this part of speech, you will first observe, that there are four classes, or descriptions, of Pronouns: first, the *Personal*; second, the *Relative*; third, the *Demonstrative*; and, fourth, the *Indefinite*.

50. In PERSONAL PRONOUNS there are four things to be considered; the person, the number, the gender, and the case.

51. There are *three persons*. The pronoun which represents, or stands in the place of the name of the person who speaks, is called the *first person*; that which stands in the place of the name of the person who is spoken to, is called the *second person*; that which stands in the place of the name of the person who is spoken of, is

called the *third person*. For example: " *I* am asking *you* about *him*."
This circumstance of *person* you will, by-and-by, find to be of great
moment; because, as you will see, the *verbs* vary their endings
sometimes to correspond with the *person* of the pronoun; and,
therefore, you ought to pay strict attention to it at the outset.

52. The *number* is either singular or plural, and the pronouns
vary their spelling to express a difference of number; as in this
table, which shows, at once, all the persons and all the numbers.

	SINGULAR.	PLURAL.
First person.	I,	We.
Second person.	Thou,	You.
Third person.	He,	They.

53. The next thing is the *gender*. The pronouns of the first and
second person have no changes to express gender; but the third
person singular has changes for that purpose: *he*, *she*, or *it*; and I
need not point out to you the cases where one of these ought to be
used instead of the other.

54. The *Case* is the last thing to be considered in personal
pronouns. The meaning of the word *case*, as used in the rules of
grammar, I have fully explained to you in Letter V, paragraph 44.
In paragraphs 45, 46, 47, and 48, in that same Letter, I have treated
of the distinction between the cases. Read all those paragraphs
again before you proceed further: for now you will find their
meaning more clearly explained to you; because the personal
pronouns, and also some of the other pronouns, have *different
endings*, or are composed of *different letters*, in order to point out the
different cases in which they are: as; *He*, *His*, *Him*.

55. The personal pronouns have, like the nouns, three cases; the
nominative, the *possessive*, and the *objective*. The following table
exhibits the whole of them at one view, with all the circumstances of
person, number, gender, and case. [*See table on p. 26.*]

56. Upon this table there are some remarks to be attended to. In
the possessive cases of *I*, *Thou*, *She*, *We*, *You*, and *They*, there are
two different words; as, *My* or *Mine*; but, you know, that the former
is used when followed by the name of the person or thing
possessed; and that the latter is used when not so followed: as,

SINGULAR NUMBER.

	Nominative.	*Possessive.*	*Objective.*
First person	I,	My, Mine,	Me.
Second person	Thou,	Thy, Thine,	Thee.
Third Pers. { Mas. Gen.	He,	His,	Him.
Femin.	She,	Her, Hers,	Her.
Neuter,	It,	Its,	It.

PLURAL NUMBER.

	Nominative.	*Possessive.*	*Objective.*
First person	We,	Our, Ours,	Us.
Second person	You,	Your, Yours,	You.
Third Pers. { Mas. Gen.	They,	Their,	Them.
Femin.	They,		
Neuter,	They,	Theirs,	

" this is *my pen*; this pen is *mine*." And, it is the same with regard to the possessive cases of *Thou, She, We, You,* and *They.*

57. *Thou* is here given as the *second person singular*; but, common custom has set aside the rules of Grammar in this case; and though we, in particular cases, still make use of *Thou* and *Thee*, we generally make use of *You* instead of either of them. According to ancient rule and custom this is not correct; but, what a whole people adopts and universally practices, must, in such cases, be deemed correct, and to be a superseding of ancient rule and custom.

58. Instead of *you* the ancient practice was to put *ye*, in the nominative case of the second person plural; but, this practice is now laid aside, except in cases, which very seldom occur; but, whenever *ye* is made use of, it must be in the *nominative*, and *never* in

the *objective*, case. I may, speaking to several persons, say, "*Ye* have injured me;" but not, "I have injured *ye*."

59. The words *self* and *selves* are sometimes added to the personal pronouns; as, *myself, thyself, himself*; but, as these compounded words are liable to no variations that can possibly lead to error, it will be useless to do any thing further than just to notice them.

60. The Pronoun *it*, though a *personal* pronoun, does not always stand for, or, at least, appear to stand for, any *noun* whatever; but is used in order to point out *a state of things*, or the *cause* of something produced. For instance: " *It* freezed hard last night, and *it* was so cold, that *it* was with great difficulty the travellers kept on their journey." Now, *what* was it that freezed so hard? Not the *frost*; because frost is the effect, and not the cause, of freezing. We cannot say, that it was the *weather* that froze; because the freezing constituted in part the weather itself. No: the pronoun *it* stands, in this place, for *state of things*, or *circumstances*; and this sentence might be written thus: "The freezing was so hard last night, and the cold was so severe, that the travellers found great difficulty in keeping on their journey." Let us take another example or two. " *It* is a frost this morning. *It* will rain to-night. *It* will be fine to-morrow." That is to say, " A state of things called frost exists this morning; a state of things called rain will exist to-night; and to-morrow a state of things called fine weather." Another example: " *It* is delightful to see brothers and sisters living in uninterrupted love to the end of their days." That is to say; " The state of things, which exhibits brothers and sisters living in uninterrupted love to the end of their days, is delightful to see." The pronoun *it* is, in this its impersonal capacity, used in a great variety of instances; but I forbear to extend my remarks on the subject here, because those remarks will find a more suitable place, when I come to another part of my instructions. I have said enough here to prevent the puzzling that might have arisen from your perceiving, that the pronoun *it* was sometimes used without your being able to trace its connexion with any noun either expressed or understood.

61. In order, however, further to illustrate this matter in this place, I will make a remark or two upon the use of the word *there*.

Example; "*There are* many men, who have been at Latin-Schools for years, and who, at last, cannot write six sentences in English correctly." Now, you know, the word *there*, in its usual sense, has reference to *place*; yet it has no such reference here. The meaning is: that " many men *are in existence*, who have been at Latin-Schools." Again: " *There never was* any thing so beautiful as that flower." That is to say; " Any thing so beautiful as that flower *never existed*, or never *was in being.*"

62. We now come to the RELATIVE PRONOUNS, of which class there are only *three*; namely, *who*, *which*, and *that*. The two latter always remain the same, through all numbers, genders, and cases; but, the pronoun *who*, changes its ending, in order to express the possessive and objective cases: as, *who*, *whose*, *whom*.

63. These pronouns are called *relative*, because they always *relate* directly to some noun or some personal pronoun, or to some combination of words, which is called the *antecedent*; that is to say, the person or thing *before going*. Thus: " The *soldier*, *who* was killed at the siege." *Soldier* is the antecedent. Again: " The *men* (if I am rightly informed,) *who* came hither last night, *who* went away this morning, *whose* money you have received, and to *whom* you gave a receipt, are natives of South America." *Men* is here the *antecedent*; and, in this sentence there are all the variations, to which this pronoun is liable.

64. *Who*, *whose*, and *whom* cannot be used correctly as relatives to any nouns or pronouns, which do not represent *men*, *women*, or *children*. It is not correct to say, the horse, or the dog, or the tree, *who* was so and so; or to *whom* was done this or that; or, *whose* colour, or any thing else, was such or such. But, the word *That*, as a relative pronoun, may be applied to nouns of all sorts; as, the *boy that* ran; the *horse that* galloped; the *tree that* was blowed down.

65. *Which*, as a relative pronoun, is confined to irrational creatures, and here it may be used, as a relative, indifferently with *that*; as, the *horse which* galloped; the *tree which* was blowed down. This application of the relative *which* solely to irrational creatures is, however, of modern date; for, in the Lord's Prayer, in the English Church Service, we say; "Our Father *which* art in Heaven." In the

American Liturgy this error has been corrected; and they say, "Our Father, *who* art in Heaven."

66. I cannot, even for the present, quit these relative pronouns without observing to you, that they are words of vast importance, and that more errors, and errors of greater consequence, arise from a misapplication of them, than from the misapplication of almost all the other classes of words put together. The reason is this, they are *relatives*, and they frequently stand as the representative of that which has gone before, and which stands in a distant part of the sentence. This will be more fully explained when I come to the *Syntax* of pronouns; but the matter is of such great moment, that I could not refrain from giving you an intimation of it here.

67. The DEMONSTRATIVE PRONOUNS are so called, because they more particularly mark, or demonstrate, the nouns, before which they are placed, or for which they sometimes stand. They are, *This*, *These*, *That*, *Those*, and *What*. The use of them is so well known, and is liable to so little error, that my chief object in giving them this separate place, is, to show you the difference between *That*, when a *relative* and when not a relative. Take an example: "*That* man is not the man, as far as I am able to discover, *that* came hither last night." The first of these *Thats* does not *relate* to the man; it merely points him out: but the latter *relates* to him, carries you back to him, and supplies the place of repetition. This same word, *That*, is sometimes a *Conjunction*: as, "*That* man is not the man, as far as I can discover, *that* came hither last night, and *that* was so ill *that* he could hardly walk." The relative is repeated in the third *That*: but, the fourth *That* is merely a conjunction, serving to *connect* the effect of the illness with the cause.

68. Perhaps a profound examination of the matter would lead to a proof of *That* being *always* a pronoun; but, as such examination would be more curious than useful, I shall content myself with having clearly shown you the difference in its offices as a *relative*, as a *demonstrative*, and as a *conjunction*.

69. *What*, together with *who*, *whose*, *whom*, and *which*, are employed in *asking questions*, and are, sometimes, ranged under a separate head, and called *interrogative* pronouns. I have thought this unnecessary; but, here is an observation of importance to attend to;

for, *which*, though, as a *relative*, it cannot be applied to the intellectual species, is, as an interrogative, properly applied to that species: as, " *which* man was it who spoke to you ?"

70. *What* sometimes stands for both noun and relative pronoun: as, " *What* I want is well known." That is to say, " *The thing which* I want is well known." Indeed, *what* has, in all cases, this extended signification; for, when, in the way of inquiry as to words which we have not clearly understood, we say, *what* ? Our full meaning is: " repeat to us *that which* you have said, or the *words which* you have spoken."

71. The INDETERMINATE PRONOUNS are so called, because they express their objects in a general and indeterminate manner. Several of them are also *adjectives*. It is only where they are employed alone, that is to say, without nouns, that they ought to be regarded as pronouns. For instance: " *One* is always hearing of the unhappiness of *one* person or *another*." The first of these *ones* is a pronoun; the last is an adjective, as is also the word *another*; for a noun is *understood* to follow, though it is not expressed. These pronouns are as follows: *One, any, each, none, some, other, every, either, many, whoever, whatever, neither*, and some few others, but all of them words invariable in their Orthography, and all of very common use.

LETTER VII.

ETYMOLOGY OF ADJECTIVES.

My Dear James,

72. In Letter III, paragraph 21, I have described what an *Adjective* is. You will, therefore, now read that paragraph carefully over, before you proceed in studying the contents of the present Letter.

73. The adjectives have no changes to express gender, or case; but, they have changes to express *degrees of comparison*. As adjectives describe the qualities and properties of nouns, and as these may be possessed in a degree higher in one case than in another, the

adjectives have degrees of comparison; that is to say, changes in their endings, to suit these varying circumstances. A tree may be *high*, but another may be *higher*, and a third may be the *highest*. Adjectives have, then, these three degrees: the first degree, or rather, the primitive word, is called the *Positive*; the second, the *Comparative*; the third, the *Superlative*. For the forming of these degrees I shall give you *four rules*; and, if you pay strict attention to these rules, you will need be told very little more about this part of speech.

74. *First Rule.* Adjectives in general, which end in a consonant, form their comparative degree by adding *er* to the positive, and form their superlative degree by adding *est* to the positive; as,

POSITIVE.	COMPARATIVE.	SUPERLATIVE.
Rich,	Richer,	Richest.

75. *Second Rule.* Adjectives, which end in *e*, add, in forming their comparative, only an *r*, and in forming their superlative, *st*: as,

POSITIVE.	COMPARATIVE.	SUPERLATIVE.
Wise,	Wiser,	Wisest.

76. *Third Rule.* When the positive ends in *d*, *g*, or *t*, and when these consonants are, at the same time, preceded by a *single vowel*, the consonant is doubled in forming the comparative and superlative: as,

POSITIVE.	COMPARATIVE.	SUPERLATIVE.
Red,	Redder,	Reddest.
Big,	Bigger,	Biggest.
Hot,	Hotter,	Hottest.

But, if the *d*, *g*, or *t*, be preceded by another consonant, or by more than one vowel, the final consonant is not doubled in the forming of the two latter degrees: as,

POSITIVE.	COMPARATIVE.	SUPERLATIVE.
Kind,	Kinder,	Kindest.
Neat,	Neater,	Neatest.

77. *Fourth Rule.* When the positive ends in *y*, preceded by a consonant, the *y* changes to *ie* in the other degrees.

POSITIVE.	COMPARATIVE.	SUPERLATIVE.
Lovely,	Lovelier,	Loveliest.
Pretty,	Prettier,	Prettiest.

78. There are some adjectives which can be reduced to no rule, and which must be considered as irregular: as,

POSITIVE.	COMPARATIVE.	SUPERLATIVE.
Good,	Better,	Best.
Bad,	Worse,	Worst.
Little,	Less,	Least.
Much,	More,	Most.

79. Some adjectives can have no degrees of comparison, because their signification admits of no augmentation: as, *all*, *each*, *every*, *any*, *several*, *very*, *some*; and all the numerical adjectives: as, *one*, *two*, *three*; *first*, *second*, *third*.

80. Adjectives which end in *most*, are superlative, and admit of no change: as, *utmost*, *uppermost*.

81. However, you will observe, that all adjectives which admit of comparison, may form their degrees by the use of the words *more* and *most*: as,

POSITIVE.	COMPARATIVE.	SUPERLATIVE.
Rich,	More rich,	Most rich.
Tender,	More tender,	Most tender.

When the positive contains but *one syllable*, the degrees are usually formed by adding to the positive according to the four rules. When the positive contains *two syllables*, it is matter of taste which method you shall use in forming the degrees. The *ear* is, in this case, the best guide. But, when the positive contains *more than two syllables*, the degrees must be formed by the use of *more* and *most*. We may say *tender* and *tenderest*, *pleasanter* and *pleasantest*, *prettier* and *prettiest*; but who could tolerate *delicater* and *delicatest*?

LETTER VIII.

ETYMOLOGY OF VERBS.

My Dear James,

82. The first thing you have to do in beginning your study as to this important part of speech, is to read again very slowly and carefully paragraphs 23, 24, 25, and 26, in Letter III. Having, by well attending to what is said in those paragraphs, learned to distinguish *Verbs* from the words belonging to other parts of speech, you will now enter, with a clear head, on an inquiry into the variations to which the words of this part of speech are liable.

83. Sorts of Verbs. Verbs are considered as *active, passive,* or *neuter.* A verb is called active when it expresses an action which is produced by the nominative of the sentence: as, " Pitt *restrained* the Bank." It is passive, when it expresses an action, which is received, or endured, by the person or thing which is the nominative of the sentence: as, " The Bank is *restrained.*" It is neuter, when it expresses simply the state of being, or of existence, of a person or thing: as, "Dick *lies* in bed;" or, when it expresses an action *confined within the actor.*

84. It is of great consequence that you clearly understand these distinctions, because I shall, by-and-by, use these terms very frequently. And, in order to give you a proof of the necessity of attending to these distinctions, I will here give you a specimen of the errors, which are sometimes committed by those who do not understand Grammar. This last-mentioned Verb, *to lie,* becomes in the past time, *lay.* Thus: " Dick *lies* on a bed now, but, some time ago, he *lay* on the floor." This verb is often confounded with the verb *to lay,* which is an *active* verb, and which becomes, in its past time, *laid.* Thus: " I *lay* my hat on the table to-day, but, yesterday, I *laid* it on the shelf." Let us take another instance in order the more clearly to explain this matter. A verb may, sometimes, be what we call a *neuter* verb, though it expresses an *action*; but this happens when the action is *confined within the actor*; that is to say, when there is no object *to which the action passes. Strike* is clearly an active verb, because something is *stricken*; a stroke is *given to,* or *put upon,*

something. But, in the case of *to rise*, though there is an *action*, it passes on to no object: as, I *rise* early. Here is no object to which the action passes. But, to *raise* is an active verb, because the action passes on to an object: as, I *raise a stick*, I *raise my hand*, I *raise my head*, and also, I *raise myself*; because, though in this last instance, the action is confined to *me*, it is understood, that my mind gives the motion to my body. These two verbs are, in speaking and writing, incessantly confounded; though one is a neuter, and the other an active verb, though one is regular and the other irregular, and though they are not, in any person, time, or mode, composed of the same letters. This confusion could never take place, if attention were paid to the *principle* above laid down.

85. Having thus given you the means of distinguishing the *sorts* of Verbs, I now proceed to matters, which are common to all the sorts. There are four things to be considered in a Verb; the *person*, the *number*, the *time*, and the *mode*.

86. THE PERSON.—Read again Letter VI on the Etymology of Pronouns. You will there clearly see the use of this distinction about *persons*; and, as I have told you, you will find that it is a matter of great consequence; because, it will now, at once, be evident to you, that, unless the distinction of person be attended to, almost every sentence must be erroneous.

87. The verb must *agree* in *person* with the *noun* or the *pronoun*, which is the nominative of the sentence. Look back at the Letter V, and at paragraphs 44, 45, 46, and 47, in order to refresh your memory as to the *nominative* and other cases. The verb, then, must *agree* with the nominative: as, " I *write*; he *writes.*" To say, " I *writes*; he *write*:" these would be both erroneous.

88. Look back at the explanation about the *persons* in the etymology of pronouns in Letter VI. There are *three persons*; but, our verbs have no variation in their spelling, except for *the third person singular*. For we say, "I *write*, you *write*, we *write*, they *write*;" and only " he, she, or it *writes.*" This, then, is a very plain matter.

89. NUMBER is a matter equally plain, seeing that our verbs do not, except in one or two instances, vary their endings, to express number. But, when several nouns, or pronouns, come together, care must be taken to make the verb *agree* with them: as, " Benbow

and Johnstone *resist* the tyrants." Not *resists*. But this will be more fully dwelt on in the Syntax.

90. THE TIME.—The verb has variations to express the *time* of an action: as, " Sidmouth *writes* a Circular Letter; Sidmouth *wrote* a Circular Letter; Sidmouth *will write* a Circular Letter." Again: " the Queen *defies* the tyrants; the Queen *defied* the tyrants; the Queen *will defy* the tyrants." The *Times* of a verb are, therefore, called the *present*, the *past* and the *future*.

91. THE MODES.—The *Modes* of verbs are the *different manners* of expressing an action, or a state of being, which manners are sometimes *positive*, sometimes *conditional*, and sometimes *indeterminate*; and there are *changes*, or *variations*, in the spelling, or writing, of the verb, or of the little words used with the verb, in order to express this difference in *manner* and sense. I will give you an instance: " He *walks* fast." " If he *walk* fast, he will fatigue himself." In most other languages, the verb changes its form very often and very much to make it express the different modes. In ours it does not; because we have little words called *signs*, which we use with the verbs instead of varying the form of the verbs themselves. To make this matter clear, I will give you an example of the English compared with the French language in this respect.

E.	F.
I march,	Je marche,
I marched,	Je marchois,
I might march,	Je marchasse,
I should march,	Je marcherois.

There are other variations in the French verb; but we effect the purposes of these variations by the use of the *signs*, *shall*, *may*, *might*, *could*, *would*, and others.

92. The modes are four in number; the *infinitive*, the *indicative*, the *subjunctive*, and the *imperative*. Besides these there are the two *participles*, of which I shall speak presently.

93. The *infinitive* mode is the verb in its primitive state: as, *to march*. And this is called the *infinitive*, because it is without bounds or limit. It merely expresses the action of marching, without any

constraint as to person or number or time. The little word, *to*, makes, in fact, a *part of the verb*. This word, *to*, is, of itself, a *preposition*; but, as prefixed to verbs, it is merely a *sign* of the Infinitive Mode. In other languages, there is no such sign. In the French, for instance, *aller*, means, *to go*; *ecrire*, means, *to write*. Thus, then, you will bear in mind, that, in English, the *to* makes a part of the verb itself, when in the *infinitive mode*.

94. The *Indicative Mode* is that, in which we express an action, or state of being, positively; that is to say, without any *condition*, or any dependant circumstance. It merely *indicates* the action or state of being, *without being subjoined to* any thing which renders the action or state of being dependant on any other action or state of being. Thus: " He *writes*." This is the indicative.

95. But, the *Subjunctive Mode* comes into use, when I say: " if he *write*, the guilty tyrants will be ready with their dungeons and axes." In this case, there is something *subjoined*; and, therefore, this is called the *subjunctive mode*. Observe, however, that, in our language, there is no very great use in this distinction of modes; because, for the most part, our little *signs* do the business, and they never vary in the letters of which they are composed. The distinction is useful only as regards the employment of verbs without the *signs*, and where the signs are left to be understood; as in the above case: " If he *should write*, the guilty tyrants would be ready." And, observe, further, that, when the *signs* are used, or understood, the verb retains its original, or primitive, form, throughout all the persons, numbers, and times.

96. The *Imperative Mode* is mentioned here merely for form's sake. It is that state of the verb which *commands*, *orders*, *bids*, *calls to*, or *invokes*: as, " *Come* hither; *be* good; *march* away; *pay* me." In other languages there are changes in the spelling of the verbs to answer to this mode: but in ours there are none of these; and, therefore, the matter is hardly worth notice, except as a mere matter of form.

97. The *Participles*, however, are different in point of importance. They are of two sorts, the *active* and the *passive*. The former ends always in *ing*, and the latter is generally the same as the *past time* of the verb out of which it grows. Thus: *working* is an active

participle, and *worked* a passive participle. They are called participles because they *partake* of the qualities of other parts of speech as well as of verbs. For instance: " I am *working*; *working* is laudable; a *working* man is more worthy of honour than a titled plunderer who lives in idleness." In the first instance, *working* is a *verb*, in the second, a *noun*, in the third, an *adjective*. So, in the case of the passive participle; "I *worked* yesterday: that is, *worked* mortar." The first is a verb, the last an adjective.

98. Thus have I gone through all the circumstances of change to which verbs are liable. I will now give you the complete *conjugation* of a verb. To *conjugate*, in its usual acceptation, means, to *join together*; and, as used by grammarians, it means, to place under one view all the *variations* in the form of a verb; beginning with the Infinitive Mode and ending with the Participle. I will now lay before you, then, the *conjugation* of the verb to *work*, exhibiting that verb in all its persons, numbers, times and modes.

INFINITIVE MODE.
To Work.

INDICATIVE MODE.

		Singular.	*Plural.*
Present Time.	1st Person.	I work,	We work,
	2d Person.	Thou workest,	You work,
	3d Person.	He, she, or it, works.	They work.
Past Time.		———I worked,	We worked,
		———Thou workedst,	You worked,
		———He worked.	They worked.
Future Time.		———I shall or will work,	We shall or will work,
		———Thou shalt or wilt work,	You shall or will work,
		———He shall or will work.	They shall or will work.

SUBJUNCTIVE MODE.

If I work, or may, might, could, would, or should, work.

If thou work, or may, ——————————— work.

If he, she, or it work, or may, ——————————— work.

If we work, or may, might, could, would, or should, work.
If you work, or may, ——————————————— work.
If they work, or may, ——————————————— work.

IMPERATIVE MODE.

Let me work,   Let us work.
Work thou,   Work you.
Let him work,   Let them work.

PARTICIPLES.

Active.—Working
Passive.—Worked.

99. Some explanatory remarks are necessary here. The third person singular of the Indicative present used to be written with *eth*: as *worketh*; but this spelling has long been disused. The *past time* may be formed by *did*: as, *did work*, instead of *worked*; and *do work* may be used in the present time; but, in fact, these little words are a great deal more than mere marks of the *times*. They are used in one time to express the negative of another, or, to affirm with more than ordinary emphasis.

100. Grammarians generally make a present and a past time under the subjunctive mode; but, the truth is, that any of the *signs* may apply to the present, past, or future of that Mode. These are little words of vast import and of constant use; and, though that use is so very difficult to be learned by foreigners, we ourselves never make mistakes with regard to it. The verb *to be* alone changes its form in order to make a past time in the Subjunctive Mode.

101. As to the *Imperative Mode*, where the pronouns *Thou* and *You* are put after the verb, we seldom do this. We make use of the verb only, which is quite sufficient.

102. Some Grammarians put in their conjugations what they call the *compound times*: as, I *have worked*, I *had worked*, I *shall have worked*, I *may have worked*, and so on. But, this can only serve to fill up a book; for all these consist merely in the introduction and use of the verb *to have* in its various parts. In the above conjugation all the *changes* or *variations* of the verb are exhibited; and it is those changes and variations, which, under the present head, form the important object of our inquiry.

103. The verbs *to have* and *to be* are of great use in our language. They are called *auxiliary verbs*. *To let* and *to do* are also called auxiliaries; but they are of far less importance than *to have* and *to be*. Before, however, I say more on the subject of these auxiliaries, I must speak of all the verbs as *regular* or *irregular*, just observing here, that the word *auxiliary* means *helper*, or *helping*.

104. Verbs are called *regular*, when they have their changes or variations according to a certain *rule* or manner. Thus: " I *walk*, I *walked*; I *work*, I *worked.*" But, I cannot say, " I *writed*." I must say, " I *wrote*." Now, observe, that we call *regular* verbs all those which end their *past time* of *the Indicative* and their *passive participle* in *ed*: and, if you now look back at the conjugation of the verb *to work*, you will find that that is a regular verb. Indeed, this is the case with almost all our verbs. But, there are some little *irregularities* even here, and they must be very well attended to, because a want of attention to them leads to very great errors even as to spelling.

105. These little irregularities I shall notice under five separate heads; and, if you should forget, at any time, what has been said on the subject, a reference to these will, in a moment, set you right. I. The verb *to work* is *perfectly* regular, for it has *ed* added to it, in order to form the *past time*, and also in order to form the *passive participle*. It is the same with the verbs to *walk*, to *turn*, to *abandon*, and numerous others. But, if the *infinitive*, that is to say, the primitive or original word, end in *e*, then *d* only is added, in the past time and participle, and *st* instead of *est* after *Thou*: as, in the case of *to move*, which becomes *moved* and *movest*. You have seen also, in the case of the verb *to work*, that we add only an *s* to form the third person singular of the present of the indicative: *he works*. But if the infinitive end in *h*, *s*, *x*, or *z*, then *es* must be added; as, *to wish*, *he wishes*; *to toss*, *he tosses*; *to box*, *he boxes*; *to buzz*, *he buzzes*.—II. When the infinitive ends in *y*, and when that *y* has *a consonant immediately before it*, the *y* is changed into *ie* to form the third person singular of the present of the indicative: as, to *reply*, he *replies*. But, (and I beg you to mark it well) if the ending *y* have *a vowel immediately before it*, the verb follows the general rule, in the formation of the third person singular of the present of the indicative: as, *to delay*, he *delays*; and not he *delaies*. It is the same in the second person

singular: as, *to reply*, thou *repliest*; *to delay*, thou *delayest*.—III. When the infinitive ends in *y*, with a consonant immediately before it, the past time of the indicative and the passive participle are formed by using an *i* instead of the *y*: as, *to reply*, he *replied*; to *deny*, it *was denied*. But, if the *y* be preceded by a vowel, *ed* is added to the *y* in the usual manner: as, to *delay*, he *delayed*.—IV. The *active participle*, which always ends in *ing*, is, in general, formed by simply adding the *ing* to the infinitive: as, to *work*, *working*; to *talk*, *talking*. But, if the infinitive end in a single *e*, the *e* is dropped: as, to *move*, *moving*. The verb *to be* is an exception to this; but, then that is an *irregular* verb. It is when the infinitive ends in a *single e* mind; for, if the *e* be double, the general rule is followed: as, to *free*, *freeing*. When the infinitive ends in *ie*, those letters are changed into *y* in the forming of the active participle; as to *lie*, *lying*.—V. When the infinitive ends in *a single consonant*, which has *a single vowel immediately before it*, the final consonant is doubled, not only in forming the active participle, but also in forming the past time of the indicative, and the passive participle: as, *to rap*, *rapping*; I *rapped*, it was *rapped*. But, observe well, this rule holds good only as to words of *one syllable*; for, if the infinitive of the verb have more than one syllable, the consonant is not doubled *unless the accent be on the last syllable*; and the accent means the main force, or weight, or sound of the voice in pronouncing the word. For instance, in the word to *open*, the accent is on the *first* syllable; and, therefore, we write *opening*, *opened*. But, when we come to the verb to *refer*, where we find the accent on the last syllable, we write *referring*, *referred*.

106. These irregularities, though very necessary to be attended to, do not prevent us from considering the verbs, which are subject to them, as *regular verbs*. The mark of a regular verb, is, that its *past time* and *passive participle* end in *ed*: every verb, which does not answer to this mark, is *irregular*.

107. There are many of these *irregular verbs*, of which I shall here insert a complete list. All the irregularities, (except the little irregularities just mentioned) which it is possible to find in an English verb (the *auxiliary verbs* excepted) are in the *past time* and the *passive participle* only. Therefore, it will be sufficient to give a List, showing, in those two instances, what are the irregularities of

each verb: and, in order to render this List convenient, and to shorten the work of referring to it, I shall make it alphabetical. With the past time of the several verbs I shall use the first person singular of the pronoun in order to make my examples as clear as possible.

LIST OF IRREGULAR VERBS.

INFINITIVE.	PAST TIME.	PARTICIPLE.
To abide,	I abode,	abode.
to be,	I was,	been.
to bear,	I bore,	borne.
to beat	I beat,	beaten.
to become,	I became,	become.
to befall,	It befell,	befell.
to beget,	I begot,	begotten.
to begin,	I began,	begun.
to behold,	I beheld,	beheld.
to bend,	I bended,	bent.
to beseech,	I besought,	besought.
to bid,	I bade,	bidden.
to bind,	I bound,	bound.
to bite,	I bit,	bitten.
to bleed,	I bled,	bled.
to break,	I broke,	broken.
to breed,	I bred,	bred.
to bring,	I brought,	brought.
to buy,	I bought,	bought.
to catch,	I caught,	caught.
to choose,	I chose,	chosen.
to cleave,	I clove,	cloven.
to come,	I came,	come.
to cost,	I cost,	cost.
to cut,	I cut,	cut.
to die,	I died,	died.
to do,	I did,	done.
to drink,	I drank,	drunk.
to drive,	I drove,	driven.
to eat,	I ate,	eaten.

To fall,	I fell,	fallen.
to feed,	I fed,	fed.
to feel,	I felt,	felt.
to fight,	I fought,	fought.
to find,	I found,	found.
to flee,	I fled,	fled.
to fling,	I flung,	flung.
to fly,	I flew,	flown.
to forbear,	I forebore,	forborn.
to forbid,	I forebade,	forbidden.
to forget,	I forgot,	forgotten.
to forgive,	I forgave,	forgiven.
to forsake,	I forsook,	forsaken.
to get,	I got,	gotten.
to give,	I gave,	given.
to go,	I went,	gone.
to grind,	I ground,	ground.
to have,	I had,	had.
to hear,	I heard,	heard.
to hide,	I hid,	hidden.
to hit,	I hit,	hit.
to hold,	I held,	held.
to hurt,	I hurt,	hurt.
to keep,	I kept,	kept.
to know,	I knew,	known.
to lay,	I laid,	laid.
to lead,	I led,	led.
to leave,	I left,	left.
to lend,	I lent,	lent.
to let,	I let,	let.
to lie,	I lay,	lain.
to lose,	I lost,	lost.
to make,	I made,	made.
to meet,	I met,	met.
to overcome,	I overcame,	overcome.
to overdo,	I overdid,	overdone.
to pass,	I passed,	past.

To pay,	I paid,	paid.
to put,	I put,	put.
to read,	I read,	read.
to rend,	I rent,	rent.
to ride,	I rode,	ridden.
to ring,	I rang,	rung.
to rise,	I rose,	risen.
to run,	I ran,	run.
to say,	I said,	said.
to see,	I saw,	seen.
to seek,	I sought,	sought.
to sell,	I sold,	sold.
to send,	I sent,	sent.
to set,	I set,	set.
to shake,	I shook,	shaken.
to shear,	I sheared,	shorn.
to shed,	I shed,	shed.
to shoe,	I shod,	shod.
to shoot,	I shot,	shotten.
to show,	I showed,	shown.
to shrink,	I shrank,	shrunk.
to shut,	I shut,	shut.
to sing,	I sang,	sung.
to sink,	I sunk,	sunk.
to sit,	I sat,	sitten.
to slay,	I slew,	slain.
to sleep,	I slept,	slept.
to slide,	I slid,	slidden.
to slit,	I slit,	slit.
to smite,	I smote,	smitten.
to speak,	I spoke,	spoken.
to speed,	I sped,	sped.
to spend,	I spent,	spent.
to spin,	I span,	spun.
to spit,	I spit,	spitten.
to spread,	I spread,	spread.
to stand,	I stood,	stood.

To steal,	I stole,	stolen.
to stick,	I stuck,	stuck.
to stink,	I stunk,	stunk.
to strike,	I struck,	stricken.
to swear,	I swore,	sworn.
to take,	I took,	taken.
to teach,	I taught,	taught.
to tear,	I tore,	torn.
to tell,	I told,	told.
to think,	I thought,	thought.
to tread,	I trod,	trodden.
to understand,	I understood,	understood.
to wear,	I wore,	worn.
to win,	I won,	won.
to wind,	I wound,	wound.
to write,	I wrote,	written.

108. It is usual with grammarians to insert several verbs in their *List of Irregulars*, which I have *not* inserted here. But, I have, in the above List, placed every verb in our language which is really irregular. However, I will here subjoin a list of those verbs, which are, by some grammarians, reckoned irregular; and, then, I will show you, not only, that they are not irregular, strictly speaking; but, that you ought, by all means, to use them in the regular form.

LIST OF VERBS, WHICH, BY SOME PERSONS, ARE
ERRONEOUSLY DEEMED IRREGULARS.

INFINITIVE.	PASSED TIME.	PARTICIPLES.
To awake,	I awoke,	awaked.
to bereave,	I bereft,	bereft.
to blow,	I blew,	blown.
to build,	I built,	built.
to burn,	I burnt,	burnt.
to burst,	I burst,	burst.
to cast,	I cast,	cast.
to chide,	I chid,	chidden.
to cling,	I clung,	clung.

To creep,	I crept,	crept.
to crow,	I crew,	crowed.
to curse,	I curst,	curst.
to dare,	I dared,	dared.
to deal,	I dealt,	dealt.
to dig,	I dug,	dug.
to dip,	I dipt,	dipt.
to draw,	I drew,	drawn.
to dream,	I dreamt,	dreamt.
to dwell,	I dwelt,	dwelt.
to freeze,	I froze,	frozen.
to geld,	I gelt,	gelt.
to gild,	I gilt,	gilt.
to gird,	I girt,	girt.
to grow,	I grew,	grown.
to hang,	I hung,	hung.
to help,	I helpt,	helpt.
to hew,	I hewed,	hewn.
to kneel,	I knelt,	knelt.
to knit,	I knit,	knit.
to lade,	I loaded,	laden.
to leap,	I leaped,	leapt.
to light,	I light,	light.
to load,	I loaded,	loaden.
to mean,	I meant,	meant.
to mow,	I mowed,	mown.
to overflow,	I overflowed,	overflown.
to saw,	I sawed,	sawn.
to shave,	I shaved,	shaven.
to shred,	I shred,	shred.
to shine,	I shone,	shone.
to sling,	I slung,	slung.
to slink,	I slunk,	slunk.
to slip,	I slipt,	slipt.
to smell,	I smelt,	smelt.
to snow,	It snowed,	snown.
to sow,	I sowed,	sown.

To spell,	I spelt,	spelt.
to spill,	I spilt,	spilt.
to spit,	I spat,	spitten.
to split,	I split,	split.
to spring,	I sprang,	sprung.
to stamp,	I stampt,	stampt.
to sting,	I stung or stang,	stung.
to strew,	I strewed,	strewn.
to strow,	I strowed,	strown.
to stride,	I strode,	stridden.
to string,	I strung,	strung.
to strip,	I stript,	stript.
to strive,	I strove,	striven.
to sweep,	I swept,	swept.
to swell,	I swelled,	swollen.
to swim,	I swam,	swum.
to swing,	I swung or swang,	swang.
to thrive,	I throve,	thriven.
to throw,	I threw,	thrown.
to thrust,	I thrust,	thrust.
to wax,	I waxed,	waxen.
to weave,	I wove,	woven.
to weep,	I wept,	wept.
to whip,	I whipt,	whipt.

109. The greater part of these verbs have become irregular by the bad practice of *abbreviating*, or *shortening*, in writing. We are always given to cut our words short; and, with very few exceptions, you find people writing *lov'd*, *mov'd*, *walk'd*; instead of *loved*, *moved*, *walked*. They wish to make the *pen* correspond with the *tongue*: but, they ought not, then, to write the word *the* at full length, nor the word *of*, nor any other little word; for, scarcely ever are these words *fully sounded* in speaking. From *lov'd*, *mov'd*, *walk'd*, it is very easy to slide into *lovt*, *movt*, *walkt*. And this has been the case with regard to *curst*, *dealt*, *dwelt*, *leapt*, *helpt*, and many others in the last inserted list. It is just as proper to say *jumpt* as it is to say *leapt*, and just as proper to say *walkt* as either; and thus we might go on, till the

orthography of the whole language were changed. When the love of contraction came to operate on such verbs as *to burst* and *to light*, it found such a clump of consonants already at the end of the words, that it could add none. It could not enable the organs even of English speech to pronounce *burst'd*, *light'd*. It, therefore, made really short work of it, and, dropping the last syllable altogether, wrote, *burst*, and *light*, in the past time and passive participle. But, is it not more harmonious, as well as more correct, to say, " the bubble is almost *bursted*," than it is to say, " the bubble is almost *burst*" ? And as to *hang*, is it not better to say, *hanged* than *hung* ? " I will be *hanged* if I do," is a very common phrase; and is it not better than it would be to say, "I will be *hung* if I do"? Many of these verbs, by being very difficult to contract, have, as in the case of *to hang*, *to swing*, and the like, reduced the shorteners to the necessity of changing almost all the letters of the words: as, to *dare*, *durst*; but, is it not better to say I *dared* than I *durst* ? This habit of contracting, or shortening, is a very mischievous habit. It leads to the destruction of all propriety in the use of letters; and, instead of *a saving of time*, it produces, by the puzzling that it gives rise to, a great *loss of time*. Hoping that what I have here said, will be a warning to you against the cutting of words short, I have only to add, on the subject of *irregular verbs*, that those in the last list are to be used in the regular form, and that the only real irregulars are those of the first list. Nay, I have, after all, left some verbs in the first list, which *may* be used in the regular form: as, *past*, which may be, in the participle, *passed*, and with full as much propriety.

110. AUXILIARY VERBS.—In the present Letter, paragraph 103, I opened this part of my subject. The word *let*, is the past time and the passive participle of the verb *to let*. It is used as an auxiliary, however, in the *present time*; and only in the *imperative mode*: as, *let me go*; *let us go*; *let him go*. That is to say, *leave me to go*, *leave us to go*, *leave him to go*. Perhaps, the meaning, *fully* expressed, would be, act in such a way that I may be left to go, or suffered to go.

111. The Auxiliary *do*, which, for the passed time, becomes *did*, is part of the verb *to do*, which in its past time is *did*, and in its passive participle *done*. In this sense, it is not an *auxiliary*, but a *principal* verb, and its meaning is equal to that of *to execute*, or *to*

perform: as, I *do my work*, I *execute my work*, I *perform my work*. As an auxiliary or *helper*, it seems to denote the *time* of the principal verb: as, I *do* walk; I *did* walk; and, we may say, I *do execute* my work, or, I *do do* my work. In this last example the first *do* is an auxiliary, and the last *do* a principal verb. However, as I said before, *do* and *did*, used as auxiliaries, do a great deal more than merely express *time*. In fact, they are not often used for that purpose only. They are used for the purpose of affirming or denying in a manner peculiarly strong: as, I *do* work, means, that I work, notwithstanding all that may be, or may have been, said, or thought, to the contrary; or it means, that I work *now*, and have not done it at some other stated, or supposed time. It is, with the exception of time, the same as to the use of *did*. These are amongst those little words of vast import, the proper force and use of which foreigners scarcely ever learn, and which we learn from our very infancy.

112. The verbs *to have* and *to be* are the two great auxiliaries. These words demand an extraordinary portion of your attention. They are *principal* verbs as well as auxiliaries. The verb *to have*, as a principal verb, signifies *possession*: as, *I have a pen*; that is to say, *I possess a pen*. Then, this is a word of very great use indeed in its capacity of principal verb; for we say, *I have a head-ache, I have a hatred* of such a thing, *I have a mind to go*; and hundreds of similar phrases. I *possess* a head-ache, has the same *meaning*; but, the other is more agreeable to the natural turn of our language. As *auxiliary* this verb is absolutely necessary in forming what are called the *compound times* of other verbs, and those times are called *compound*, because they are formed of *two* or *more verbs*. Suppose the subject to be of *my working*; and, that I want to tell you, that my work is *ended*; that I have *closed* my work. I cannot, in a short manner, tell you this without the *help* of the verb *to have*. To say, *I work*, or, *I worked*, or, *I will work*: these will not answer my purpose. No: I must call in the *help* of the verb *to have*, and tell you I *have* worked. So, in the case of the past time, I must say, I *had* worked; in the future, I *shall have* worked; in the subjunctive mode, I must say, I may, might, could, or should *have* worked. If you reflect a little you will find *a clear reason* for employing the verb *to have* in this way; for, when I say, " I *have* worked," my words amount to this; that the *act*

of working is now *in my possession*. It is *completed*. It is a thing *I own*, and, therefore, I say, *I have* it.

113. The verb *to be* signifies *existence* when used as a principal verb. " *To be* ill, *to be* well, *to be* rich, *to be* poor," mean, to *exist* in illness, in health, in riches, in poverty. This verb, in its *compound times* requires the *help* of the verb, *to have*: as, I *have been*, I *had been*, I *shall have been*, and so on. As *auxiliary*, this verb is used with the *participles* of other verbs: as, *to be* working, he *is* working, it *is* worked. Now, you will perceive, if you reflect, that these phrases mean as follows; *existing in work, he exists in work, it exists in a worked state*. Both these verbs are sometimes used, at one and the same time, as auxiliaries to other principal verbs: as, *I have been writing*: *I have been imprisoned*; and so on; and, upon patient attention to what has already been said, you will find, that they retain, upon all occasions, their full meaning, of *possession* in the one case, and of *existence* in the other.

114. Now, my dear James, if I have succeeded in making clear to you the *principle*, out of which the use of these words, as auxiliaries, has arisen, I have accomplished a great deal; for, if well grounded in that *principle*, all the subsequent difficulties will speedily vanish before you.

115. I now proceed to close this long and important Letter by presenting to you the conjugation of these two verbs, both of which are *irregular*, and every irregularity is worthy of your strict attention.

INFINITIVE MODE.
To have.

INDICATIVE MODE.

		Singular.	Plural.
Pr. Time.		1st Person, I have,	We have,
		2d Person, Thou hast,	You have,
		3d Person, He, she, or it has or hath.	They have.
PastT.		——I had,	We had,
		——Thou hadst,	You had,
		——He, she, or it had.	They had.

Fu. Time.
—I shall, or will, have,	We shall, or will, have,
—Thou shalt, or wilt, have,	You shall, or will, have,
—He, she, or it, shall, or will, have.	They shall, or will, have.

SUBJUNCTIVE MODE.

If I have, or may, might, would, could, or should, have.
If thou have, or may, ——————————————— have.
If he, she, or it, have, or may,——————————— have.
If we have, or may,————————————————— have.
If you have, or may, ——————————————— have.
If they have, or may,————————————————— have.

IMPERATIVE MODE.

Let me have,	Let us have,
Have thou,	Have you,
Let him, her, or it have.	Let them have.

PARTICIPLES.

Active.—Having.
Passive.—Had.

116. Though I have inserted *hath* in the third person singular of the present of the indicative, it is hardly ever used. It is out of date, and ought to be wholly laid aside.

117. The verb *to be* is still more irregular, but, a little attention to its irregularities will prevent all errors in the use of it.

INFINITIVE MODE.
To be.

INDICATIVE MODE.

	Singular.	*Plural.*
	1st Person, I am,	We are,
Pres. Time.	2d Person, Thou art,	You are,
	3d Person, He, she, or it is.	They are.
	—I was,	We were,
Past Time.	—Thou wast,	You were,
	—He, she, or it, was.	They were.
	—I shall, or will, be,	We shall, or will, be,
Future Time.	—Thou shalt, or wilt, be,	You shall, or will, be,
	—He, she, or it, shall, or will, be.	They shall, or will, be.

SUBJUNCTIVE MODE.

Pres.
Time.
> If I be, or may, might, would, could, or should, be.
> If Thou be, or may, ——————————————— be.
> If He, she, or it, be, or may, ——————— be.
> If We be, or may, ————————————— be.
> If You be, or may, ————————————— be.
> If They be, or may, ———————————— be.

Past Time.
> If I were,
> If Thou wert,
> If He, she, or it were.
> If We were,
> If You were,
> If They were.

IMPERATIVE MODE.

Let me be,   Let us be,
Be thou,   Be you,
Let him, she, or it, be,   Let them be.

118. In the Subjunctive Mode, I have made use of the conjunction *if*, throughout all the conjugations of verbs. But, a verb may be in that Mode without an *if* before it. The *if* is only *one* of the marks of that mode. A verb is always in that Mode, when the *action* or *state of being* expressed by the verb is expressed *conditionally*; or when the action or state of being is, in some way or other, *dependent* on some other action or state of being. But, of this I shall speak more at large when I come to the *Syntax* of Verbs.

119. There remain a few words to be said about the *signs*, the *defective verbs*, and the *impersonal verbs*. The signs, *may*, *might*, *can*, *could*, *will*, *would*, *shall*, *should*, and *must*, have all, originally, been verbs, though they are now become defective in almost all their parts, and serve only as signs to other verbs. *Will*, indeed, is part of a regular verb: as, *to will*, *they willed*, they are *willing*, they *will be willing*. The word *would* is certainly the past time and passive participle of the same verb; and, indeed, it is used as a principal verb now, in certain cases: as, " *I would* he were rich." That is to say, I *desire*, or am *willing*, or, it is *my will*, that he *should be* rich. But, deep inquiries regarding the origin of these words are more curious

than useful. A mere idea of the nature of their origin is enough. The word *ought* is a verb defective in most of its parts. It certainly, however, is no other than a part of the verb *to owe*, and is become *ought* by corruption. For instance; " I *ought* to write to you," means, that "I *owe* the performance of the act of writing to you." *Ought* is made use of only in the *present time*, and, for that reason, a great deal has been lost to our language by this corruption. As to the verbs, which some Grammarians have called *impersonal*, there are, in fact, no such things in the English language. By *impersonal verb* is meant, a verb that has no *noun* or *pronoun* for its nominative case; no person or thing that is the actor, or receiver of an action, or that is in being. Thus: "It *rains*," is by some called an *impersonal* verb; but the pronoun *it* represents the person. Look again at Letter VI, and at paragraphs 60 and 61. You will there find what it is that this *it*, in such cases, represents.

120. Thus I have concluded my Letter on the Etymology of verbs, which is by far the most important part of the subject. Great as have been my endeavours to make the matter clear to you, I am aware, that after the *first reading* of this Letter, your mind will be greatly confused. You will have had a glimpse at every thing in the Letter, but will have seen nothing clearly. But, my dear James, lay the book aside for a day or two. Then read the whole Letter again and again. Read it early, while your mind is clear, and while sluggards are snoring. Write it down. Lay it aside for another day or two. Copy your own writing. *Think* as you proceed; and, at the end of your copying, you will understand clearly all the contents of the Letter. Do not attempt to study the Letter *piece by piece*. In your readings as well as in your copyings go clean throughout. If you follow these instructions, the remaining part of your task will be very easy and pleasant.

LETTER IX.

ETYMOLOGY OF ADVERBS.

121. In Letter III, and in paragraphs 27 and 28, you will find a description of this part of speech. Read again those two paragraphs, in order to refresh your memory. There is not much to be said about adverbs under the head of Etymology. They are words liable to few variations. Adverbs are very numerous, and may be divided into five principal classes; that is to say, Adverbs of *time*, of *place*, of *order*, of *quality*, and of *manner*. This last class, which is the most numerous, is composed of those which are derived, immediately, from adjectives, and which end in *ly*: as, *especially*, *particularly*, *thankfully*.

122. These adverbs, ending in *ly*, are, for the most part, formed by simply adding *ly* to the adjective: as *especial* becomes *especially*; but, if the adjective end in *y*, that *y* is changed into *i* in forming the adverb: as, *happy*, *happily*; *steady*, *steadily*. If the adjective end in *le*, the *e* is dropped in forming the adverb: as, *possible*, *possibly*.

123. Some few adverbs have *degrees of comparison*: as, *often*, *oftener*, *oftenest*; and those which are derived from irregular adjectives, are irregular in forming their degrees of comparison: as *well*, *better*, *best*.

124. Some adverbs are *simple*, or *single*: others *compound*. The former consist of *one word*, the latter of *two*, or more words: as, *happily*; *at present*, *now-a-days*; which last means, *at the days that now are*. Another adverb of this description is, *by-and-by*; which is used to express, *in a short time*; and literally it means, *near and near*; because *by* itself, as an adverb, means *near*, *close beside*. When adverbs are compound, the words composing them ought to be connected by a *hyphen*, or hyphens, as in the above examples of *now-a-days* and *by-and-by*.

LETTER X.

ETYMOLOGY OF PREPOSITIONS.

125. LETTER III, paragraphs 29 and 30, has taught you of what description of words *Prepositions* are. The chief use of them is to express the different *relations* or *connexions*, which nouns have with each other, or, in which nouns stand with regard to each other: as, John gives money *to* Peter; Peter receives money *from* John. It is useless to attempt to go into curious inquiries as to the *origin* of prepositions. They never change their endings; they are always written in the same manner. Their *use* is the main thing to be considered; and that will become very clear to you, when you come to the syntax.

126. There are two *abbreviations*, or *shortenings*, of prepositions, which I will notice here, because they are in constant use, and may excite doubts in your mind. They are *a* and *o'*: as, I am *a* hunting; he is *a* coming; it is one *o'clock*. The *a* thus added, is *at* without doubt; as, I am *at* hunting; he is *at* coming. Generally this is a vulgar and redundant manner of speaking; but it is *in use*. In mercantile accounts you will frequently see this *a* made use of in a very odd sort of way: as, "six bales marked 1 *a* 6." The merchant means, "six bales marked from 1 *to* 6." But, this I take to be a relick of the Norman French, which was once the law and mercantile language of England; for, in French, *a*, with an accent, means *to* or *at*. I wonder that merchants, who are generally men of sound sense, do not discontinue the use of this mark of affectation. And, I beg you, my dear James, to bear in mind, that the *only* use of words is *to cause our meaning to be clearly understood*; and that the best words are those, which are familiar to the ears of the greatest number of persons. The *o'*, with the mark of elision, means, *of*, or *of the*, or *on*, or *on the*: as, *two o'clock*, is the same as to say two *of the* clock, or two *according to* the clock, or two *on the* clock.

127. As to the prepositions, which are joined to verbs or other words: as, to *outlive*, to *undervalue*, to be *overdone*, it would be to waste our time to spend it in any statements about them; for, these are *other words* than to *live*, to *value*, to be *done*. If we were to go, in

this way, into the subject of the *composition* of words, where should we stop? Thank*ful*, thank*less*, with*out*, with*in*. These are all *compound* words, but, of what *use* to us to enter on, and spend our time in, inquiries of mere curiosity? It is for monks, and for Fellows of English Colleges, who live by the sweat of other people's brows, to spend their time in this manner, and to call the result of their studies *learning*; for you, who will have to earn what you eat and what you drink and what you wear, it is to avoid every thing that tends not to real utility.

LETTER XI.

ETYMOLOGY OF CONJUNCTIONS.

128. IN Letter III, paragraph 31, you have had a description of this sort of words, and also some account of the *uses* of them. Some of them are called *copulative* conjunctions, and others *disjunctive*. They all serve to *join together* words, or parts of sentences; but, the former express *an union* in the actions, or states of being, expressed by the verb: as you *and* I talk. The latter a *disunion*: as, you talk, *but* I act. The words of this part of speech never vary in their endings. They are always spelled in one and the same way. In themselves they present no difficulty; but, as you will see by-and-by, to use them properly, with other words, in the forming of sentences, demands a due portion of your attention and care.

LETTER XII.

CAUTIONARY REMARKS.

MY DEAR JAMES,

129. BEFORE we enter on SYNTAX, let me give you a *caution*

or two with regard to the contents of the foregoing LETTERS.

130. There are some words, which, under different circumstances, belong to more than one part of speech, as, indeed, you have seen, in the *Participles*. But, this is by no means confined to that particular description of words. I *act*. Here *act* is a verb; but the *act* performed by me shows the very same word in the capacity of a noun. The message was sent *by* him; he stood *by* at the time. In the first of these examples *by* is a preposition; in the last an adverb. Mind, therefore, that it is *the sense in which the word is used, and not the letters of which it is composed*, that determines what is the part of speech to which it belongs.

131. Never attempt to *get by rote* any part of your instructions. Whoever falls into that practice soon begins to esteem the powers of *memory* more than those of *reason*; and the former are despicable indeed when compared with the latter. When the fond parents of an eighth wonder of the world call him forth into the middle of the parlour to repeat to their visitors some speech of a play, how angry would they be, if any one were to tell them, that their son's endowments equalled those of a parrot or a bull-finch! Yet, a German bird-teacher would make either of these more perfect in this species of oratory. It is this mode of teaching, which is practised in the great schools, that assists very much in making dunces of Lords and Country Squires. They "*get their lesson*;" that is to say, they repeat the *words* of it; but, as to its *sense* and *meaning*, they seldom have any understanding. This operation is sometimes, for what reason I know not, called getting a thing *by heart*. It must, I should think, mean *by hear't*; that is to say, by *hear it*. That a person may get and retain and repeat a lesson in this way, without any effort of the mind, is very clear from the fact, of which we have daily proof, that people sing the words and tune of a song with perfect correctness, at the very time when they are most seriously thinking and debating in their minds about matters of great importance to them.

132. I have cautioned you before against studying the foregoing instructions piece-meal; that is to say, *a little bit* at a time. Read a Letter *all through* at once; and, now that you have come to the end of my instructions on Etymology, read all the Letters through at

once; do this repeatedly; taking care to proceed slowly and carefully; and, at the end of a few days, all the matters treated of will form a connected whole in your mind.

133. Before you proceed to the Syntax, *try yourself a little*, thus: copy a short sentence from any book. Then write down the words, one by one, and write against each what part of speech *you think* it belongs to. Then look for each word in the dictionary, where you will find the several parts of speech denoted by little letters after the word: *s.* is for substantive, or noun; *pro.* for pronoun; *a.* for article; *v. a.* for verb active; *v. n.* for verb neuter; *adj.* for adjective; *adv.* for adverb; *pre.* for preposition; *con.* for conjunction; *int.* for interjection. It will give you great pleasure and encouragement when you find that you are right. If you be sometimes wrong, this will only urge you to renewed exertion. You will be proud to see, that, without any one at your elbow, you have really acquired something which you can never lose. You will begin, and with reason, to think yourself learned; your sight, though the objects will still appear a good deal confused, will dart into every part of the science; and, you will pant to complete what you will be convinced you have successfully begun.

═══

LETTER XIII.

SYNTAX GENERALLY CONSIDERED.

MY DEAR JAMES,

134. IN Letter II, paragraph 9, I shortly explained to you the meaning of the word SYNTAX, as that word is used in the teaching of grammar. Read that paragraph again.

135. We are, then, now entering upon this branch of your study; and it is my object to teach you how to give all the words you make use of their proper situation when you come to put them into sentences. Because, though every word that you make use of may be correctly spelled; that is to say, may have all the letters in it that it

ought to have, and no more than it ought to have; and though all the words may, at the same time, be the fit words to use in order to express what you wish to express; yet, for want of a due observance of the principles and rules of Syntax, your sentences may be incorrect, and, in some cases, they may not express what you wish them to express.

136. I shall, however, carry my instructions a little further than the construction of independent sentences. I shall make some remarks upon the manner of *putting sentences together*; and on the things necessary to be understood, in order to enable a person to write a series of sentences. These remarks will show you the use of figurative language, and will, I hope, teach you how to avoid the very common error of making your writing confused and unintelligible.

===

LETTER XIV.

SYNTAX.

The Points and Marks made use of in writing.

My Dear James,

137. There are, as I informed you in paragraph 9, Letter II, *Points* made use of in the making, or writing, of sentences; and, therefore, we must first notice these; because, as you will soon see, the sense, or meaning, of the words is very much dependent upon the points which are used along with them. For instance: " *you will be rich if you be industrious, in a few years.*" Then again: " *you will be rich, if you be industrious in a few years.*" Here, though in both sentences, the words and also the order of the words are precisely the same, the meaning of one of the sentences is very different from that of the other. The first sentence means, that you will, *in a few years' time*, be rich, if you be industrious *now*. The second means, that you will be rich, *some time or other*, if you be industrious *in a few years from this time*. And all this great difference in meaning is, as

you must see, produced solely by the difference in the situation of the *comma*. Put another comma after the last word *industrious*, and the meaning becomes *dubious*. A memorable proof of the great importance of attending to *points* was given to the English nation in the year 1817. A Committee of the House of Lords made a report to the House, respecting certain political clubs. A secretary of one of those clubs presented a petition to the House, in which he declared positively, and offered to prove at the bar, that a part of the report was *totally false*. At first their Lordships blustered: their high blood seemed to boil: but at last, the Chairman of the Committee apologized for the report by saying, that there ought to have been *a full point* where there was only a *comma*! and that it was this, which made that false, which would otherwise have been, and which was intended to be, true!

138. These points being, then, things of so much consequence in the forming of sentences, it is necessary that I explain to you the use of them, before I proceed any further. There are four of them: the *Full-Point*, or *Period*; the *Colon*; the *Semi-Colon*; the *Comma*.

139. The *Full-Point* is a single dot, thus [.], and it is used at the end of every complete sentence. That is to say, at the end of every collection of words, which makes a full and complete meaning, and is not necessarily connected with other collections of words. But a sentence may consist of several *members*, or *divisions*, and then it is called a *compound* sentence. When it has no division, it is called a *simple* sentence; thus: "The people suffer great misery." This is a simple sentence; but, " The people suffer great misery, and daily perish for want," is a compound sentence; that is to say, it is compounded, or made up, of two simple sentences.

140. The *Colon*, which is written thus [:], is next to the Full-Point in requiring a complete sense in the words. It is, indeed, often used when the sense is complete, but when there is something still behind, which tends to make the sense fuller or clearer.

141. The *Semi-Colon* is written thus [;], and it is used to set off, or divide simple sentences, in cases where the Comma is not quite enough to keep the meaning of the simple sentences sufficiently distinct.

142. The *Comma* is written thus [,], and is used to mark the

shortest pauses in reading, and the smallest divisions in writing. It
has, by some grammarians, been given as a rule, to use a comma to
set off every part of a compound sentence, which part has in it a *verb*
not in the infinitive mode; and, certainly, this is, in general, proper.
But, it is not always proper: and, besides, commas are used, in
numerous cases, to set off parts which have no verbs in them; and
even to set off single words, which are not verbs; and of this the very
sentence, which I am now writing, gives you ample proof. The
comma marks the shortest pause that we make in speaking; and it is
evident, that, in many cases, its use must depend upon taste. It is
sometimes used to give *emphasis*, or *weight*, to the word after which it
is put. Observe, now, the following two sentences: "I was very well
and cheerful last week; *but*, am rather feeble and low-spirited now."
" I am very willing to yield to your kind requests; *but*, I will set your
harsh commands at defiance." Commas are made use of, when
phrases, that is to say, portions of words, are throwed into a
sentence, and which are not absolutely necessary to assist in its
grammatical construction. For instance: " There were, *in the year*
1817, petitions from a million and a half of men, who, *as they
distinctly alleged*, were suffering the greatest possible hardships."
The two phrases, in *italicks*, may be left out in the reading, and still
the sentence will have its full grammatical construction.

143. Let us now take a compound sentence or two, containing all
the four points. " In a land of liberty it is extremely dangerous to
make a distinct order of the profession of arms. In absolute
monarchies this is necessary for the safety of the prince, and arises
from the main principle of their constitution, which is that of
governing by fear; but in free states the profession of a soldier,
taken singly and merely as a profession, is justly an object of
jealousy. In these no man should take up arms, but with a view to
defend his country and its laws: he puts off the citizen when he
enters the camp; but it is because he is a citizen, and would
continue *so*, that he makes himself for a while a soldier. The laws
therefore and constitution of these kingdoms know no such state as
that of a perpetual standing soldier, bred up to no other profession
than that of war: and it was not till the reign of Henry VII, that the
Kings of England had so much as a guard about their persons."

This passage is taken from Blackstone's Commentaries, Book I, Chap. 13. Here are four complete sentences. The first is a simple sentence. The other three are compound sentences. Each of these latter has its members, all very judiciously set off by points. The word *so*, in the third sentence, ought to be *such*, or the words *a citizen* ought to be repeated. But, with this trifling exception, these are very beautiful sentences. Nothing affected or confused in them: all is simple, clear, and harmonious.

144. You will now see, that it is quite impossible to give any *precise rules* for the use of these several points. Much must be left to taste: something must depend upon the weight which we may wish to give to particular words, or phrases; and something on the seriousness, or the levity, of the subject, on which we are writing.

145. Besides these points, however, there are certain grammatical signs, or marks, which are made use of in the writing of sentences: the mark of *parentheses*, the mark of *interrogation*, the mark of *exclamation*, the *apostrophe*, otherwise called the mark of elision, and the *hyphen*.

146. The mark of *parentheses* consists of two curved strokes drawn across the line of writing, or of print. Its use is to enclose a phrase, throwed in hastily to assist in elucidating our subject, or to add force to our assertions or arguments. But, observe, the parentheses ought to be very sparingly used. It is necessarily an *interrupter*: it breaks in upon the regular course of the mind: it tends to divert the attention from the main object of the sentence. I will give you, from Mr. TULL, Chap. XIII, an instance of the omission of the parentheses, and also of the proper employment of it. "PALLADIUS thought also, with others of the ancients, that Heaven was to be frightened with red cloth, with the feathers or the heart of an owl, *and a multitude of such ridiculous scarecrows*, from spoiling the fruits of the fields and gardens. The ancients, having no rational principles, or theory of agriculture, placed their chief confidence in magical charms and enchantments, which he, who has the patience or curiosity to read, may find, under the title aforementioned, in CATO, in VARRO (*and even* COLUMELLA *is as fulsome as any of them*), all written in very fine language; which is most of the erudition that can be acquired, as to field husbandry, from the Greek and Latin

writers, whether in verse or prose." For want of the mark of
parentheses in the first of these sentences, we almost think, at the
close of it, that the author is speaking of the *crows*, and not of *Heaven*
being frightened from spoiling the fruits of the fields and the
gardens. But, with regard to the use of the parentheses, I shall
speak, perhaps, more fully by-and-by; for the employment of it is a
matter of some importance.

147. The mark of *interrogation*, which is written thus [?], is used
when a question is asked: as, " *Who has my pen? What man is that?*"
In these and numerous other cases, the mark is not necessary to our
clearly comprehending the meaning of the writer. But, this is not
always the case. " What does he say? Put the horse into the
stable." Again: " What does he say? Put the horse into the
stable? " In *speaking*, this great difference in the meaning, in this
instance, would be fully expressed by the voice and manner of the
speaker; but, in writing, the mark of interrogation is, you see,
absolutely necessary in order to accomplish the purpose.

148. The mark of *exclamation*, or *admiration*, is written thus [!],
and, as its name denotes, is used to distinguish words or sentences
that are exclamatory, from such as are not: "*What do you say*! *What
do you say?* " The difference in the sense is very obvious here.
Again: "*He is going away to-night*! *He is going away tonight*."
The last simply states the fact; but, the first, besides stating the fact,
expresses *surprise* at it.

149. The *Apostrophe*, or mark of *elision*, is a comma, placed above
the line, thus [']. Elision means a *striking out*; and this mark is used
for that purpose: as, *don't*, for *do not*; *tho'*, for *though*; *lov'd*, for *loved*.
I have mentioned this mark, because it is used properly enough in
poetry; but, I beg you never to use it in prose in one single instance
during your whole life. It ought to be called the mark not of *elision*,
but of *laziness* and *vulgarity*. It is necessary as the mark of the
possessive case of nouns, as you have seen in Letter V, paragraph
47. That is its use, and any other employment of it is an abuse.

150. The *Hyphen* or *Conjoiner*, is a little line, drawed to connect
words, or parts of words: as in *sea-fish*; *water-rat*. For, here are two
distinct words, though they, in these instances, make but one.
Sometimes the Hyphen is used to connect many words together:

" The never-to-be-forgotten cruelty of the Borough-tyrants."
When, in writing or in printing, a line ends with part of a word, a
hyphen is placed after that part, in order to show that that part is to
be joined, in the reading, with that which begins the next line.

151. These are all the *grammatical* marks; but, there are others,
used in writing for the purpose of saving time and words. The
mark of *quotation*, or of *citing*. This mark consists of *two commas*
placed thus: "There were many men." It is used to enclose words,
taken from other writings, or from other persons' discourse; and,
indeed, it is frequently used to enclose certain sentences, or words,
of the writer, when he wishes to mark them as wholly distinct from
the general course of any statement that he is making, or of any
instruction that he is giving. I have, for instance, in the writing of
these Letters to you, set off many of my examples by marks of
quotation. In short, its use is to notify to the reader that such and
such words, or such and such sentences, are not to be looked upon
as forming part of the regular course of those thoughts which are at
the present time coming from the mind of the writer.

152. This mark [¶] is found in the Bible. It stands for
Paragraph. This [§] is sometimes used instead of the word *Section*.
As to stars [*] and the other marks which are used for the purpose
of leading the eye of the reader to *Notes*, in the same page, or at the
end of the book, they are perfectly arbitrary. You may use for this
purpose any marks that you please. But, let me observe to you
here, that *Notes* ought seldom to be resorted to. Like parentheses,
they are *interrupters*, and much more troublesome interrupters,
because they generally tell a much longer story. The employing of
them, arises, in almost all cases, from confusion in the mind of the
writer. He finds the matter *too much for him*. He has not the talent
to work it all up into one lucid whole; and, therefore, he puts part of
it into *Notes*. Notes are seldom *read*. If the text, that is to say, the
main part of a writing, be of a nature to engage our earnest
attention, we have not time to stop to read the notes; and, if our
attention be not earnestly engaged by the text, we soon lay down the
volume, and, of course, read neither notes nor text.

153. As a mark of *Abbreviation*, the full point is used: as, " Mr.
Mrs." But, I know of hardly any other words that ought to be

abbreviated; and if these were not, it would be all the better. People may indulge themselves in this practice, until at last, they come to write the greater part of their words in single letters. The frequent use of abbreviations is always a mark of slovenliness and of vulgarity. I have known Lords abbreviate almost the half of their words: it was, very likely, because they did not know how to spell them to the end. Instead of the word *and*, you often see people put &. For *what reason* I should like to know. But to this & is sometimes added a *c*; thus, *&c. And* is, in Latin, *et*, and *c* is the first letter of the Latin word *cætera*, which means *the like*, or *so on*. Therefore this *&c.* means *and the like*, or *and so on*. This abbreviation of a foreign word is a most convenient thing for such writers as have too much indolence or too little sense to say fully and clearly what they ought to say. If you *mean* to say *and the like*, or, *and so on*, why not say it? This abbreviation is very frequently made use of without the writer having any idea of its import. A writer on grammar says; " When these words are joined to *if*, *since*, *&c.* they are adverbs." But, where is *the like* of *if*, or of *since*? The best way to guard yourself against the committing of similar errors is *never* to use this abbreviation.

154. The use of CAPITALS and *italicks* I will notice in this place. In the books, printed before the middle of the last century, a capital letter was used as the first letter of *every noun*. Capitals are now used more sparingly. We use them at the beginning of every paragraph, let the word be what it may; at the beginning of every sentence, which follows a full-point; at the beginning of all *proper names*; at the beginning of all adjectives growing out of the names of countries, or nations: as, the *English* language; the *French* fashion; the *American* government. We use capitals, besides, at the beginning of *any* word, when we think the doing of it likely to assist in elucidating our meaning, but in general, we use them as above stated. The use of *italick* characters, in print, is to point out, as worthy of particular attention, the words distinguished by those characters. In writing with a pen, a stroke is drawed under such words as we wish to be considered to be in *italicks*. If we wish words to be put in SMALL CAPITALS, we draw two strokes under them; if in FULL CAPITALS, we draw three strokes under them.

155. The last thing I shall mention, under this head, is the *caret* [A], which is used to point upwards to a part which has been omitted, and which is inserted between the line, where the caret is placed, and the line above it. Things should be called by their right names, and this should be called the *blunder-mark*. I would have you, my dear James, scorn the use of this thing. *Think* before you write; let it be your *custom* to write *correctly* and in a *plain hand*. Be as careful that neatness, grammar, and sense prevail, when you write to a blacksmith about shoeing a horse, as when you write on the most important subjects and when you expect what you write to be read by persons whose good opinion you are most anxious to obtain or secure. Habit is powerful in all cases: but its power in this case is truly wonderful. When you write, bear constantly in mind, that some one is *to read* and *to understand* what you write. This will make your hand-writing, and also your meaning, *plain*. Never think of *mending* what you write. Let it *go*. No patching; no *after-pointing*. As your pen moves, bear constantly in mind, that it is making strokes which are to remain *for ever*. Far, I hope, from my dear James, will be the ridiculous, the contemptible affectation, of writing in a slovenly or illegible hand; or, that of signing his name otherwise than in plain letters.

156. In concluding this Letter let me caution you against the use of what, by some, is called the *dash*. The dash is a stroke along the line: thus: "I am rich—I was poor—I shall be poor again." This is wild work indeed! Who is to know what is intended by the use of these *dashes*? Those who have thought proper, like Mr. Lindley Murray, to place *the dash* amongst the *grammatical points*, ought to give us some rule relative to its different longitudinal dimensions in different cases. The *inch*, the *three quarter-inch*, *the half-inch*, the *quarter-inch*: these would be something determinate; but, " *the dash*," without measure, must be a most perilous thing for a young grammarian to handle. In short, " *the dash*," is a cover for ignorance as to the use of points, and it can answer no other purpose. A dash is very often put, in crowded print, in order to save the room that would be lost by the breaks of distinct paragraphs. This is another matter. Here the dash comes *after a full point*. It is the using of it in the body of a sentence against which I caution you.

LETTER XV.

MY DEAR JAMES,

157. BEFORE you proceed to my instructions relative to the employing of articles, you will do well to read again all the paragraphs in Letter IV. Our articles are so few in number, and they are subject to so little variation in their orthography, that very few errors can arise in the use of them. But, still, errors may arise; and it will be necessary to guard you against them.

158. You will not fall into very gross errors in the use of the articles. You will not say, as in the erroneous passage cited by DOCTOR LOWTH, " and I persecuted this way unto *the* death," meaning *death generally*; but you may commit errors less glaring. " The Chancellor informed the Queen of it, and she immediately sent for *the* Secretary and Treasurer." Now, it is not certain, here, whether the Secretary and Treasurer be not one and the same person; which uncertainty would have been avoided by a repetition of the article: " *the* Secretary and *the* Treasurer:" and, you will bear in mind, that, in every sentence, the very first thing to be attended to, is *clearness as to meaning*.

159. Nouns which express the whole of a species do not, in general, take the definite article: as, " *grass* is good for horses, and *wheat* for men." Yet, in speaking of the appearance of the face of the country, we say, " *the* grass looks well; *the* wheat is blighted." The reason of this, is, that, we are, in this last case, limiting our meaning to *the* grass and *the* wheat, which are on the ground at this time. " How do *hops* sell? *Hops* are dear; but *the* hops look promising." In this respect there is a passage in Mr. TULL, which is faulty. " Neither could weeds be of any prejudice to *corn*." It should be " *the* corn;" for, he does not mean corn universally, but *the* standing corn, and *the* corn amongst which weeds grow; and, therefore, the definite article is required.

160. " Ten shillings *the* bushel," and like phrases, are perfectly correct. They mean, " ten shillings *by the* bushel, or *for the* bushel." Instead of this mode of expression we sometimes use, " ten shillings

a bushel;" that is to say, ten shillings *for a* bushel, or a bushel *at a time*. Either of these modes of expression is far preferable to *per* bushel; for, the *per* is not English, and is, to the greater part of people, a mystical sort of word.

161. The indefinite article *a*, or *an*, is used with the words, day, month, year, and others: as, once *a* day; twice *a* month; *a* thousand pounds *a* year. It means *in a* day, *in a* month; *in*, or, *for*, *a* year; and though *per annum* means the same as this last, the English phrase is, in all respects, the best. The same may be said of *per cent*. that is *per centum*, or, in plain English, *the hundred* or *a hundred*: by ten *per centum* we mean ten *for the hundred*, or, ten *for a hundred*; and why can we not, then, say, in plain English, what we mean?

162. When there are several nouns following the indefinite article, care ought to be taken, that it *accord with them*: " *a* dog, cat, owl, and sparrow." *Owl* requires *an*; and, therefore, the article must be repeated in this phrase; as, " *a* dog, *a* cat, *an* owl, and *a* sparrow."

163. Nouns signifying fixed and settled collections of individuals: as, *thousand*, *hundred*, *dozen*, *score*, take the indefinite article, though they are of plural meaning. It is a certain *mass*, or *number*, or *multitude*, called a *score*; and so on; and the article agrees with these understood words, which are in the singular number.

—

LETTER XVI.

SYNTAX, AS RELATING TO NOUNS.

MY DEAR JAMES,

164. READ again Letter V, the subject of which is the Etymology of Nouns. Nouns are *governed*, as it is called, by verbs and prepositions; that is to say, these latter sorts of words *cause nouns to be in such or such a case*; and there must be a *concord*, or an *agreement*, between the nouns and the other words, which, along with the nouns, compose a sentence.

165. But these matters will be best explained when I come to the *Syntax of Verbs*; for, until we take the verb into account, we cannot go far in giving rules for the forming of sentences. Under the present head, therefore, I shall content myself with doing little more than to give some further account of the manner of using the *Possessive Case* of nouns; that being the only case to denote which of our nouns *vary their endings*.

166. This possessive case was pretty fully spoken of by me in the Letter just referred to; but, there are certain other observations to make with regard to the using of it in sentences. When the noun, which is in the possessive case, is expressed by a circumlocution; that is to say, by many words in lieu of one, the sign of the possessive case is joined to the last word: as, "*John*, the old farmer's, wife. *Oliver*, the spy's, evidence." It is, however, much better to say, " the wife of *John*, the old farmer. The evidence of *Oliver*, the spy."

167. When two or more nouns in the possessive case follow each other and are joined by a conjunctive conjunction, the sign of the possessive case is, when the thing possessed is the same, put to the last noun only: as, " Peter, Joseph, and Richard's estate." In this example the thing possessed being one and the same thing, the sign applies equally to each of the three possessive nouns. But, " Peter's, Joseph's and Richard's estate," implies that *each* has an estate; or, at least, it will admit of that meaning being given to it, while the former phrase will not.

168. Sometimes the sign of the possessive case is left out, and a *hyphen* is used in its stead: as, "Edwards, the *government-spy*." That is to say, "the government's spy;" or "the spy *of the* government." These two words, joined in this manner, are called a *compound* noun; and, to this compounding of nouns our language is very prone. We say, "*chamber-floor, horse-shoe, dog-collar*;" that is to say, *chamber's* floor, *horse's* shoe, *dog's* collar.

169. This is an advantage peculiar to our language. It enables us to say much in few words, which always gives strength to language; and, after *clearness*, strength is the most valuable quality that writing or speaking can possess. " The Yorkshire-men flew to arms." If we could not compound our words, we must say, " the

men of the shire of York flew to arms." When you come to learn
French, you will soon see how much the English language is better
than the French in this respect.

170. You must take care, when you use the possessive case, not
to use after it words which create a confusion in meaning. HUME
has this sentence: " They flew to arms and attacked *Northumberland's* house, *whom* they put to death." We know what is *meant*,
because *whom* can relate to *persons* only; but, if it had been an attack
on Northumberland's *men*, the meaning would have been, that the
men were put to death. However, the sentence, as it stands, is
sufficiently incorrect. It should have been: "They flew to arms,
attacked the house of Northumberland, and put him to death."

171. A passage from DOCTOR HUGH BLAIR, the author of
Lectures on Rhetoric, will give you another instance of error in the use
of the possessive case. I take it from the 24th Lecture: "In
comparing Demosthenes and Cicero, most of the French critics are
disposed to give the preference to the latter. P. Rapin the jesuit, in
the parallels which he has drawn between some of the most eminent
Greek and Roman writers, uniformly decides in favour of the
Roman. For the preference which he gives to Cicero, he assigns,
and lays stress on one reason of a pretty extraordinary nature, viz.
that Demosthenes could not possibly have so clear an *insight* as
Cicero *into* the manners and passions of men; Why? because *he* had
not the advantage of *perusing Aristotle's Treatise of Rhetoric*, wherein,
says our critic, *he* has fully laid open *that mystery*: and to support this
weighty argument, *he* enters into a controversy with A. Gellius, in
order to prove that Aristotle's Rhetoric was not published till after
Demosthenes had spoken, *at least*, his most considerable orations."
It is surprising that the Doctor should have put such a passage as
this upon paper, and more surprising that he should leave it in this
state after having perused it with that care, which is usually
employed in examining writings that are to be put into print, and
especially writings in which every word is expected to be used in a
proper manner. In Bacon, in Tull, in Blackstone, in Hume, in
Swift, in Bolingbroke; in all writers, however able, we find errors.
Yet, though many of their sentences will not stand the test of strict
grammatical criticism, the *sense* generally is clear to our minds: and

we read on. But, in this passage of Doctor Blair, *all is confusion*: the mind is puzzled: we, at last, hardly know *whom* or *what* the writer is talking about; and we fairly come to a stand.

172. In speaking of the many faults in this passage, I shall be obliged to make here observations which would come under the head of pronouns, verbs, adverbs, and prepositions. The first two of the three sentences are, in themselves, rather obscure, and are well enough calculated for ushering in the complete confusion that follows. The *he* which comes immediately after the word *because* may relate to Demosthenes; but to what noun does the second *he* relate? It would, when we first look at it, seem to relate to the same noun as the first *he* relates to; for, the Doctor cannot call *Aristotle's Treatise of Rhetoric* a *he*. No: in speaking of this the Doctor says, " *wherein*;" that is to say, *in which*. He means, I dare say, that the *he* should stand for *Aristotle*; but it does not stand for Aristotle. This noun is not a *nominative* in the sentence; and it cannot have the pronoun relating to it as such. This *he* may relate to *Cicero*, who may be supposed to have laid open a mystery in the perusing of the treatise; and the words which follow the *he* would seem to give countenance to this supposition: for *what* mystery is meant by the words " *that* mystery?" Is it the mystery of *Rhetoric*, or the mystery *of the manners and passions of men*? This is not all, however; for the Doctor, as if bewitched by the love of confusion, must tack on another long member to the sentence, and bring forward another *he* to stand for *P. Rapin*, whom and whose argument we have, amidst the general confusion, wholly forgotten. There is an error also in the use of the active participle, *perusing*. " Demosthenes could not have so complete an insight as Cicero, because he *had not* the advantage of *perusing*." That is to say, the advantage of being engaged *in perusing*. But this is not what is meant. The Doctor means, that he *had not had* the advantage *of perusing*; or, rather, that he *had not* the advantage *of having perused*. In other words, that Demosthenes could not have, or possess, a certain kind of knowledge, at the time when he made his orations, because, at that time, he had not, or did not possess, the advantage of *having perused*, or having *finished to peruse*, the treatise of Aristotle. Towards the close of the last sentence the adverb, " *at least*," is put in a wrong place.

The Doctor means, doubtless, that the adverb should apply to *considerable*, and not to *spoken*; but, from its being improperly placed, it applies to the latter, and not to the former. He means to say, that Demosthenes had spoken the most considerable, *at least*, of his orations; but, as the words now stand, they mean, that he had *done the speaking part to them*, if he had done nothing more. There is an error in the use of the word " *insight*," followed, as it is, by " *into*." We may have a *look*, or *sight*, *into* a house; but not an *insight*. This would be to take an *inside view of an inside*.

173. We have, here, a pretty good proof, that a knowledge of the Greek and Latin is not sufficient to prevent men from writing bad English. Here is a *profound scholar*, a teacher of rhetoric, discussing the comparative merits of Greek and Latin writers, and disputing with a French critic: here he is, writing English in a manner more incorrectly than you will, I hope, be liable to write it at the end of your reading of this little book. Lest it should be supposed, that I have taken great pains to hunt out this erroneous passage of Doctor Blair, I will inform you, that I have hardly looked into his book. Your brothers, in reading it through, marked a great number of erroneous passages, from amongst which I have selected the passage just cited. With what propriety, then, are the Greek and Latin languages called the " *learned* languages?"

LETTER XVII.

SYNTAX, AS RELATING TO PRONOUNS.

My Dear James,

174. You will now read again Letter VI. It will bring you back to the subject of pronouns. You will bear in mind that personal pronouns *stand for*, or in the *place of*, nouns; and, that the greatest care ought always to be taken in using them; because, being small words, and in frequent use, the proper weight of them is very often unattended to.

175. You have seen, in the passage from Doctor Blair, quoted in the foregoing Letter, what confusion arises from the want of taking care, that the pronoun relate *clearly* to its nominative case, and that it be not left to be understood to relate to any thing else. Little words, of great and sweeping influence, ought to be used with the greatest care; because errors in the using of them make such great errors in point of meaning. In order to impress, at the out-set, these precepts on your mind, I will give you an instance of this kind of error from ADDISON; and, what is well calculated to heighten the interest you ought to feel upon the occasion, is, that the sentence, which contains the error, is, by Doctor Blair, held forth to students of language, in the University of Edinburgh, as *a perfect model of correctness and of elegance.* The sentence is from Addison's Spectator, Number 411. " There are, indeed, but very few, who know how to be idle and innocent, or have a relish of any pleasures that are not criminal; every diversion *they* take, is at the expense of some one virtue or other, and *their* very first step out of business is into vice or folly." Doctor Blair says: " Nothing can be more elegant, or more finely turned, than this sentence. It is neat, *clear*, and musical. We could hardly alter one word, or displace one member, without spoiling it. Few sentences are to be found more finished, or more happy." See Blair's 20th Lecture on Rhetoric.

176. Now, then, my dear little James, let us see whether we, plain English scholars, have not a little more judgment than this professor in a *learned* University, who could not, you will observe, be a *Doctor*, until he had preached a Sermon in the Latin language. What does the pronoun *they* mean in this sentence of Mr. Addison? What noun does it *relate to*, or *stand for*? What noun is the *nominative* of the sentence? The nominative of the sentence is the word *few*, meaning *few persons*. Very well, then, the pronoun, *they*, relates to this nominative; and the meaning of the sentence is this: " that but few persons know how to be idle and innocent; that *few persons* have a relish of any pleasures that are not criminal; that every diversion *these few persons* take is at the expense of some one virtue or other, and that the very first step *of these few persons* out of business is into vice or folly." So that the sentence says *precisely the contrary* of what the author meant; or, rather, the whole is perfect

nonsense. All this arises from the misuse of the pronoun, *they*. If, instead of this word, the Author had put, *people in general* or *most people*, or *most men*, or any word, or words, of the same meaning, all would have been right.

177. I will take another instance of the consequence of being careless in the use of personal pronouns. It is from JUDGE BLACKSTONE, Book II, Chapter 6. "For, the custom of the manor has, in both cases, so far superseded the will of the Lord, that, provided the services be performed, or stipulated for by fealty, he cannot, in the first instance, refuse to admit the heir of *his* tenant upon *his* death; nor, in the second, can *he* remove *his* present tenant so long as *he* lives." Here are *lord*, *heir*, and *tenant*, all confounded. We may *guess* at the Judge's meaning; but, we cannot say, that we *know* what it is: we cannot say that we are *certain whose* life, or *whose* death, he is speaking of.

178. Never write a personal pronoun, without duly considering *what noun* it will, upon a reading of the sentence, be *found to relate to*. There must be a noun, expressed or understood, to which the pronoun clearly relates, or you will not write sense. "The *land-holder* has been represented as a monster which must be hunted down, and the *fund-holder* as a still greater evil, and both have been described as rapacious creatures, who take from the people fifteenpence out of every quartern loaf. *They* have been told that Parliamentary Reform is no more than a half-measure, changing only one set of thieves for another: and that *they* must go to the land, as nothing short of that would avail *them*." This is taken from the memorable report of a committee of the House of Lords, in 1817, on which report the cruel dungeon-bill was passed. Now, to *what nouns* do these pronouns relate? Who are the *nominatives* in the first sentence? The *land-holder* and the *fund-holder*, to be sure; and, therefore, to them do the pronouns relate. These Lords mean, doubtless, that the *people* had been told, that the *people* must go to the land; that nothing else would avail the *people*: but, though they *mean* this, they do not *say* it; and this part of their report is as false in Grammar as other parts of the report were in fact.

179. When there are two or more nouns, connected by a copulative conjunction, and when a personal pronoun is made use

of to relate to them, or stand for them, you must take care that the
personal pronoun *agree* with them in number. " He was fonder of
nothing than of *wit* and *raillery*; but, he is far from being happy in
it." This Doctor Blair, in his XIXth Lecture, says of Lord
Shaftesbury. Either *wit* and *raillery* are one and the same thing, or
they are different things: if the former, one of the words is used
unnecessarily; if the latter, the pronoun ought to have been, *them*,
and not *it*.

180. When, however, the nouns take the disjunctive conjunction, *or*, the pronoun must be in the singular: as, " When he shoots
a partridge, a pheasant, or a woodcock, he gives *it* away."

181. Nouns of numbers, or multitude, such as *Mob*, *Parliament*,
Rabble, *House of Commons*, *Regiment*, *Court of King's Bench*, *Den of
Thieves*, and the like, may have pronouns agreeing with them either
in the singular or in the plural number; for, we may, for instance,
say of the House of Commons, " *they* refused to hear evidence
against Castlereagh, when Mr. Maddox accused him of having sold
a seat; or, *it* refused to hear evidence." But, we must be uniform in
our use of the pronoun in this respect. We must not, in the same
sentence, and applicable to the same noun, use the singular in one
part of the sentence and the plural in another part. We must not, in
speaking of the House of Commons, for instance, say, " *they*, one
year, voted unanimously, that cheap corn was an evil, and, the next
year, *it* voted unanimously, that dear corn was an evil." There are
persons, who pretend to make very nice distinctions as to the cases
when these nouns of multitude ought to take the singular, and when
they ought to take plural, pronoun; but these distinctions are too
nice to be of any real use. The rule is this: that nouns of multitude
may take *either* the singular, or the plural, pronoun; but not *both* in
the same sentence.

182. As to *gender*, it is hardly possible to make a mistake. There
are no terminations to denote gender, except in the third person
singular, *he*, *she*, or *it*. We do, however, often *personify* things.
Speaking of a *nation* we often say *she*; of the *sun*, we say *he*; of the
moon, we say *she*. We may personify things at our pleasure; but, we
must take care to be consistent, and not call a thing *he*, or *she*, in one
part of a sentence, and *it* in another part. The occasions when you

ought to personify things, and when you ought not, cannot be stated in any *precise rule*. Your own taste and judgment will be your best guides. I shall give you my *opinion* about figures of speech in a future Letter.

183. Nouns which denote sorts, or kinds, of living creatures, and which do not of themselves distinguish the male from the female, such as *rabbit*, *hare*, *hog*, *cat*, *pheasant*, *fowl*, take the neuter pronoun, unless we happen to know the gender of the individual we are speaking about. If I see you with a cock pheasant in your hand, I say, " where did you shoot *him*," but, if you tell me you have shot *a pheasant*, I say, " where did you shoot *it*."

184. The personal pronouns in their *possessive case* must, of course, agree in number and gender with their correspondent nouns or pronouns: " John and Thomas have been so foolish as to sell *their* land and to purchase what is called stock; but their sister, who has too much sense to depend on a bubble for her daily bread, has kept *her* land: *theirs* is gone for ever; but *hers* is safe." So they must also, in their *objective case*: " John and Thomas will lose the interest of their money, which will soon cease to be paid to *them*. The rents of their sister will regularly be paid to *her*; and Richard will also enjoy his income, which is to be paid to *him* by *his* sister." If there be nouns of both genders used before pronouns, care must be taken, that no confusion, or obscurity arise from the misuse of the pronoun. HUME says; "they declared it treason to attempt, imagine, or speak evil of the king, queen, or *his* heirs." This has, at least, a meaning, which shuts out the heirs of the queen. In such cases the noun should be *repeated*.

185. Take care, in using the personal pronouns, not to employ the *objective case* where you ought to employ *the nominative*; and take care also of the *opposite error*. "Him strikes I: Her loves he." These offend the ear at once. But, when a number of words come in between the discordant parts, the ear does not detect the error. " It was some of those, who came hither last night, and went away this morning, who did the mischief, and not my brother and *me*." It ought to be " my brother and *I*." For, I am not, in this instance, the *object*, but the *actor*, or supposed actor. " Who broke that glass? It was *me*." It ought to be *I*; that is to say, " it was *I who*

broke it." Fill up the sentence with all the words that are understood; and, if there be errors you will soon discover them. After the words *than* and *as* this error, of putting the objective for the nominative is very frequently committed: as, " John was very rich, but Peter was richer than *him*; and, at the same time, as learned as *him* or any of his family." It ought to be richer than *he*: as learned as *he*: for, the full meaning here, is, " richer than *he was*: as learned as *he was*." But, it does not always happen, that the nominative case comes after *than*, or, *as*: " I love you more than *him*: I give you more than *him*: I love you as well as *him*." That is to say, I love you more than *I love him*: I give you more than *I give to him*: I love you as well as *I love him*. Take away *him* and put *he*, in all these cases, and the grammar is just as good, only the *meaning is quite different*. "I love you as well as *him*," means that I love you as well *as I love him*; but, " I love you as well as *he*," means, that I love you as well *as he loves you*.

186. You see, then, of what importance this distinction of *cases* is. But, you must not look for *this word*, or *that word*, coming before or coming after, to be *your guide*. It is *reason* which is to be your sole guide. When the person or thing represented by the pronoun is the *object*, then it must be in the objective case: when it is the *actor*, or when it is merely the person or thing said *to be* this or that, then it must be in the nominative case. Read again paragraphs 46, 47, and 48, of Letter V.

187. The errors, committed with regard to the confounding of cases, arise most frequently, when the pronouns are placed, in the sentences, at a great distance from the words which are connected with them, and which determine the case. " *He* and his sister, and not their uncle and cousins, the estate was given *to*." Here is nothing that *sounds* harsh; but, bring the pronoun close to the preposition that demands the objective case: say, the estate was given *to he*; and then, you perceive the grossness of the error in a moment. " The work of national ruin was pretty effectually carried on *by* the ministers; but more effectually by the paper-money makers than *they*." This does not hurt the ear; but, it ought to be *them*: "more effectually than *by them*."

188. The pronouns *mine, thine, theirs, yours, hers, his,* stand

frequently by themselves; that is to say, not followed by any noun. But, then, the noun is *understood*. "This is *hers*." That is to say, her *property*; her *hat*, or whatever else. No difficulty can arise in the use of these words.

189. But, the use of the personal pronoun *it* is a subject of considerable importance. Read again paragraphs 60 and 61, Letter VI. Think well upon what you find there; and, when you have done that, proceed with me. This pronoun, with the verb *to be*, is in constant use in our language. To say, " your uncle *came* hither last night," is not the same thing as to say " *it was* your uncle *who came* hither last night," though the *fact* related be the same. "*It is I* who write," is very different from " *I write*," though, in both cases, my being writing is the fact very clearly expressed, and is one and the same fact. " *It is those men,* who deserve well of their country," means a great deal more than, " *Those men* deserve well of their country." The principal verbs are the same: the propositions are the same; but the real meaning is different. " *It is* the dews and showers *that* make the grass grow," is very different from merely observing, that " *Dews and showers make* the grass grow."

190. DOCTOR LOWTH has given it as his opinion, that it is *not correct* to place plural nouns, or pronouns, after the *it*, thus used; an opinion which arose from the want of a little more reflection. The *it* has nothing to do, grammatically speaking, with the rest of the sentence. The *it*, together with the verb to be, express *states of being*, in some instances, and in others this phrase serves to mark, in a strong manner, *the subject*, in *a mass*, of what is about to be affirmed, or denied. Of course, this phrase, which is in almost incessant use, may be followed by nouns and pronouns in the singular, or in the plural, number. I forbear to multiply examples, or to enumerate the various ways in which this phrase is used, because one grain of reasoning is worth whole tons of memory. The *principle* being once in your mind, it will be ready to be applied to every class of cases, and to every particular case of each class.

191. For want of a reliance on principles, instead of examples, how the latter have swelled in number, and grammar-books in bulk! But, it is much easier to quote examples than to lay down principles. For want of a little thought, as to the matter immediately before us,

some grammarians have found out " *an absolute case*," as they call it; and Mr. LINDLEY MURRAY gives an instance of it in these words: " Shame *being* lost, all virtue is lost." The full meaning of this sentence is this: " *It being,* or *the state of things being such*, that shame *is* lost, all virtue is lost."

192. Owing to not seeing the use and power of this *it* in their true light, many persons, after long puzzling, think they must make the pronouns, which immediately follow, conform to the cases, which the verbs and prepositions of the sentence demand. " It is *them*, and not the people, whom I address myself *to.*" " It was *him*, and not the other man, that I sought *after.*" The prepositions, *to* and *after*, demand an objective case; and they have it in the words *whom* and *that*. The pronouns which follow the *it* and the verb *to be*, must *always* be in the *nominative case*.

193. This *it* with its verb *to be* is sometimes employed with the preposition *for*, with singular force and effect. " *It is for* the guilty to live in fear, to skulk and to hang their heads; but *for* the innocent *it is* to enjoy ease and tranquillity of mind, to scorn all disguise, and to carry themselves erect." This is much more forcible than to say: " The guilty generally live in fear," and so on, throughout the sentence. The word *for*, in this case, denotes appropriateness, or fitness; and, the full expression would be this: " To the *state of being*, or *state of things* called guiltiness, to live in fear *is fitting*, or is *appropriate*." If you pay attention to the *reason*, on which the use of these words is founded, you will never be at a loss to use them properly.

194. The word *it* is the greatest troubler that I know of in language. It is so small, and so convenient, that few are careful enough in using it. Writers seldom spare this word. Whenever they are at a loss for either a nominative or an objective, to their sentence, they, without any kind of ceremony, clap in an *it*. A very remarkable instance of this pressing of poor *it* into actual service, contrary to the laws of Grammar and of sense, occurs in a piece of composition, where we might, with justice, insist on correctness. This piece is on the subject of grammar; it is a piece written by *a Doctor of Divinity*, and read by him to students in grammar and language in an academy; and the very sentence that I am now about

to quote is selected by the author of a grammar, as testimony of high authority in favour of the excellence of his work. Surely, if correctness be ever to be expected, it must be in a case like this. I allude to two sentences in the " Charge of the REVEREND DOCTOR ABERCROMBIE to the senior class of the Philadelphia Academy, published in 1806," which sentences have been selected and re-published by Mr. LINDLEY MURRAY, as a testimonial of the *merits* of his Grammar; and which sentences are, by Mr. MURRAY, given to us in the following words: " The unwearied *exertions* of this gentleman *have* done more towards elucidating the obscurities, and embellishing the structure, of our language, than any *other writer* on the subject. *Such a work* has long been wanted; and, from the success with which *it* is executed, cannot be too highly appreciated."

195. As, in the learned Doctor's opinion, obscurities can be elucidated, and, as, in the same opinion, Mr. Murray is an able hand at this kind of work, it would not be amiss were the grammarian to try his skill upon this article from the hand of his dignified eulogist: for here is, if one may use the expression, a constellation of obscurities. Our poor, oppressed *it*, which we find forced into the Doctor's service, in the second sentence, relates to " *such a work*," though this work is nothing that has an existence, notwithstanding it is said to be " *executed*." In the first sentence, the "exertions" become, all of a sudden, a "*writer*:" the *exertions* have done more than " any *other* writer:" for, mind you, it is not the *gentleman* that has done any thing; it is " the *exertions* that *have* done " what is said to be done. The word *gentleman* is in the possessive case, and has nothing to do with the action of the sentence. Let us give the sentence a turn, and the Doctor and the Grammarian will hear how it will sound. "This gentleman's *exertions* have done more than any *other writer*." This is upon a level with " this gentleman's *dog* has killed more hares than any *other sportsman*." No doubt, DOCTOR ABERCROMBIE *meant* to say: " the exertions of this gentleman have done more *than those* of any other writer. Such a work as this gentleman's has long been wanted; his work, seeing the successful manner of its execution, cannot be too highly commended." *Meant*! No doubt at all of that! And, when

we hear a Hampshire plough-boy say: "Poll Cherrycheek have giv'd I thick hankecher," we know very well that he *means* to say, "Poll Cherrycheek has given me this handkerchief:" and yet, we are but too apt to *laugh at him*, and to call him *ignorant*; which is wrong; because he has no pretensions to a knowledge of grammar, and he may be very skilful as a plough-boy. However, we will not laugh at DOCTOR ABERCROMBIE, whom I knew, many years ago, for a very kind and worthy man, and who baptized your elder brother and elder sister. But, if we may, in any case, be allowed to laugh at the ignorance of our fellow-creatures, that case certainly does arise, when we see a professed grammarian, the author of voluminous precepts and examples on the subject of grammar, producing, in imitation of the possessors of invaluable medical secrets, testimonials vouching for the efficacy of his literary panacea, and when, in those very testimonials, we find most flagrant instances of bad grammar.

196. However, my dear James, let this strong and striking instance of the misuse of the word *it* serve you in the way of caution. Never put an *it* upon paper without thinking well of what you are about. When I see many *its* in a page, I always tremble for the writer.

197. We now come to the second class of pronouns; that is to say, the RELATIVE PRONOUNS, of which you have had some account in Letter VI, paragraphs, 62, 63, 64, 65, and 66; which paragraphs you should now read over again with attention.

198. *Who*, which becomes *whose* in the possessive case, and *whom* in the objective case, is, in its use, confined to rational beings: for, though some writers do say; "the country *whose* fertility is great," and the like, it is not correct. We must say; "the country, the fertility of *which*." But, if we *personify*; if, for instance, we call a nation a *she*, or the sun a *he*, we must then, if we have need of relative pronouns, take these, or the word *that*, which is a relative applicable to rational as well as irrational and even inanimate beings.

199. The errors which are most frequent, in the use of these relative pronouns, arise from not taking care to use *who* and *whom* when they are respectively demanded by the verbs or prepositions.

" *To who* did you speak? *Whom* is come to-day?" These sentences are too glaringly wrong to pass from our pens to the paper. But, as in the case of personal pronouns, when the relatives are placed, in the sentence, at a distance from their antecedents, or verbs, or prepositions, the ear gives us no assistance. " *Who*, of all the men in the world, do you think I *saw*, the other day? *Who*, for the sake of his numerous services, the office was given to." In both these cases it ought to be *whom*. Bring the verb, in the first, and the preposition in the second, case closer to the relative; as, *who I saw*: *to who the office was given*; and, you see the error at once. But, take care! " *Whom* of all the men in the world, do you think *was* chosen to be sent as an ambassador? *Whom*, for the sake of his numerous services *had* an office of honour bestowed upon him." These are nominative cases, and ought to have *who*: that is to say, " *who was chosen*; *who had an office*." I will not load you with numerous examples. Read again about the *nominative* and *objective* cases in Letter V. Apply your *reason* to the subject. *Who* is the nominative, and *whom* the objective. Think well about the matter, and you will want no more examples.

200. There is, however, an erroneous way of employing *whom* which I must point out to your particular attention, because it is so often seen in very good writers, and because it is very deceiving. " The duke of Argyle, *than whom* no man was more hearty in the cause. Cromwell, *than whom* no man was better skilled in artifice." A hundred such phrases might be collected from HUME, BLACK-STONE, and even from Doctors BLAIR and JOHNSON. Yet, they are bad grammar. In all such cases, *who* should be made use of: for, it is *nominative* and not objective. " No man was more hearty in the cause *than he was*: no man was better skilled in artifice *than he was*." It is a very common parliament-house phrase, and, therefore, presumptively *corrupt*: but, it is a Doctor Johnson phrase, too: . " Pope, *than whom* few men had more vanity." The Doctor did not say, " Myself, *than whom* few men have been found more base, having, in my Dictionary, described a pensioner as a slave of state, and having afterwards myself become a pensioner."

201. I differ, as to this matter, from Bishop Lowth, who says, that " the relative *who*, having reference to no verb or preposition

understood, but only to its antecedent, when it follows *than*, is *always in the objective case*; even though the pronoun, if substituted in its place, would be in the nominative." And, then, he gives an instance from Milton. " Beelzebub, *than whom*, Satan except, none higher sat." It is curious enough, that this sentence of the Bishop is, itself, ungrammatical! Our poor, unfortunate *it* is so placed as to make it a matter of doubt whether the Bishop meant *it* to relate to *who*, or to *its antecedent*. However, we know his meaning; but, though he says, that *who*, when it follows *than*, is always in the objective case, he gives us no *reason* for this departure from a clear general principle: unless we are to regard as a reason, the example of Milton, who has committed many hundreds, if not thousands, of grammatical errors, many of which the Bishop himself has pointed out. There is a sort of side-wind attempt at a reason in the words, " having reference to no *verb* or *preposition* understood." I do not see the *reason* even if this could be; but, it appears to me impossible, that a noun or pronoun can exist in a grammatical state without having reference to some *verb* or *preposition*, either expressed or understood. What is meant by Milton? "Than Beelzebub none *sat* higher, except Satan." And, when, in order to avoid the repetition of the word Beelzebub, the relative becomes necessary, the full construction must be, " no devil sat higher *than who* sat, except Satan;" and not " no devil sat higher *than whom* sat." The supposition that there can be a noun, or pronoun, which has reference to *no verb*, and *no preposition*, is certainly a mistake.

202. *That*, as a relative, may, as we have seen, be applied either to persons or things; but it has no possessive case, and no change to denote the other two cases. We say, "The man *that gives*, and the man *that* a thing is given *to*." But, there are some instances, when it can hardly be called proper to use *that* instead of *who*, or *whom*. Thus; directly after a proper name, as in HUME: "The queen gave orders for taking into custody the Duke of Northumberland, who fell on his knees to the Earl of Arundel, *that* arrested him." *Who* would have been much better, though there was a *who* just before the sentence. In the same author: "Douglas, *who* had prepared his people, and *that* was bent upon taking his part openly." This never ought to be, though we see it continually. *Either* may

do; but *both* never ought to be relatives of the same antecedent in the same sentence. And, indeed, it is very awkward, to say the least of it, to use *both* in the same sentence, though relating to different antecedents, if all these be names of rational beings. " The Lords, *who* made the first false report, and the Commons, *that* seemed to vie with their Lordships in falsehood, became equally detested." *That*, as a relative, cannot take the preposition or verb immediately before it: as, "the man *to whom* I gave a book;" but I cannot say, "the man *to that* I gave a book;" nor "the knife *to that* I put a handle." "Having defeated *whom*, he remained quiet;" but, we cannot, in speaking of persons, say, "having defeated *that*, he remained quiet."

203. *Which*, as a relative pronoun, is applied to irrational beings only, and, as to those beings, it may be employed indifferently with *that*, except in the cases, where the relative comes directly after a *verb* or a *preposition*, in the manner just spoken of. We say " the town, the horse, the tree, *which*; or *to which*;" and so on. And we say, " the town, the tree, the horse, *that*;" but not *to* or *for that*.

204. We may, in speaking of nouns of multitude, when the multitude consists of rational creatures, and when we choose to consider it as a *singular* noun, make use of *who* or *whom*, or of *which*, just as we please. We may say, " the *crowd*, *which* was going up the street; or, the crowd, *who* was going up the street;" but we cannot make use of both in the same sentence and relating to the same noun. Therefore, we cannot say, " the crowd *who* was going up the street and *which* was making a great noise." We must take the *who*, or the *which*, in both places. If such noun of multitude be used in the *plural number*, we then go on with the idea of the rationality of the individuals in our minds; and, therefore, we make use of *who* and *whom*. " The assembly, *who* rejected the petition, but, to *whom* another was immediately presented."

205. *Who*, *whose*, *whom*, and *which*, are employed in asking questions; to which, in this capacity, we must add, *what*. "*Who* is in the house? *Whose* gun is that? *Whom* do you love best? *What* has happened to-day?" *What* means generally, as a relative, "*the thing which*:" as, " give me *what* I want." It may be used in the nominative and in the objective case: " What happens to-day, may

happen next week; but I know not *to what* we shall come at last:" or, "*the thing which* happens to-day, may happen next week; but I know not *the thing which* we shall come to at last."

206. *Which*, though, in other cases, it cannot be employed as a relative with nouns which are the names of rational beings, is, with such nouns, employed in asking questions: as, " the tyrants allege, that the petition was disrespectful. *Which* of the tyrants?" Again: "one of the petitioners had his head cleaved by the yeomanry. *Which*?" That is to say, "which of the petitioners was it?"

207. *What*, when used in asking for a repetition of what has been said: as, *what*? means, " tell me *that which*, or *the thing which*, you have said." This word is used, and with great force, in the way of exclamation: " What! rob us of our right of suffrage, and, then, when we pray to have our right restored to us, shut us up in dungeons!" The full meaning is this: " *What do they do*? They rob us of our right."

208. It is not, in general, advisable to crowd these relatives together; but, it sometimes happens that it is done. " *Who, that* has any sense, can believe such palpable falsehoods? *What, that* can be invented, can disguise these falsehoods? By *whom, that* you ever heard of, was a pardon obtained from the mercy of a tyrant? Some men's rights have been taken from them by force and by genius, but *whose, that* the world ever heard of before, were taken away by ignorance and stupidity?"

209. *Whosoever, whosesoever, whomsoever, whatsoever, whichsoever*, follow the rules applicable to the original words. The *so* is an adverb, which, in its general acceptation, means *in like manner*; and *ever*, which is also an adverb, means, at *any time*, at *all times*, or *always*. These two words, thus joined in *whosoever*, mean, *who, in any case that may be*; and so of the other three words. We sometimes omit the *so*, and say, *whoever, whomever, whatever*, and even *whosever*. It is a mere abbreviation. The *so* is understood; and, it is best not to omit to write it. Sometimes the *soever* is separated from the pronoun: "*What* man *soever* he might be." But, the main thing is, to understand the *reason* upon which the use of these words stands; for, if you understand that, you will always use the words properly.

210. The DEMONSTRATIVE PRONOUNS have been described in Letter VI, paragraph 67; and, I have very little to add to what is there said upon the subject. They never change their endings, to denote gender or case; and the proper application of them is so obvious, that it requires little to be said about it. However, we shall hear more of these pronouns, when we come to the syntax of *verbs*. One observation I will make here, however, because it will serve to caution you against the commission of a very common error. You will hardly say, " *Them* that write;" but, you may say, as many do, "We ought always to have a great regard *for them*, who are wise and good." It ought to be, " *for those*, who are wise and good;" because the word *persons* is understood: " *those persons* who are wise and good:" and it is bad grammar to say, " *them persons* who are wise and good." But, observe, in *another sense*, this sentence would be correct. If I be speaking of *particular persons*, and, if my object be to make you understand, that they are *wise and good*, and also, that *I love them*, then, I say, very correctly, "I love *them*, who are wise and good." Thus: " The father has two children: he loves *them*, who are wise and good; and they love him, who is very indulgent." It is the *meaning* that must be your guide; and *reason* must tell you what is the meaning. " *They*, who can write, save a great deal of bodily labour," is very different from " *Those* who can write, save a great deal of bodily labour." The *those* stands for *those persons*; that is to say, *any persons, persons in general*, who can write; whereas, the *they*, as here used, relates to some particular persons; and the sentence means, that these particular persons *are able to write*, and, by that means, *they* save a great deal of bodily labour. DOCTOR BLAIR, in his 21st Lecture, has fallen into an error of this sort: thus, "These two paragraphs are extremely worthy of Mr. ADDISON, and exhibit a style which *they*, who can successfully imitate, may esteem themselves happy." It ought to be *those* instead of *they*. But, this is not the only fault in this sentence. Why say "*extremely* worthy?" *Worthiness* is a quality which hardly admits of *degrees*, and, surely, it does not admit of *extremes*. Then again, at the close: to *esteem* is to *prize*, to *set value on*, to *value highly*. How, then, can men "*esteem* themselves happy?" How can they "*prize* themselves happy?" How can they "*highly value themselves happy*?" My dear

James, let chamber-maids and members of the House of Commons, and learned Doctors, write thus: be you content with plain words which convey your meaning: say that a thing is *quite worthy* of a man; and that men may *deem* themselves happy.

211. The INDETERMINATE PRONOUNS have been enumerated in Letter VI, paragraph 71. They are sometimes *adjectives*, as is stated in that paragraph. *Whoever*, *Whatever*, and *Whichever* (that is, *whosoever*, *whatsoever*, *whichsoever*,) though *relatives*, are indeterminate too. But, indeed, it signifies little how these words are *classed*. It is the *use* of them that we ought to look to. *Every*, which I have reckoned amongst these pronouns, is never, now-a-days, used *without* a *noun*, and is, therefore, in fact, an *adjective*. The error that is most frequently committed in using these pronouns is, the putting of the *plural* verb, or *plural* pronoun, after nouns preceded by *every*, *each* or *either*; especially in the case of *every*: as "*every* man; *every* body; *every* house." These are understood to mean, all the *men*, all the *people*, all the *houses*; but, only *one man*, *one body*, *one house*, is spoken of, and, therefore, the verb ought to be in the singular: as, "every body *is* disgusted;" and not "every body *are* disgusted."

212. Before you use any of these words, you should think well on their *true meaning*; for, if you do this, you will seldom commit errors in the use of them. Doctor Johnson, in his Rambler, Number 177, has this passage. "*Every one* of these virtuosos looked on all his associates as wretches of depraved taste and narrow notions. *Their* conversation was, *therefore*, fretful and waspish, *their* behaviour brutal, *their* merriment bluntly sarcastick, and *their* seriousness gloomy and suspicious." Now these *theirs* certainly relate to *every one*, though the author meant, without doubt, that they should relate to *the whole body of virtuosos*, including the every one. The word *therefore*, adds to the confusion. The virtuosos were, *therefore*, fretful and waspish. *What for*? Was it because *every one* saw his associates in a bad light? How can my thinking meanly of others make *their* conversation fretful? If the Doctor had said: "*These virtuosos looked on each other*. . . ." the meaning would have been clear.

213. The pronoun *either*, which means *one of two*, is very often

improperly employed. It is used to denote one of *three* or *more*, which is always incorrect. We say, " *either* the *dog* or the *cat*;" but not, " *either* the *dog*, the *cat*, or the *pig*." Suppose some one to ask me, which I choose to have, mutton, veal, or woodcock, I answer *any one* of them; and not *either* of them. Doctor Blair has used *any one* where he ought to have used *either*. " The *two words* are not altogether synonymous; yet, in the present case, *any one* of them would have been sufficient."

214. In concluding this Letter on the Syntax of Pronouns, I must observe, that I leave many of these indeterminate pronouns un-noticed in a particular manner. To notice every one individually could answer no purpose except that of swelling the size of a book; a thing which I most anxiously wish to avoid.

LETTER XVIII.

SYNTAX, AS RELATING TO ADJECTIVES.

215. By this time, my dear James, you will hardly want to be reminded of the nature of Adjectives. However, it may not be amiss for you to read again attentively the whole of Letter VII.

216. Adjectives, having no relative effect, containing no repre-sentative quality, have not the dangerous power, possessed by pronouns, of throwing whole sentences into confusion, and of perverting or totally destroying the writer's meaning. For this reason, there is little to be said respecting the using of Adjectives.

217. When you make use of an Adjective in the way of compari-son, take care that there be a congruity, or fitness, in the things or qualities compared. Do not say that a thing is *deeper* than it is *broad* or *long*; or that a man is *taller* than he is *wise* or *rich*. HUME says, "The principles of the Reformation were *deeper* in the prince's mind than to be *easily eradicated*." This is *no comparison* at all. It is nonsense.

218. When Adjectives are used as *nouns*, they must, in all

respects, be treated as nouns. " The guilty, the innocent, the rich, the poor, are mixed together." But, we cannot say, " *a* guilty," meaning to use the word *guilty* as a noun.

219. If two or more Adjectives be used as applicable to the same noun, there must be a comma, or commas, to separate them: as, " a poor, unfortunate man;" unless *and* or *or* be made use of, for then a comma, or commas may be omitted: as, " a lofty and large and excellent house."

220. Be rather sparing than liberal in the use of Adjectives. One, which expresses your meaning, is better than two, which can, at best, do no more than express it, while the additional one may, possibly, do harm. But, the error most common in the use of Adjectives, is the endeavouring to strengthen the Adjective by putting an adverb before it, and which adverbs convey the notion, that the quality or property expressed by the Adjective admits of degrees: as, " *very* honest, *extremely* just." A man may be *wiser* than another *wise* man, an act may be *more wicked* than another *wicked* act; but, a man cannot be *more honest* than another: every man, who is *not honest*, must be *dishonest*; and every act which is *not just* must be *unjust*. " *Very* right," and " *very* wrong," are very common expressions, but they are both incorrect. Some express-ions may be *more common* than others; but, that which is *not right* is *wrong*; and that which is *not wrong* is *right*. There are here no intermediate degrees. We should laugh to hear a man say: " you are *a little* right, I am *a good deal* wrong; that person is honest in *a trifling degree*; that act was *too* just." But, our ears are accustomed to the adverbs of exaggeration. Some writers deal in these to a degree that tires the ear and offends the understanding. With them, every thing is *excessively* or *immensely* or *extremely* or *vastly* or *surprisingly* or *wonderfully* or *abundantly*, or the like. The notion of such writers is, that these words give *strength* to what they are saying. This is a great error. Strength must be found in the *thought*, or, it will never be found in the *words*. Big-sounding words, without thoughts corresponding, are effort without effect.

221. Care must be taken, too, not to use such Adjectives as are improper to be applied to the nouns along with which they are used. "*Good* virtues; *bad* vices; *painful* tooth-achs; *pleasing* pleasures."

These are staringly absurd; but, amongst a select society of empty heads, " *moderate* Reform" has long been a fashionable expression; an expression which has been well criticised by asking the gentlemen who use it, how they would like to obtain *moderate justice* in a court of law, or to meet with *moderate chastity* in a wife.

222. To secure yourself against the risk of committing such errors, you have only to take care to ascertain the full meaning of every word you employ.

———

LETTER XIX.

SYNTAX, AS RELATING TO VERBS.

223. LET us, my dear James, get well through this Letter; and, then, we may, I think, safely say, that we know something of Grammar: a little more, I hope, than is known by the greater part of those, who call themselves Latin and Greek scholars, and who dignify their having studied those languages with the name of " *Liberal Education.*"

224. There can be no sentence, there can be no sense in words, unless there be *a verb*, either expressed or understood.   Each of the other parts of speech may, alternately, be dispensed with; but the verb never can.   The verb being, then, of so much importance, you will do well to read again, before you proceed further, paragraphs 23, 24, 25, and 26 in Letter III, and the whole of Letter VIII.

225. Well, then, we have now to see how verbs are used in sentences, and how a misuse of them affects the meaning of the writer.   There must, you will bear in mind, always be a verb, expressed or understood.   One would think, that this was not the case in the direction written on a post letter.   To John Goldsmith, Esq. Hambledon, Hampshire.   But, what do these words really mean?   Why, they mean: " This letter *is to be delivered* to John Goldsmith, who *is* an Esquire, who *lives* at Hambledon, which *is* in Hampshire."   Thus, there are no less than five verbs, where we

thought there was no verb at all. " Sir, I beg you to give me a bit of bread." The sentence, which follows the *Sir*, is complete; but the *Sir* appears to stand wholly without connexion. However, the full meaning is this: " I beg you, who are *a* Sir, to give me a bit of bread." " What, John?" That is to say, " What *is* said by you, whose name *is* John?" Again, in the date of a letter: "Long Island, 25 March, 1818." That is: " *I am now writing* in Long Island; this *is* the twenty-fifth day of March, and this month *is* in the one thousand eight hundred and eighteenth year of the Christian era."

226. Now, if you take time to reflect a little on this matter, you will never be puzzled for a moment by those detached words, to suit which grammarians have invented *vocative cases*, and *cases absolute*, and a great many other appellations, with which they puzzle themselves, and confuse and bewilder and torment those who read their books.

227. We *almost always*, whether in speaking or in writing, leave out some of the words, which are necessary to a *full expression* of our meaning. This leaving out is called the *Ellipsis*. *Ellipsis* is, in geometry, an *oval* figure; and, the compasses, in the tracing of the line of this figure, do not take their full sweep all round, as in the tracing of a *circle*, but they make *skips* and *leave out* parts of the area, or surface, which parts would be included in the circle. Hence it is, that the *skipping over*, or leaving *out*, in speaking or in writing, is called the *Ellipsis*; without making use of which, we, as you will presently see, scarcely ever open our lips or move our pens. " He told me, that he had given John the gun, which the gunsmith brought the other night." That is: " He told *to* me, that he had given *to* John the gun, which the gunsmith brought *to this place*, or hither, *on* the other night." This would, you see, be very cumbrous and disagreeable; and, therefore, seeing that the *meaning* is quite clear without the words, marked by italicks, we *leave these words out*. But, we may easily go too far in this elliptical way, and say: "He told me, he had given John the gun, the gunsmith brought the other night." This is leaving the sentence too bare, and making it to be, if not nonsense, hardly sense.

228. Reserving some further remarks, to be made by-and-by, on

the Ellipsis, I have now to desire, that, always, when you are examining a sentence, you will take into your view the words that are *left out*. If you have any doubt as to the correctness of the sentence, fill it up by putting in the left-out words, and, if there be an error, you will soon discover it.

229. Keeping in mind these remarks on the subject of *understood words*, you will now listen attentively to me, while I endeavour to explain to you the manner in which *verbs* ought to be used in sentences.

230. The first thing is, to come at a clear understanding with regard to the *cases* of nouns and pronouns as connected, in use, with *verbs* and *prepositions*; for, on this connection, depends a great deal. Verbs *govern*, as it is called, nouns and pronouns; that is to say, they sometimes cause, or make, nouns or pronouns to be in a certain case. *Nouns* do not vary their endings to denote different cases; but *pronouns* do; as you have seen in Letter VI. Therefore, to illustrate this matter, I will take the pronoun personal of the third person singular, which in the nominative case, is, *he*, possessive case, *his*, objective case, *him*.

231. When *a man* (it is the same with regard to any other person or thing) is the *actor*, or *doer*, the *man* is in the nominative case, and the corresponding pronoun is, *he*: " *He* strikes." The same case exists when the man is the *receiver* or *endurer*, of an action. " *He* is stricken." It is still the same case when the man is said *to be* in any state or condition. " *He* is unhappy." Indeed, there is no difference in these two latter instances; for, " *he* is stricken," is no other than to say that " he *is* in a state, or condition, called *stricken*." Observe, too, that, in these two latter instances, the *he* is followed by the verb *to be*: he *is* stricken, he *is* unhappy; and, observe moreover, that whenever the verb *to be* is used, the *receiver*, or *be-er*, (if I may make a word) is, and must be, in the *nominative case*. But, now, let me stop a little to guard you against a puzzle. I say, " the verb *to be*;" but, I do not mean *those two words* always. When I say, the verb *to be*, I may mean as in the above examples, *is*. This is the verb *to be*, in the third person singular. " I *write*." I should say, that here is the pronoun *I* and the verb *to write*; that is to say, it is the verb *to write* in one of its forms. The *to* is the sign of the infinitive mode;

and the verb in that state, is the root, or the foundation, from which all the different parts or forms proceed. Having guarded ourselves against this puzzler, let us come back to our nominative case. The *actor*, the *doer*, the *receiver of an action*, the *be-er*, must always be in the nominative case; and, it is called nominative case, because it is that state, or situation, or case, in which the person, or thing, is *named* without being pointed out as the *object*, or *end*, of any foregoing action or purpose: as, " *he* strikes; *he* is stricken; *he* is happy." This word *nominative* is not a good word; *acting and being* case, would be much better. This word, nominative, like most of the terms used in teaching grammar, has been taken from the Latin. It is bad; it is inadequate to its intended purpose; but, it is *used*; and, if we understand its meaning, or, rather, what it is designed to mean, its intrinsic insufficiency is of no consequence. Thus, I hope, then, that we know what the *nominative* is. " He writes; he sings; he is sick; he is well; he is smitten; he is good;" and so on, always with a *he*.

232. But (and now pay attention) if the *action pass* from the *actor to a person or thing acted upon*, and, if there be no part of the verb, *to be*, employed; then the person or thing acted upon is in the *objective* case; as, " he smites *him*; he strikes *him*; he kills *him*." In these instances we wish to show, not only an action that is performed and the person who performs it, but also the person *upon whom* it is performed. Here, therefore, we state the *actor*, the *action*, and the *object*; and, the person or thing which is the object, is in the *objective case*. The verb is said, in such instances, to *govern* the noun or pronoun; that is to say, to make it, or force it, to be in the objective case; and, to make us use *him* instead of *he*.

233. However, I remember, that I was very much puzzled on account of these cases. I saw, that when " Peter was *smitten*," Peter was in the *nominative case*; but, that, when any person or thing " *had smitten* Peter," Peter was in the *objective case*. This puzzled me much; and the loose and imperfect definitions of my grammar-book yielded me no clue to a disentanglement. Reflection on the *reason* for this apparent inconsistency soon taught me, however, that, in the first of these cases, Peter is merely *named*, or *nominated*, as the *receiver* of an action: and that, in the latter instance, Peter is

mentioned as the *object* of the action *of some other person* or thing, expressed or understood. I perceived, that, in the first instance, " *Peter is smitten*," I had a complete sense. I was informed as to the person who had received an action, and also as to what sort of action he had received. And, I perceived, that, in the second instance, " *John has smitten Peter*," there was an actor who took possession of the use of the verb, and made Peter the object of it: and that this actor, *John*, now took to the *nominative*, and put Peter in the objective case.

234. This puzzle was, however, hardly got over, when another presented itself: for, I conceived the notion, that Peter was in the nominative *only because no actor was mentioned at all in the sentence*; but, I soon discovered this to be an error: for, I found that, " Peter is smitten *by John*," still left Peter *in the nominative*; and that, if I used the pronoun, I must say, " *he* is smitten by John;" and not " *him* is smitten by John."

235. Upon this puzzle I dwelt a long time: a whole week, at least. For, I was not content unless I could reconcile every thing to *reason*; and, I could see no reason for this. Peter, in this last instance, appeared to be the *object*, and there was the *actor*, John. My *ear*, indeed, assured me, that it was right to say, " *he* is smitten by John;" but my reason doubted the information and assurances of my ear.

236. At last, the little insignificant word, *by*, attracted my attention. This word, in this place, is a *preposition*. Ah! That is it! prepositions *govern* nouns and pronouns: that is to say, *make them to be in the objective case*! So that, John, who had plagued me so much, I found to be in the objective case; and, I found, that, if I put him out, and put the pronoun in his place, I must say, " Peter is smitten *by him*".

237. Now, then, my dear James, do you clearly understand this? If you do not, have patience. Read and think, and weigh well every part of what I have here written: for, as you will immediately see, a clear understanding with regard to the *cases* is one of the main inlets to a perfect knowledge of grammar.

238. Verbs, of which there must be one at least, expressed or understood, in every sentence, must *agree* in *person* and in *number*

with the nouns or pronouns, which are the *nominatives* of the sentence; that is to say, the verbs must be of the same person and same number as the nominatives are. Verbs frequently change their forms and endings to make themselves *agree* with their *nominatives*. How necessary is it, then, to know what is, and what is not, a nominative in a sentence! Let us take an example. " John smite Peter." What are these words? *John* is a noun, *third person*, singular number, nominative case. *Smite* is a verb, *first person*, singular number. *Peter* is a noun, third person, singular number, objective case. Therefore the sentence is incorrect; for the *nominative*, *John*, is in the *third* person, and the verb is in the *first*: while both ought to be in the *same person*. The sentence ought to be, " John *smites* Peter;" and not " John *smite* Peter."

239. This is, to be sure, a very glaring error: but still it is no more than an error, and is, in fact, as excusable as any other grammatical error. " The men lives in the country." Here, the verb, *lives*, is in the *singular* number, and the noun *men*, which is the nominative, is in the *plural* number. "The men *live* in the country," it ought to be. These errors stare us in the face. But, when the sentences become longer, and embrace several nominatives and verbs, we do not so readily perceive the errors that are committed. " The intention of the act of parliament, and not its several penalties, *decide* the character of the corrupt assembly by whom it was passed." Here the noun, *penalties*, comes so near to the verb, *decide*, that the ear deceives the judgment. But, the noun, *intention*, is the nominative to the verb, which, therefore, ought to be, *decides*. Let us take a sentence still more deceiving. "Without the aid of a fraudulent paper money, the tyrants never could have performed any of those deeds, by which their safety *have been* endangered, and which *have*, at the same time, made them detested." *Deeds*, is the nominative to the *last have* and its principal verb: but *safety* is the nominative to the *first have*; and therefore, this first *have* ought to have been *has*. You see, that the error arises from our having the plural noun, *deeds*, in our eye and ear. Take all the rest of the sentence away, and leave " *safety have* been " standing by itself, and then the error is as flagrant as " *John smite Peter*." Watch me, now, in the next sentence. " It must be

observed, that land fell greatly in price as soon as the cheats began to draw in their paper money. In such cases the quantity and quality of the land is the same as it was before; but, the price is reduced, all of a sudden, by a change in the value and power of the money, which becomes very different from what it was." Here are two complete sentences, which go very glibly off the tongue. There is nothing in them that offends the ear. The first is, indeed, correct; but, the last is a mass of error. *Quantity and quality*, which are the *nominative* in the first member of the sentence, make, together, a *plural*, and should have been followed, after the word *land*, by *are* and not by *is*; and, the *it was*, which follows, should, of course, have been, *they were*. In the second member of the sentence, *value and power* are the nominative of *becomes*, which, therefore, should have been, *become*; and, then, again, there follows an *it was* instead of *they were*. We are misled, in such cases, by the nearness of the singular noun, which comes in between the nominatives and the verbs. We should not be likely to say, "quantity and quality *is*; value and power *becomes*." But when a singular noun comes in between such nominatives and the verbs, we are very apt to be thinking of that noun, and to commit error. When we once begin, we keep on; and, if the sentence be long, we get together, at last, a fine collection of verbs and pronouns, making as complete nonsense as heart can wish. Judge Blackstone in the 4th Book, Chapter 33, says, "The very *scheme and model* of the administration of common justice between party and party, *was* entirely settled by this king; and *has* continued nearly the same to this day." *Administration of common justice* was full upon the Judge's ear: down he clapped, *was*; and, *has*, naturally followed: and, thus, my dear son, in grammar, as in moral conduct, one fault almost necessarily produces others.

240. Look, therefore, at your *nominative*, before you put a *verb* upon paper; for, you see, it may be *one word*, or *two*, or *more words*. But, observe, if there be two, or more singular nouns or pronouns, separated by *or*, which, you know is a *disjoining* conjunction; then, the verb must be in the singular; as, "a soldier *or* a sailor, who *has* served his country faithfully, *is* fairly entitled to a pension; but who will say, that a prostituted peer,

a pimp, *or* a buffoon, *merits* a similar provision from the public?"

241. It sometimes happens, that there are, in the nominative, two or more nouns, or pronouns, and that they are in *different numbers*, or in *different persons*: as, " *The minister*, or *the Borough-tyrants*." These nouns cannot have the verb to *agree* with them *both*. Therefore, if it be the conspiring of these wretches against the liberties of the people, of which we have to speak, we cannot say, "The minister, or the borough-tyrants, *conspire*;" because the verb would then not *agree* in number with the noun, *minister*; nor can we say, *conspires*; because the verb would not agree with the noun, *borough-tyrants*. Therefore, we must not write such sentences: we must say, " The minister *conspires*, or the borough-tyrants *conspire* against the liberties of the people." Repetition is, sometimes, disagreeable to the ear; but, it is better to repeat, be it ever so often, than to write bad grammar, which is only another term for nonsense.

242. When nominatives are separated by *nor*, the rule of *or* must be followed. " Neither man *nor* beast *is* safe in such weather;" and not *are* safe. And, if nominatives of different numbers present themselves, we must not give them a verb which *disagrees* with either the one or the other. We must not say: "Neither the halter *nor* the bayonets *are* sufficient to prevent us from obtaining our rights." We must avoid this bad grammar by using a different form of words: as, " We are to be prevented from obtaining our rights by neither the halter nor the bayonets." And, why should we *wish* to write bad grammar, if we can express our meaning in good grammar?

243. If *or* or *nor* disjoin nouns and pronouns of different *persons*, these nouns and pronouns, though they be all of the same *number*, cannot be the nominative of one and the same verb. We cannot say "They or *I am* in fault; I, or they, or he, *is* the author of it; George or I *am* the person." Mr. Lindley Murray says, that we *may* use these phrases; and, that we have only to take care that the verb agree with that person, which *is placed nearest* to it; but, he says also, that it would be *better* to avoid such phrases by giving a different turn to our words. I do not like to leave any thing to chance or to discretion, when we have a clear principle for our guide. Fill up

the sentences; and, you will see what pretty work here is. " They *am* in fault or I *am* in fault; I *is* the author, or they *is* the author, or he *is* the author: George *am* the person, or *I am* the person." Mr. Murray gives a similar latitude as to the verbs used with a mixture of plurals and singulars, as mentioned in the foregoing paragraph. The truth, I suspect, is, that Mr. Murray, observing that great writers frequently committed these errors, thought it prudent to give up the cause of grammar, rather than seem to set himself against such formidable authority. But, if we follow this course, it is pretty clear, that we shall very soon be left with no principle and no rule of grammar.

244. The nominative is frequently a noun of *multitude*; as *mob*, *parliament*, *gang*. Now, where this is the case, the verb is used in the singular or in the plural, upon precisely the same principles, that the pronouns are so used; and as these principles, together with ample illustrations in the way of example, have been given you in Letter XVII, paragraph 181, I need say nothing more of the matter. I will just observe, however, that *consistency*, in the use of the verb, in such cases, is the main thing to keep in view. We may say: "The gang of borough-tyrants *is* cruel:" or, that " the gang of borough-tyrants *are* cruel;" but, if we go on to speak of their notoriously brutal ignorance, we must not say: " The gang of borough-tyrants *is* cruel, and *are* also notoriously as ignorant as brutes." We must use *is* in both places, or *are* in both places.

245. In looking for the nominative of a sentence, take care that the *relative pronoun* be not a stumbling block, for relatives have no changes to denote *number* or *person*; and, though they may some-times appear to be, of themselves, nominatives, they never can be such. " The men *who are* here: the man *who is* here; the cocks *that* crow, the cock *that crows*." Now, if the relative be the nominative, why do the verbs *change*, seeing that here is *no change in the relative*? No: the verb, in pursuit of its nominative, runs through the relatives to come at their antecedents, *men*, *man*, *cocks*, *cock*. Bishop Lowth says, however, that " the relative is the nominative when no other nominative comes between it and the verb;" and Mr. Murray has very faithfully copied this erroneous observation. " *Who is* in the house? *Who are* in the house? *Who strikes* the iron? *Who strike* the

iron? *Who was* in the street? *Who were* in the street? Now, here is, in all these instances, no other nominative between the relative and the verb; and yet the verb is continually varying. Why does it vary? Because it disregards the relative and goes and finds the antecedent, and accommodates its number to that antecedent. The antecedents are, in these instances, understood; "What *person is* in the house? What *persons are* in the house? What *person strikes* the iron? What *persons strike* the iron? What *person was* in the street? What *persons were* in the street?" The Bishop seems to have had a misgiving in his mind, when he gave this account of the nominative functions of the *relative*; for he adds, " the relative is of the *same person* as the antecedent: and the verb *agrees with it* accordingly." Oh, oh! But, the relative is *always the same*, and is of *any* and of *every number* and *person*. How, then, can the verb, when it makes *its changes* in number and person, be said to *agree* with the relative? Disagree, indeed, with the relative the verb cannot any more than it can with a preposition; for the relative has, like the preposition, no changes to denote cases; but, the danger is, that, in certain instances, the relative may be *taken for a nominative*, without your looking after the antecedent, which is the real nominative, and that, thus, not having the number and person of the antecedent clearly in your mind, you may give to the verb a wrong number or person. It is very seldom, that those who lay down erroneous rules furnish us with examples by the means of which we are enabled to detect the error of these rules: yet, Mr. Murray has, in the present case, done this most amply. For, in another part of his book, he has these two examples: " I am the general, *who give* the orders to-day. I am the general, *who gives* the orders to-day." Here the antecedents as well as the relatives are precisely the same; the order of the words is the same; and yet the verbs are different. *Why?* Because, in the first example, the pronoun *I* is the nominative, and, in the second, the noun *general*. The first means, " *I*, who am the general here, *give* the orders to-day." The second means, " The general, who *gives* the orders to-day, is I." Nothing can more clearly show, that the relative cannot be the nominative, and that, to consider it as a nominative must lead to error and confusion. You will observe, therefore, that, when I, in the Etymology and Syntax as relating to relative pronouns, speak of relatives *as being in the nominative case*, I mean, that they relate *to nouns or to personal pronouns, which are in that case*. The same observation applies to the other cases.

246. We are sometimes embarrassed to fix precisely on the nominative, when a sort of *addition* is made to it by words expressing persons or things that accompany it: as, "The Tyrant, with the Spy, *have* brought Peter to the block." We hesitate to determine, whether the *Tyrant* alone, is the nominative, or whether the nominative includes the Spy; and, of course, we hesitate which to employ, the *singular* or the *plural* verb; that is to say, *has* or *have*. The meaning must be our guide. If we mean, that the act has been *done* by the Tyrant *himself*, and that the spy has been a mere *involuntary* agent, then we ought to use the singular; but, if we believe, that the spy has been a *co-operator*; an *associate*; an *accomplice*; then we must use the plural of the verb. "The Tyrant, with his Proclamation, *has* produced great oppression and flagrant violations of law." *Has*, by all means, in this case; because the Letter is a mere instrument. Give the sentence a turn: "The Tyrant *has* produced great oppression and flagrant violations of the law with his Proclamation." This is good; but, the Tyrant "*has* brought Peter to the block *with* the spy," is bad. It sounds badly; and it is bad sense. It does not say what we mean it should say. "A leg of mutton, with turnips and carrots, *is* very good." If we mean to say, that a leg of mutton, when cooked with these vegetables, is good, we must use *is*; but, if we be speaking of the goodness of a leg of mutton *and* these vegetables taken all together, we must use *are*. When *with* means *along with*, *together with*, *in company with*, and the like, it is nearly the same as *and*; and then the plural verb must be used. "*He*, with his bare hand, *takes* up hot iron." Not, "he, with his bare hand, *take* up." "He, with his brothers, *are* able to do much." Not "*is* able to do much." If the pronoun be used instead of *brothers*, it will be in the objective case: "He, with *them*, are able to do much." But, this is no impediment to the including of the noun (represented by *them*) in the nominative. *With*, which is a preposition, takes the objective case after it; but, if the persons, or things, represented by the words coming after the preposition, form part of the actors in a sentence, the under-

stood nouns make part of the nominatives. "The bag, with the guineas and dollars in it, *were* stolen." For, if we say, *was* stolen, it is *possible* for us to mean, that *the bag only* was stolen. "Sobriety, with great *industry* and *talent*, *enable* a man to perform great deeds." And not *enables*: for, sobriety *alone* would not enable a man to do great things. "The borough-tyranny, with the paper-money makers, *have* produced misery and starvation." And, not *has*; for we mean that the two have *co-operated*. "Zeal, with discretion, *do* much;" and not "does much;" for, we mean, on the contrary, that it *does nothing*. It is the meaning that must determine which of the numbers we ought, in all such cases, to employ.

247. The verb *to be* sometimes comes between two nouns of different numbers. " The great evil *is* the borough-debt." In this instance there is nothing to embarrass us; because *evil* and *borough-debt* are both in the singular. But: " the great evil *is* the *taxes*," is not so clear of embarrassment. The embarrassment is the same, when there is a singular noun on one side and two or more singulars or plurals on the other side: as, " the curse of the country *is* the profligacy, the rapacity, the corruption of the law-makers, the base subserviency of the administrators of the law, and the frauds of the makers of paper-money." Now, we mean, here, that these things *constitute*, or *form*, or *make up*, a curse. We mean, that the curse *consists* of these things; and, if we *said* this, there would be no puzzling. " The evil *is* the taxes." That is, the taxes constitute the evil; but, we cannot say, " the *evil are* the taxes;" nor can we say, that " the *curse are* these things." Avoid, then, the use of the verb *to be*, in all such cases. Say, the curse of the country consists *of*, or arises *from*, or is produced *by*. Doctor Blair, in his 19th Lecture, says: "a feeble, a harsh, *or* an obscure style, *are* always faults." The *or* required the singular verb, *is*; but *faults* required *are*. If he had put *is* and *faulty*, there would have been no doubt of his being correct. But, as the sentence now stands, there is great room for doubt, and that, too, as to more than one point: for fault means *defect*, and a style, which is a *whole*, cannot well be called a *defect*, which means a want of goodness in *a part*. Feebleness, harshness, obscurity, are *faults*. But, to call the style itself, to call the *whole thing*, a *fault*, is more than the Doctor meant. The style may be

faulty, and yet it may not be a fault. The Doctor's work is faulty: but, surely, the work is not a *fault*!

248. Lest you should be, in certain instances, puzzled to find your nominative case, which, as you must now see, constitutes the main spring and regulator of every sentence, I will here point out to you some instances, wherein there is used, apparently, neither verb nor nominative. " *In general*, I dislike to drink wine." This *in general* is no more, in fact, than *one word*. It means *generally*. But, sometimes, there is a verb comes in; " generally speaking." Thus: " The borough-tyrants, generally *speaking*, are great fools as well as rogues." That is to say, " when *we* speak generally;" or, " if *we* are speaking generally;" or, " when *men*, or *people*, speak general-ly." For observe, that there *never can be* a sentence without a verb, expressed or understood, and that there *never can be* a verb without a nominative case expressed or understood.

249. Sometimes not only two or more nouns, or pronouns, may be the nominative of a sentence; but *many other words* along with them may assist in making a nominative: as, " Pitt, Rose, Steel, and their associates, giving to Walter a sum of the public money as a reward for libelling the sons of the king *was* extremely profligate and base." That is to say, this act of Pitt and his associates *was* extremely profligate and base. It is, when you come to inquire, the *act* which is the nominative, and all the other words only go to describe the origin and end of the act.

250. You must take care, that there *be* a nominative, and that it *be* clearly expressed or understood. " The Attorney General, Gibbs, whose malignity induced him to be extremely violent, and *was* listened to by the Judges." The first verb, *induced*, has a nomina-tive, namely, the *malignity* of the Attorney General, Gibbs: but the *was* has no nominative, either expressed or clearly understood; and, we cannot, therefore, tell, what or who it was that was listened to: whether the *malignity* of Gibbs, or *Gibbs himself*. It should have been, and *who*, or, and *he*, was listened to; and then we should have known, that it was Gibbs himself that was listened to. The omitting of the nominative, five hundred instances of which I could draw from Judge Blackstone and Doctor Johnson, arises very often from a desire to avoid a repetition of the noun or

pronoun; but, repetition is always to be preferred before obscurity.

251. Now, my dear James, I hope, that I have explained to you sufficiently, not only *what the nominative is*, but what are its powers in every sentence; and that I have imprinted deeply on your mind the necessity of keeping the nominative constantly in your eye. For want of doing this, Judge Blackstone has, in Book IV, Chap. 17, committed some most ludicrous errors. " Our ancient Saxon *laws* nominally punished theft with death, if above the value of twelve-pence; but the criminal was permitted to redeem *his* life by a pecuniary ransom; as among *their* German *ancestors*." What confusion is here! Whose ancestors? *Theirs*. Who are *they*? Why, the *criminal*. *Theirs*, if it relate to any thing, must relate to *laws*; and then the *laws* have *ancestors*. Then, *what* is it that was to be of above the value of twelvepence? The *death* or the *theft*? By, "*if above the* value of twelvepence," the Judge without doubt, meant, "*if the thing stolen were* above the value of twelvepence;" but he says no such thing; and the meaning of the words is, if *the death* were above the value of twelvepence. The sentence should have stood thus: "Our ancient Saxon laws nominally punished theft with death, if the thing stolen were above the value of twelvepence; but the criminals were permitted to redeem their lives by a pecuniary ransom; as amongst their German ancestors." I could quote, from the same author, hundreds of examples of similar errors; but, were there only this one to be found in a work, which is composed of matter, which was read, in the way of Lectures, by a professor of law to students in the University of Oxford, even this one ought to be sufficient to convince you of the importance of attending to the precepts, which I have given you relative to this part of our subject.

252. As to the *objective case* it has nothing to do with *verbs*; because, a noun which is not in the nominative must be in the *objective*; and because verbs do never vary their endings to make themselves *agree* with the objective. This case has been sufficiently explained under the head of *personal pronouns*, which have endings to denote it.

253. The *possessive case*, likewise, has nothing to do with verbs, only, you must take care, that you do not, in any instance, look upon it as a nominative. "The quality of the apples *were* good." No: it

must be *was*; for *quality* is the nominative and *apples* the possessive. "The want of learning, talent, and sense, *are* more visible in the two houses of parliament, than in any other part of the nation." Take care upon all such occasions. Such sentences are, as to grammatical construction, very deceiving. It should be " *is* more visible;" for *want* is the nominative; and *learning*, *talent*, and *sense*, are in the possessive. The want *of learning*, and so on.

254. You now know all about the *person* and *number* of verbs. You know the reasons upon which are founded their variations with regard to these two circumstances. Look, now, at the *conjugation* in Letter VIII, paragraph 98; and, you will see, that there remain the *Times* and *Modes* to be considered.

255. Of *Times* there is very little to be said here. All the fanciful distinctions of, *perfect*, *present*, *more past*, and *more perfect past*, and numerous others, only tend to bewilder, confuse, and disgust the learner. There can be but *three* times, the *present*, the *past*, and the *future*; and, for the expressing of these, our language provides us with words and terminations the most suitable that can possibly be conceived. In some languages, which contain no little words such as our signs, *will*, *shall*, *may*, and so on, the verbs themselves change their form in order to express what we express by the help of these signs. There are *two past times* in French, for instance: I will give you an example in order to explain this matter. " The working men every day *gave* money to the tyrants, who, in return, *gave* the working men dungeons and axes." Now here is our word *gave*, which is the passed time of the verb *to give*. It is the same word, you see, in both instances; but you will see it different in the French. "Tous les jours les ouvriers *donnoient* de l'argent aux tyrans, qui, en retour, *donnèrent* aux ouvriers des cachots et des haches." You see, that, in one place, our *gave* is translated by *donnoient*, and, in the other place, by *donnèrent*. One of these is called, in French, the *past imperfect*, and the other, the *past perfect*. This distinction is necessary in the French; but similar distinctions are wholly unnecessary in English.

256. In the Latin language, the verbs change their endings so as *to include in the verbs themselves* what we express by our auxiliary verb *to have*. And they have as many changes, or different endings, as are required to express all those various circumstances of time that

we express by, *work, worked, shall work, may work, might work, have worked, had worked, shall have worked, may have worked, might have worked*; and so on. It is, therefore, necessary for the Latins to have distinct appellations to suit these various circumstances of time, or states of an action; but, such distinction of appellations can be of no use to *us*, whose verbs never vary their endings, to express time, except the single variation from the *present* to the *past*; for, even as to the *future*, the *signs* answer our purpose. In our compound times, that is to say, such as, I *have worked* there is the verb *to have*, which becomes *had*, or *shall have*, and so on.

257. Why, then, should we perplex ourselves with a multitude of artificial distinctions, which cannot, by any possibility, be of any use in practice? These distinctions have been introduced from this cause: those who have written English Grammars, have been taught Latin; and, either unable to divest themselves of their Latin rules, or unwilling to treat with simplicity that, which, if made somewhat of a mystery, would make them appear more *learned* than the mass of the people, they have endeavoured to make our simple language turn and twist itself so as to become as complex in its principles as the Latin language is.

258. There are, however, some few remarks to be made with regard to the *times* of verbs; but, before I make them, I must speak of the *participles*. Just cast your eye again on Letter VIII, paragraphs 97 and 102. Look also at the conjugations of the verbs, *to work, to have* and *to be*, in that same letter. These *participles*, you see, with the help of *to have* and *to be*, form our *compound times*. I need not tell you, that *I was working* means the same as *I worked*, only that the former supposes that something else was going on at the same time, or that something happened at the time I was work-ing, or that, at least, there is some circumstance of action or of existence *collateral with my working*: as, "I was working *when he came*; *I was sick* while I was *working*; *it rained while* I was working; *she scolded while* I was working." I need not tell you the use of *do* and *did*; I need not say, that I *do work* is the same as, I *work*, only the former expresses the action more positively, and adds some degree of force to the assertion; and that *did work* is the same as *worked*, only the former is, in the past time, of the same use as *do* is in the

present. I need not dwell here on the uses of *will*, *shall*, *may*, *might*, *should*, *would*, *can*, *could*, and *must*: which uses, various as they are, are as well known to us all as the uses of our teeth and our noses; and to misapply which words argues, not only a deficiency in the reasoning faculties, but almost a deficiency in instinctive discrimination. I will not, my dear James, in imitation of the learned doctors, pester you with a philological examination into the origin and properties of words, with regard to the use of which, if you were to commit an error in conversation, your brother Richard, who is four years old, would instantly put you right. Of all these little words I have said quite enough before; but, when the verbs *to have* and *to be* are used *as auxiliaries to principal verbs*, and, especially when the sentences are long, errors of great consequence may be committed; and, therefore, against these it will be proper to guard you.

259. *Time* is so plain a matter; it must be so well known to us, whether it be the *present*, the *past*, or the *future* that we mean to express, that, we shall hardly say " we *work*," when we are speaking of our *having worked last year*. But you have seen, in Letter XVI, paragraph 171 (look at it again), that Doctor Blair could make a mistake in describing *the time of an action*. Doctor Blair makes use of, " it *had* been better omitted." Meaning, that it, " *would have been* better to omit it." This is a sheer vulgarism, like, " I *had* as lief be killed as enslaved." Which ought to be, " I *would* as lief." But, the most common error is, the using of the verb *to have* with the passive participle, when the *past time*, simply, of the verb ought to be used. " Mr. Speaker, I *expected*, from the former language, and positive promises of the Noble Lord and the Right Honourable the Chancellor of the Exchequer, to *have seen* the Bank paying in gold and silver." This is House-of-Commons' language. Avoid it as you would avoid all the rest of their doings. I expected *to see*, to be sure, and not to *have seen*, because the *have seen* carries *your act of seeing back beyond the period*, within which it is supposed *to have been expected to take place*. " I *expected to have ploughed* my land last *Monday*." That is to say, " I *last Monday* was in the act of expecting to have ploughed my land *before that day*." But, this is not what the writer means. He means to say, that, last Monday, or before that day, he was in the act of expecting *to plough* his land on that day. "I

called on him and *wished to have submitted* my manuscript to him."
Five hundred of such errors are to be found in Dr. Goldsmith's
works. " I wished, *then*, and *there*, *to submit* my manuscript to him."
I wished *to do* something *there*, and did not *then* wish that I had *done*
something before.

260. When you use the *active participle*, take care that the *times* be
attended to, and that you do not, by misapplication, make confusion
and nonsense. " I had not the pleasure of *hearing* his sentiments,
when I wrote that letter." It should be of *having heard*; because the
hearing must be supposed to have been wanted *previous* to the act of
writing. This word *wanted*, and the word *wanting*, are frequently
misused. " All that was *wanting* was honesty." It should be
wanted. "The Bank is weighed in the balance and found wanting,"
and not *wanted*. Found to be *wanting*, or *in want*: in want of money
to pay its notes.

261. I will not fatigue your memory with more examples relating
to the *times* of verbs. Consider well what you *mean*; what you *wish
to say*. Examine well into the true meaning of your words; and you
will never make a mistake as to the times. " *I thought to have heard*
the Noble Lord produce something like proof." No! My dear
James will never fall into the use of such senseless gabble! You
would think of *hearing* something; you would think of *to hear*, not *to
have heard*. You would be *waiting to hear*, and not, like these men,
be waiting to have heard. " *I should have liked to have been informed* of
the amount of the Exchequer Bills." A phraseology like this can be
becoming only in those Houses, where it was proposed to relieve
the distresses of the nation by setting the labourers to dig holes one
day and fill them up the next.

262. It is erroneous to confound the *past time* with the *passive
participle* of the verb. But, now, before I speak of this very common
error, let us see a little more about the *participles*. You have seen, in
Letter VIII, what the participles are: you have seen, that *working* is
the active participle, and *worked* the passive participle. We shall
speak fully of the active by-and-by. The passive participle and the
verb *to be*, or some part of that verb, make what is called the *passive
verb*. This is not a verb which, *in its origin*, differs from an active
verb, in like manner as a *neuter* verb differs from an active verb. To

sleep is neuter in its origin, and must, in all its parts, be neuter; but, every active verb *may* become a *passive verb*. The passive verb is, in fact, that state of an active verb which expresses, as we have seen above, the action as being *received*, or *endured*; and it is called *passive*, because, the *receiver* or *endurer* of the action is *passive*; that is to say, *does nothing*. " John *smites*; John is *smitten*." Thus, then, the passive verb is no other than the passive participle, used along with some part of the verb *to be*.

263. Now, then, let us see a specimen of the errors, of which I spoke at the beginning of the last paragraph. When the verb is *regular*, there can be no error of this sort; because the past time and the passive participle are written in the same manner: as " John *worked*; John *is worked*." But, when the verb is *irregular*, and when the past time and the passive participle are written in a manner different from each other, there is room for error, and error is often committed: " John *smote*; John *is smote*." This is gross. It offends the ear; but, when a company, consisting of men who have been enabled, by the favour of the late William Pitt, to plunder and insult the people, meet under the name of a Pitt Club, to celebrate the birth-day of that corrupt and cruel minister, those who publish accounts of their festivities, always tell us, that such and such toasts *were drank*; instead of *drunk*. I *drank* at my dinner to-day; but the milk and water, which I *drank*, *were drunk* by me. In the lists of irregular verbs, in Letter VIII, the differences between the past times and the passive participles are all clearly shown. You often hear people say, and see them write, " We *have spoke*; it *was spoke* in my hearing;" but, " we *have came*; *was did*," are just as correct.

264. *Done* is the passive participle of *to do*, and it is very often misused. This *done* is frequently a very great offender against Grammar. *To do* is the *act of doing*. We often see people write: " I *did* not speak, yesterday, so well as I wished to have *done*." Now, what is meant by the writer? He means to say, that he *did* not speak so well as he then *wished*, or was wishing, *to speak*. Therefore, the sentence should be: " I did not speak yesterday so well as I wished *to do*." That is to say, " so well as I wished to do it;" that is to say, to do, or to perform, *the act of speaking*.

265. Take great care not to be too free in your use of the verb *to*

do in any of its times or modes. It is a nice little *handy* word, and, like our oppressed *it*, it is made use of very often, when the writer is at a *loss* for what to put down. *To do* is to *act*, and, therefore, it never can, in any of its parts, supply the place of a *neuter* verb. Yet, to employ it for this purpose is very common. Dr. Blair, in his 23rd Lecture, says: " It is somewhat unfortunate, that this Number of the Spectator did not *end*, as it might very well have *done*, with the former beautiful period." That is to say, " done *it*." And, then, we ask: done what? Not the *act of ending*: because, in this case, there is *no action* at all. The verb means *to come to an end*; *to cease*; *not to go any further*. This same verb, *to end*, is, sometimes, an active verb: " I *end* my sentence;" and then the verb *to do* may supply its place: as, " I have not ended my sentence so well as I might have *done*;" that is, done *it*; that is, done, or performed, the *act of ending*. But, the Number of the Spectator was no *actor*: it was expected to *perform* nothing: it was, by the Doctor, wished to have *ceased* to proceed. "Did not *end*, as it very well might have *ended*, ..." This would have been correct; but the Doctor wished to avoid the *repetition*, and thus he fell into bad grammar. " Mr. Speaker, I do not *feel* so well satisfied as I should have *done*, if the Right Honourable Gentleman had explained the matter more fully." You constantly hear talk like this amongst those whom the Boroughs make law-givers. To *feel* satisfied is, when the satis-faction is to arise from conviction produced by fact or reasoning, a senseless expression; and, to supply its place, when it is, as in this case, a neuter verb, by *to do*, is as senseless. Done *what*? Done *the act of feeling*? "I do not *feel* so well satisfied as I should have *done*, or *executed*, or *performed*, the *act of feeling*!" What incomprehensible words! Very becoming in the creatures of corruption, but ridicu-lous in any other persons in the world.

266. But, do not misunderstand me. Do not confound *do* and *did*, as parts of a *principal* verb with the same words, as parts of an *auxiliary*. Read again Letter VIII, paragraph 111. *Do* and *did*, as *helpers*, are used with neuter as well as with active verbs; for here it is not their business to *supply the place* of other verbs, but merely to add strength to affirmations and negations, or to mark time: as, " The sentence *does end*; I *do feel* easy." But *done*, which is the

passive participle of the active verb *to do*, can never be used as an auxiliary. The want of making this distinction has led to the very common error, of which I spoke in the last paragraph, and against which I am very desirous to guard you.

267. In sentences, which are *negative*, or *interrogative*, *do* and *did* express *time*: as, " You *do* not *sleep*; *did* you not *feel*?" But they do not here *supply the place* of other verbs: they merely help; and their assistance is useful only as to the circumstance of time; for we may say; " you *sleep* not; *felt* you not?" And if, in answer to this question, I say, " I *did*," the word *feel* is understood: " I *did feel*."

268. Well, then, I think, that, as far as relates to the active verb, the passive verb, and the passive participle, enough has now been said. You have seen, too, something of the difference between the functions of the active verb and those of the *neuter*; but, there are a few remarks to be made with regard to the latter. A neuter verb cannot have a noun or pronoun in the objective case after it; for though we say, " I *dream* a *dream*," it is understood that my mind has been engaged *in* a dream. " I *live* a good *life*," means that I am living *in* a good manner. " I *walk* my horse about," means, that I *lead*, or conduct my horse in the pace called a *walk*. Nor, can a neuter verb become *passive*; because a passive verb is no other than a verb describing *an action received*, or *endured*. " The Noble Earl, on returning to town, found that the Noble Countess *was eloped* with his Grace." I read this very sentence in an English newspaper not long ago. It should be *had eloped*; for *was eloped*, means that *somebody* had *eloped the Countess*; it means, that she had *received*, or *endured*, from some actor, *the act of eloping*, whereas, she is the actress, and the act is confined to *herself*. The verb is called neuter because the action does not pass over to any thing. There are verbs which are *inactive*: such as to *sit*, to *sleep*, to *exist*. These are also neuter verbs, of course. But, *inactivity* is not necessary to the making of a verb neuter. It is sufficient, for this purpose, that the action do not pass from the actor to any object.

269. In the instance just mentioned, the error is flagrant: " *Was eloped*," is what few persons would put down in writing: yet, any body might do it *upon the authority of Doctor Johnson*: for he says, in his Dictionary, that *to elope* is an *active verb*, though, he says that it is

synonymous with *to run away*, which, in the same Dictionary, he says is a *neuter verb*. However, let those who prefer Doctor Johnson's authority to the dictates of reason and common sense, say, that " his Grace *eloped the Countess*; and, that, accordingly, the Countess *was eloped*."

270. The danger of error, in cases of this kind, arises from the circumstance of there being many verbs, which are active in one sense and neuter in another. The verb to *endure*, for instance, when it means to *support*, to *sustain*, is active: as, "I *endure pain*." But, when it means *to last*, to *continue*, it is neuter: as, "The earth *endures* from age to age." In the first sense we can say, the pain is *endured*; but, in the last, we cannot say the earth *is endured* from age to age. We say, indeed, I *am fallen*; the colt *is grown*, the trees *are rotten*, the stone *is crumbled*, the post *is mouldered*, the pitcher *is cracked;* though to grow, to rot, to crumble, to moulder, to crack, are, all of them, *neuter verbs*. But it is clearly understood here, that we mean, that the colt *is in a grown*, or *augmented state*; that the trees *are in a rotten state*; and so on: and, it is equally clear, that we could not mean, that the Countess was *in an eloped state*. " The Noble Earl found that the Countess *was gone*." This is correct, though *to go* is a neuter verb. But, *gone*, in this sense, is not the participle of the verb *to go*: it is merely an *adjective*, meaning *absent*. If we put any word after it, which gives it a verbal signification, it becomes erroneous. " He found that the Countess *was gone out of the house*." That is to say, was *absent out of the house*; and this is nonsense. It must, in this case, be, " He found, that the Countess *had gone out of the house*."

271. Much more might be said upon this part of my subject; many niceties might be stated and discussed; but, I have said quite enough on it to answer every useful purpose. Here, as every where else, take time to *think*. There is a *reason* for the right use of every word. Have your *meaning* clear in your mind; know the *meaning* of all the words you employ; and, then, you will seldom commit errors.

272. There remains to be noticed the use of the *active participle*, and then we shall have a few, and only a few, words to say upon the subject of the *Modes* of verbs. As to the active participle, paragraph 97, in Letter VIII, will have told you nearly all that is necessary. We

know well, that *I am working*, means that *I work*, and so on. There is great nicety in distinguishing the circumstances which call for the use of the one from those which call for the use of the other; but, like many other things, though very difficult to explain by words, these circumstances are perfectly well understood, and scrupulously attended to, by even the most illiterate persons. The active participle is, you know, sometimes a *noun* in its functions: as "*working* is good for our health." Here it is the *nominative* case to the verb *is*. Sometimes it is an adjective, as, " the *working* people." As a noun it may be in any of the three cases: as, *working* is good; the advantage *of working*; *I like working*." It may be in the singular, or in the plural: "The *working* of the mines: the *workings* of corruption." Of course it requires *articles* and *prepositions* as nouns require them. More need not be said about it; and, indeed, my chief purpose in mentioning the active participle in this place is to remind you, that it may be a *nominative case* in a sentence.

273. The *Modes* have been explained in Letter VIII, paragraphs 92, 93, 94, 95, and 96. Read those paragraphs again. The *infinitive mode* has, in almost all respects, the powers of a *noun*. "*To work* is good for our health." Here it is the nominative of the sentence. " To eat, to drink, and to sleep *are* necessary." It cannot become a plural; but it may be, and frequently is, in the objective case; as, " I want *to eat*." The *to* is, in some few cases, omitted, when the infinitive is the objective case: as, " *I dare write*." But, " I dare *to* write," is just as neat, and *more* proper. The *to* is omitted by the use of the *Ellipsis*; as, " I like *to* shoot, hunt, and course." But, care must be taken not to leave out the *to*, if you thereby make the *meaning doubtful*. Repetition is, sometimes, disagreeable, and tends to enfeeble language; but, it is always preferable to obscurity.

274. If you cast your eye once more on the *conjugation* of the verb *to work* in Letter VIII, you will see that I have there set down the three other Modes with all their persons, numbers, and times. The *Imperative Mode* I dispatched very quietly by a single short paragraph; and, indeed, in treating of the other two Modes, the *Indicative* and the *Subjunctive*, there is nothing to do but to point out the trifling variations that our verbs undergo in order to make them

suit their forms to the differences of *Mode*. The Indicative Mode is that manner of using the verb which is applied when we are speaking of an action without any other action being at all connected with it so as to make the one a *condition* or *consequence* of the other. " He *works* every day; he *rides* out;" and so on. But, there may be a condition or a consequence dependent on this working and riding; and, in that case, these verbs must be in the subjunctive mode; because the action they express *depends* on something else, going before, or coming after. " If he *work* every day, *he shall be paid* every day; if he *ride* out, he will not be at home by supper-time." The *s* is dropped at the end of the verbs here; and the true cause is this, that there is a *sign* understood. If filled up, the sentence would stand thus: " if he *should work*; if he *should ride* out." So that, after all, the verb has, in reality, *no change of termination to denote what is called mode*. And all the fuss, which Grammarians have made about the *potential* modes and other fanciful distinctions of the kind, only serve to puzzle and perplex the learner.

275. Verbs in general, and, indeed, all the verbs, except the verb *to be*, have always the *same form* in the *present time of the indicative* and in that of *the subjunctive*, in all the persons, save the second and third person singular. Thus we say, in the present of the indicative, *I work, we work, you work, they work*; and, in the subjunctive, the same. But, we say, in the former, *thou workest, he works*; while, in the subjunctive we say, *thou work, he work*; that is to say, thou *mayest work*, or mightest, or shouldest (and so on) work; and he *may* work, or might, or should; as the sense may require. Therefore, as to all verbs, except the verb *to be*, it is *only in these two persons* that any thing can happen to render any distinction of mode necessary. But, the verb *to be*, has more of variation than any other verb. *All other verbs* have the same form in their indicative *present time* as in their *infinitive mode*, with the trifling exception of the *st* and *s* added to the second and third person singular: as, to *have*, to *write*, to *work*, to *run*; I *have*, I *write*, I *work*, I *run*. But, the verb *to be*, becomes in its present time of the indicative; I *am*, thou *art*, he *is*, we *are*, you *are*, they *are*; which are great changes. Therefore, as the subjunctive, in all its persons, takes the infinitive of the verb without any change

at all, the verb *to be* exhibits the use of this mode most clearly; for, instead of I *am*, thou *art*, he *is*, we *are*, the subjunctive requires, I *be*, thou *be*, he *be*, we *be*: that is to say, I *may* be, or *might* be; and so on. Look now at the *conjugation* of the verb *to be*, in Letter VIII, paragraph 117; and then come back to me.

276. You see, then, that this important verb, the verb *to be*, has a form, in some of its persons, appropriated to the *subjunctive mode*. This is a matter of consequence. Distinctions, without differences in the things distinguished, are fanciful, and, at best, useless. Here is a real difference; a practical difference; a difference in the form of the word. Here is a *past time* of the subjunctive; a past time distinguished, in some of its persons, by a different manner of spelling, or writing, the word. If I *be*; if I *were*; if he *were*: and not if I *was*, if he *was*. In the case of other verbs, the past of the indicative is the same as the past of the subjunctive; that is to say, the verb is written in the same letters; but, in the case of the verb *to be*, it is otherwise. If I *worked*, if I *smote*, if I *had*. Here the verbs are the same as in, I *worked*, I *smote*, I *had*; but, in the case of the verb *to be*, we must say, in the past of the indicative, I *was*, and in that of the subjunctive, if I *were*.

277. The question, then, is this. *What are the cases*, in which we ought to use the subjunctive form? Bishop Lowth, and on his authority, Mr. Lindley Murray, have said, that *some* conjunctions have a *government* of verbs; that is to say, *make them or force them to be in the subjunctive mode*. And then these gentlemen mention particularly the conjunctions, *if*, *though*, *unless*, and, some others. But (and these gentlemen allow it) the verbs which follow these conjunctions are not *always* in the subjunctive mode; and, the using of that mode must depend, *not upon the conjunction*, but upon the sense of the whole sentence. How, then, can the conjunctions *govern* the verb? It is the sense, the meaning of the whole sentence, which must govern: and of this you will presently see clear proof. " *If* it *be* dark, do not come home. *If* eating *is* necessary to man, he ought not to be a glutton." In the first of these sentences, the matter expressed by the verb *may be* or *may not be*. There exists an *uncertainty* on the subject. And, if the sentence were filled up, it would stand thus: " If it *should be* dark, do not come home." But, in the second

sentence, there exists no such uncertainty. We know, and all the world knows, that *eating is necessary to man*. We could not fill up the sentence with *should*. And, therefore, we make use of *is*. Thus, then, the conjunction *if*, which, you see, is employed in both cases, has nothing at all to do with the government of the verb. It is the sense which governs.

278. There is a great necessity for care as to this matter; for, the meaning of what we write is very much affected, when we make use of the modes indiscriminately. Let us take an instance. " *Though* her chastity *be* right and becoming, it gives her no claim to praise; because she would be criminal, *if* she *were* not chaste." Now, by employing the subjunctive in the first member of the sentence, we leave it *uncertain* whether it be *right*, or *not*, for her to be chaste; and, by employing it, in the second, we express a *doubt as to the fact* of her chastity. We mean neither of these; and, therefore, notwithstanding that here are a *though* and an *if*, both the verbs ought to be in the indicative. " Though her chastity *is* right and becoming, it gives her no claim to praise; because, she would be criminal, *if* she *was* not chaste." Fill up with the signs. " Though her chastity *may be* right; if she *should not be* chaste:" and, then, you see, at once, what a difference there is in the meaning.

279. The subjunctive is necessarily always used where a *sign* is *left out*: as, " Take care, that *he come* to-morrow, that *you be* ready to receive him, that *he be* well received, and that *all things be* duly prepared for his entertainment." Fill up with the *signs*, and you will see the *reason* for what you write.

280. The verb *to be* is sometimes used thus: " *Were he* rich, I should not like him the better. *Were it* not dark, I would go." That is to say, *if* he *were*; *if* it *were*. " *It were* a jest indeed, to consider a set of seat-sellers and seat-buyers as a lawful legislative body. *It were* to violate every principle of morality to consider honesty as a virtue, when not to be honest is a crime which the law punishes." The *it* stands for a great deal here. "Ridiculous, indeed, would the state of our minds be, if it *were* such as to exhibit a set of seat-sellers and seat-buyers as a lawful legislative body." I mention these instances, because they appear *unaccountable*: and, I never like to slur things over. Those expressions, for the

using of which we cannot give *a reason*, ought not to be used at all.

281. As to instances, in which authors have violated the principles of Grammar, with respect to the use of the modes, I could easily fill a book much larger than this with instances of this kind from Judge Blackstone and Doctor Johnson. One only shall suffice. I take it from the Judge's first Book. " Therefore, *if* the king *purchases* lands of the nature of gavelkind, where all *the sons inherit equally*: yet, upon the king's demise, *his eldest son* shall succeed to these lands *alone*." Here is fine confusion, not to say something inclining towards high treason; for, if the king's son be to inherit these *lands alone*, he, of course, is *not to inherit the crown*. But, it is the verb *purchases*, with which we have to do at present. Now, it is very notorious, that the king *does not* purchase lands in gavelkind, nor any other lands; whereas, from the form of the verb, it is taken for granted, that he does it. It should have been, " If the king *purchase* lands;" that is to say, if *he were to purchase*, or if he *should purchase*.

282. Thus, my dear James, have I gone through all that appeared to me of importance, relating to verbs. Every part of the Letter ought to be carefully read, and its meaning ought to be well weighed in your mind; but, always recollect, that, in the using of verbs, that which requires your first and most earnest care, is the ascertaining of the *nominative* of the sentence; for, out of every hundred grammatical errors, full fifty, I believe, are committed for want of due attention as to this matter.

―――

LETTER XX.

SYNTAX, AS RELATING TO ADVERBS, PREPOSITIONS, AND CONJUNCTIONS.

283. AFTER what has been said, my dear James, on the subject of the verb, there remains little to be added. The *Adverbs*, *Prepositions*, and *Conjunctions* are all words, which never *vary their endings*.

Their uses have been sufficiently illustrated in the letters on the SYNTAX of Nouns, Pronouns, and Verbs. In a letter, which is yet to come, and which will contain specimens of *false grammar*, the misuse of many words belonging to these inferior parts of speech will be noticed; but, it would be a waste of your time to detain you by an elaborate account of that which it is, by this time, hardly possible for you not to understand.

284. Some grammarians have given *lists* of adverbs, prepositions, and conjunctions. For what *reason* I know not, seeing that they have not attempted to give lists of the words of other parts of speech. These lists must be *defective*, and, therefore, worse than no lists. To find out the meaning of single words, the *Dictionary* is the place. The business of grammar is to show the connection between words, and the manner of using words properly. The sole cause of this dwelling upon these parts of speech appears to me to have been a notion, that they would seem to be *neglected*, unless a certain number of pages of the book were allotted to each. To be sure each of them is a part of speech, as completely as the little finger is a part of the body; but, few persons will think, that, because we descant very frequently, and at great length, upon the qualities of the head and heart, we ought to do the same with regard to the qualities of the little finger.

285. I omitted in the Letter on verbs, to notice the use of the word *thing*; and I am not sorry that I did, because, by my noticing it in this concluding paragraph, the matter may make a deeper impression on your mind. *Thing* is, of course, a *noun*. A *pen* is a thing, and every animal, or creature, animate or inanimate, is a *thing*. We apply it to the representing of every creature in the universe, except to men, women, and children; and a *creature* is that which has been *created*, be it living, like a *horse*, or dead like *dirt*, or *stones*. The use of the word *thing* as far as this goes, is plainly reconcilable to reason; but, " to get drunk is a beastly *thing*." Here is neither human being, irrational animal, nor inanimate creature. Here is merely *an action*. Well, then, this action is the *thing*; for, as you have seen in Letter XIX, paragraph 273, a verb in the infinitive mode, has, in almost all respects, the functions and powers of *a noun*. " It was a most atrocious *thing* to uphold the Bank of

England in refusing to give gold for its promissory notes, and to compel the nation to submit to the wrong that it sustained from that refusal." The meaning is, that the whole of these measures, or transactions, constituted a most atrocious *deed* or *thing*.

LETTER XXI.

SPECIMENS OF FALSE GRAMMAR, TAKEN FROM THE WRITINGS OF DOCTOR JOHNSON AND FROM THOSE OF DOCTOR WATTS.

MY DEAR JAMES,

THE chief object of this Letter is to prove to you the necessity of using great care and caution in the construction of your sentences. When you see writers like Doctor Johnson and Doctor Watts committing grammatical errors, and, in some instances, making their words amount to nonsense, or, at least, making their meaning doubtful; when you see this in the author of a grammar and of a dictionary of the English Language, and in the author of a work on the subject of Logic; and when you are informed that these were two of the most learned men that England ever produced, you cannot fail to be convinced, that constant care and caution are necessary to prevent you from committing not only similar, but much greater, errors.

Another object, in the producing of these specimens, is to convince you, that a knowledge of the Latin and Greek Languages does not prevent men from writing bad English. Those Languages are, by impostors and their dupes, called, " the *learned* languages;" and those who have paid for having studied them are said to have received " a *liberal* education." These appellations are false, and, of course, they lead to false conclusions. *Learning*, as a noun, means *knowledge*, and *learned* means *knowing*, or *possessed of knowledge*. Learning is, then, to be acquired by *conception*; and, it is shown in *judgment*, in *reasoning*, and in the various modes of employing it. What, then, can *learning* have to do with any particular tongue? Good grammar, for instance, written in Welsh, or in the language of the Chipewaw Savages, is more *learned* than bad grammar written in Greek. The learning is in the *mind* and not on the *tongue*: learning consists of *ideas*, and not of the *noise* that is made by the mouth. If, for instance, the Reports, drawn up by the House of Commons, and which are compositions discovering, in every sentence, ignorance the most profound, were written in Latin, should we then call them *learned*? Should we say, that the mere change of the words from one tongue into another, made that learned which was before unlearned? As well may we say, that a falsehood written in English would have been truth if written in Latin; and as well may we say, that a certain hand-writing is a *learned* hand-writing, or, that certain sorts of ink and paper, are *learned* ink and paper, as that a language, or tongue, is a learned language, or tongue.

The cause of the use of this false appellation, " learned languages," is this, that those who teach them in England have, in consequence of their teaching, *very large estates in house and land*, which are public property, but which are now used for the sole benefit of those teachers, who are, in general, the relations or dependents of the Aristocracy. In order to give a colour of reasonableness to this species of appropriation, the languages taught by the possessors are called " the *learned* languages;" and, which appellation is, at the same time, intended to cause the mass of the people to believe, that the professors and learners of these languages are, in point of wisdom, far superior to other men; and, to establish the opinion that all but themselves are *unlearned* persons. In short, the appellation, like many others, is a trick which fraud has furnished for the purpose of guarding the snug possessors of the property against the consequences of the people's understanding the matter.

It is curious enough, that this appellation of " learned languages " is confined to the English nation, and the American, which inherits it from the English. Neither in France, in Spain, in Italy, nor in Germany, is this false and absurd appellation in use. The same motives have not existed in those countries. There the monks and other priests have plundered by open force. They had not any occasion to resort to this species of imposition. But, in England, the thing required to be glossed over. There was something or other required in that country as an apology for taking many millions a year from the public to keep men to do no apparently useful thing.

Seeing themselves unable to maintain the position, that the Latin and Greek are more " *learned* languages" than others, the impostors and their dupes tell us, that this is not what they mean. They mean, they say, not that those languages are, *in themselves*, more learned than others; but that, to possess a knowledge of them is a proof that the possessor is *a learned man*. To be sure, they do not offer us any argument in support of this assertion; while it would be easy to show, that the assertion must, in every case, be false. But, let it suffice, for this time, that we show, that the possession of the knowledge of those languages, does not prevent men from committing numerous grammatical errors when they write in their native language.

I have, for this purpose, fixed upon the writings of Doctor Johnson and of Doctor Watts; because, besides its being well known, that they were deeply skilled in Latin and Greek, it would be difficult to find two men with more *real* learning. I take also the two works, for which they are, respectively, the most celebrated: the RAMBLER of Doctor Johnson and the LOGIC of Doctor Watts. These are works of very great learning. The RAMBLER, though its general tendency is to spread a gloom over life and to damp all enterprise, private as well as public, displays a vast fund of knowledge in the science of morals; and the LOGIC, though the religious zeal of its pious, sincere, and benevolent author, has led him into the very great error of taking his examples of self-evident propositions from amongst those, many of which, great numbers of men think not to be self-evident, is a work wherein profound learning is conveyed in a style the most simple and in a manner the most pleasing. It is impossible to believe that the Logic was not revised with great care; and, as to the Rambler, the biographer of its author tells us, that the Doctor made *six thousand* corrections and alterations before the work was printed in volumes.

The RAMBLER is in *Numbers*; therefore, at the end of each extract from it, I shall put the letter R. and the *Number*. The LOGIC is divided into *Parts* and *Chapters*. At the end of each extract from it, I shall put L.; and then add the *Part* and *Chapter*. I shall range the extracts under the names of the Parts of Speech, to which the erroneous words respectively belong.

ARTICLES.

" I invited her to spend a day in viewing *a* seat *and gardens*."—R. No. 34.

" For all our speculative acquaintance with things should be made subservient to our better conduct in *the* civil and religious life."—L. Introduction.

The indefinite Article, *a*, cannot, you know, be put before a *plural* noun. We cannot say *a gardens*; but, this is, in fact, said in the above extract. It should have been "a seat and *its* gardens." "*Civil and religious life*" are general and indefinite in the second extract. The article, therefore, was unnecessary, and is improperly used. Look back at the use of Articles, Letter IV.

NOUNS.

" Among the innumerable historical *authors*, *who* fill every nation with accounts of *their ancestors*, or undertake to transmit to futurity the events of *their* own time, the greater part, when fashion and novelty have ceased to recommend *them*, are of no *other use* than *chronological memorials*, which necessity may sometimes require to be consulted."—R. No. 122.

This is all confusion. *Whose* ancestors? The *nation's* ancestors are meant; but, the *author's* are expressed. The two *theirs* and the *them* clearly apply to the *same noun*. How easily all this confusion would have been avoided by considering the nation as a singular, and saying *its ancestors*! In the latter part of the sentence, the *authors* are called *chronological memorials*; and though we may, in some cases, use the word *author* for *author's work*; yet, in a case like this, where we are speaking of the authors as *actors*, we cannot take such a liberty.

" Each of these *classes* of the human race has desires, fears, and conversation, peculiar to *itself*; cares which *another* cannot feel, and pleasures which *he* cannot partake."—R. No. 160.

The noun of multitude, *classes*, being preceded by *each*, has the pronoun, *itself*, properly put after it; but the *he* does not correspond with these. It should have been *it*. With regard to these two extracts, see paragraph 181.

" His great ambition was to shoot flying, and he, therefore, spent whole days in the woods, pursuing *game*, which, before he was near enough to see *them*, his approach frighted away."—R. No. 66.

Game is not a noun of *multitude*, like *Mob*, or *House of Commons*. There are different *games*, or *pastimes*; but, this word, as applied to the describing of *wild animals*, has no plural; and, therefore, cannot have a plural pronoun to stand for it.

" The obvious duties of piety towards God and love towards man, with the *governments* of all our inclinations and passions."—L. Part 4.

This plural is so clearly wrong, that I need not show *why* it is wrong.

" And by *this mean* they will better judge what to choose."—L. Part 4.

Mean, as a noun, is never used in the *singular*. It, like some other words, has broken loose from all principle and rule. By universal acquiescence, it is become always a plural, whether used with singular or plural pronouns and articles, or not. Doctor Watts, in other instances, says, *this means*.

" Having delayed to buy a coach myself, till I should have the lady's *opinion*, for *whose* use it was intended."—R. No. 34.

We know that *whose* relates to *lady*, according to the Doctor's meaning; but, grammatically, it does not. It relates to *opinion*. It should have been " the opinion of *the lady*, for whose use." See Syntax of Nouns, Letter XVI, paragraphs 170 and 171.

PRONOUNS.

" Had *the opinion* of my censurers been unanimous, *it* might have overset my resolution; but, since I find *them* at variance with each other, I can, without scruple, neglect *them*, and follow my own imagination."—R. No. 23.

You see, the Doctor has, in the last member of the sentence, the *censurers* in his eye, and he forgets his nominative, *opinion*. It is the opinion that was *not unanimous*, and not the censurers who were not unanimous; for, they were unanimous in censuring.

" *They* that frequent the chambers of the sick, will generally find the sharpest pains, and most stubborn maladies, among *them whom* confidence in the force of nature formerly betrayed *to* negligence or irregularity; and that superfluity of strength, which was at once *their* boast and their *snare*, has often, in the end, no other effect, than that it continues *them* long in impotence and anguish."—R. No. 38.

The *They* and the first *them* ought to be *those*; the *to* ought to be *into*. The two *theirs* and the last *them* are not absolutely faulty, but they do not clearly enough relate to their antecedent.

" METISSA brought with her an old maid, recommended by her mother, *who* taught *her* all the arts of domestick management, and was, on every occasion, her chief agent and directress. *They* soon invented one reason or other to quarrel with all my servants, and either prevailed on me to turn *them* away, or treated *them* so ill, that *they* left me of themselves, *and always supplied their places* with some brought from my wife's family.—R. No. 35.

Here is perfect confusion and pell-mell! *Which* of the two, the *old maid* or the *mother*, was it that taught the arts of domestick management? And which of the two was taught, *Metissa* or the *old maid*? " *They* soon invented." Who are *they*? Are there two, or all the three? And, *who* supplied the places of the servants? The meaning of the *words* clearly is, that *the servants themselves supplied the places*. It is very rarely that we meet with so bad a sentence as this.

" I shall not trouble you with a history of the stratagems practised upon my judgment, or the allurements tried upon my heart, which, if you have, in any part of your life, been acquainted with *rural politicks*, you will easily conceive. *Their* arts have no great variety, *they think* nothing worth *their care* but money."—R. No. 35.

" Their arts:" but *whose* arts? There is no antecedent, except " *rural politicks*;" and, thus, all this last sentence is perfect nonsense.

" But the fear of not being approved as just *copiers* of human manners is not the most important concern that *an author* of this sort ought to have before *him*."—R. No. 4.

An author cannot be said to fear not to be approved as just *copiers*. The word *author* ought to have been in the plural and *him* ought to have been *them*.

" The wit, whose vivacity condemns slower tongues to silence; the *scholar*, whose knowledge allows *no man* to think *he* instructs *him*."—R. No. 188.

Which of the two is allowed? The *scholar*, or the *no man*? Which of the two does *he* relate to? Which of the two does the *him* relate to? By a little *reflection* we may come at the Doctor's meaning; but, if we must stop to discover the grammatical meaning of an author's *words*, how are we to imbibe the science which he would teach us?

" The state of the possessor of humble virtues, to the affecter of great excellences, is that of a small cottage of stone, to the palace raised with ice by the empress of Russia; *it* was for a time, splendid and luminous, but the first sunshine melted it to nothing."—R. No. 21.

Which, instead of *it*, would have made clear that which is now dubious; for *it* may relate to *cottage* as well as to *palace*; or it may relate to *state*.

" The *love of retirement* has, in all ages, adhered closely to those minds, which have been most enlarged by knowledge, or elevated by genius. Those who enjoyed *every thing* generally supposed to confer happiness, have been forced to seek *it* in the shades of privacy."—R. No. 7.

To seek *what*? The *love of retirement*, or *every thing*? The Doctor means *happiness*, but his *words* do not mean it.

" Yet there is a certain race of men, *that* make it their duty to hinder the reception of every work of learning or genius, *who* stand as sentinels in the avenues of fame, and value themselves upon giving ignorance and envy the first notice of *a prey*."—R. No. 3.

That, or *who*, may, as we have seen, be the relative of a noun, which is the name of a rational being or beings; but *both* cannot be used, as applicable to the *same noun* in the same sentence. Nor is " *a prey* " proper. *Prey* has *no plural*. It is like *fat, meat, grease, garbage*, and many other words of that description.

" For, among all the *animals*, upon *which* nature has impressed *deformity* and *horror*, there was none *whom* he durst not encounter rather than a beetle."—R. No. 126.

Here are *whom* and *which* used as the relatives to the *same noun*; and, besides, we know, that *whom* can, in no case, be a relative to irrational creatures, and, in this case, the author is speaking of such creatures only. " *Horror* " is not a thing that can be impressed upon another thing so as to be seen. Horror is a *feeling of the mind*; for, though we say, " horror was *visible on his countenance*," we clearly mean, that, the outward *signs* of horror were visible. We cannot *see* horror as we can *deformity*. It should have been " *deformity* and *hideousness*."

" To cull from the mass of *mankind* those individuals, upon *which* the attention ought to be most employed."—R. No. 4.

The antecedent belongs to *rational* beings, and, therefore, the *which* should have been *whom*.

" This determination led me to Metissa, the daughter of Chrysophilus, *whose person* was at least without deformity."—R. No. 35.

The person of *which* of the two? Not of the old Papa, to be sure; and yet this is what the *words* mean.

" To persuade *them who* are entering the world, that all are equally vicious, is not to awaken judgment."—R. No. 119.

Those persons, who are entering the world, and not any *particular* persons of whom we have already been speaking. We cannot say, *them persons*; and, therefore, this sentence is incorrect.

" Of these pretenders it is fit to distinguish *those who* endeavour to deceive from *them who* are deceived."—R. No. 189.

" I have, therefore, given a place to what may not be useless *to them whose* chief ambition is to please."—R. No. 34.

The *thems* in these two sentences should be *those*. But, *them who are deceived* has another sort of error attached to it, for the *who*, remember, is not, of itself, a *nominative*. The antecedent, as you have seen, must be taken into view. This antecedent, must be, *the persons*, understood; and then we have *them persons are deceived*.

" Reason, as to the power and principles *of it*, is the common gift of God to man."—L. Introduction.

The *it* may relate to *power* as well as to *reason*. Therefore, it would have been better to say, " Reason, as to *its* power and principles;" for if clearness is always necessary, how necessary must it be in the teaching of Logic?

" All the prudence that *any man* exerts in *his* common concerns of life."—L. Introduction.

Any man means, here, the same as *men in general*, and the concerns mean, the concerns common to men in general; and, therefore, the article *the* should have been used instead of the pronoun *his*.

" It gives pain to the mind and memory, and exposes the unskilful *hearer* to mingle the superior and inferior particulars together; it leads *them* into a thick wood instead of open day-light, and places *them* in a labyrinth instead of a plain path."—L. Part 4, Chap. 2.

The *grammar* is clearly bad; and the *rhetoric* is not quite free from fault. *Labyrinth* is the opposite of *plain path*, but *open day-light* is not the opposite of a *thick wood*. *Open plain* would have been better than *open day-light*; for open day-light may exist along with a thick wood.

VERBS.

" There are many things which we every day see others unable to perform, and, perhaps, have even miscarried ourselves in attempting; and yet *can* hardly *allow* to be difficult."—R. No. 122.

This sentence has in it one of the greatest of faults. The *nominative case* of *can allow* is not clear to us. This is a manner *too elliptical*. " *We* can hardly allow *them*," is what was meant.

" A man's eagerness *to do that good, to which he is not called*, will betray him into crimes."—R. No. 8.

The man is not called *to the good*, but to *do* the good. It is not my business, at this time, to criticise the *opinions* of Doctor Johnson; but, I cannot refrain from just remarking upon this sentence, that it contains the sum total of *passive obedience* and *non-resistance*. It condemns all disinterested zeal and every thing worthy of the name of patriotism.

" We are not compelled to toil through half a folio to be convinced, that the author has *broke* his promise."—R. No. 1.

" The muses, when they *sung* before the throne of Jupiter."—R. No. 3.

In the first of these, the *passed time* is used where the *passive participle* ought to have been used; and, in the second, the *passive participle* is used in place of the *passed time*. *Broken* and *sang* were the proper words.

" My purpose *was*, after ten months more spent in commerce, to *have withdrawn* my wealth to a safer country."—R. No. 120.

The *purpose* was *present*, and therefore, it *was* his purpose *to withdraw* his wealth.

" A man may, by great attention, persuade others, that he really has the qualities that he presumes to boast; but, the hour *will come* when he *should* exert them, and then whatever he *enjoyed in praise*, he *must suffer in reproach*."—R. No. 20.

Here is a complete confounding of times. Instead of *should*, it should be *ought to*; and instead of *enjoyed*, it should be, *may have enjoyed*. The sense is bad too; for, how can a man *suffer in reproach what he has enjoyed in praise*?

" He had taught himself to think riches more valuable than nature *designed them*, and to expect from them . . . . "—R. No. 120.

" I could prudently *adventure an inseparable union*."—R. No. 119.

" I propose *to endeavour the entertainment* of my countrymen."—R. No. 1.

" He may, by *attending the remarks*, which every paper will produce."—R. No. 1.

In each of these four sentences, a *neuter* verb has the powers of an *active* verb given to it. " Designed them *to be*; adventure *on*; endeavour to *entertain*; attending *to*." To *design a thing* is to draw it; to *attend a thing* is to wait on it. No case occurs to me at present, wherein *adventure* and *endeavour* can be active verbs; but, at any rate, they ought not to have assumed the active office here.

" *I was not condemned* in my youth to solitude, either by indigence or deformity, *nor passed* the earlier part of life without the flattery of courtship."—R. No. 119.

The verb cannot change from a *neuter* to an *active* without a repetition of the *nominative*. It should have been, nor *did I pass*; or, nor *passed I*.

" ANTHEA *was content* to call a coach, and *crossed* the brook."—R. No. 34.

It should be " *she* crossed the brook."

" He will be welcomed with ardour, *unless* he *destroys* those recommendations by his faults."—R. No. 160.

"*If* he *thinks* his own judgment not sufficiently enlightened, he may rectify his opinions."—R. No. 1.

" *If* he *finds*, with all his industry, and all his artifices, that he cannot deserve regard, or cannot obtain it, he may let the design fall."—R. No. 1.

The subjunctive mode ought to be used in all these three sentences. In the first, the meaning is, " unless he *should* destroy." In the two last, the Doctor is speaking of his own undertaking; and, he means, " the author, if he *should* think, if he *should* find; may then rectify his opinions; may then let fall his design." He therefore, should have written, " if he *think*; if he *find*."

" Follow solid argument wherever *it leads* you."—L. Part 3.

Wherever it *may lead* you, or *shall lead* you, is meant: and, therefore, the subjunctive mode was necessary. It should have been: " wherever it *lead* you."

" See, therefore, that your general definitions, or descriptions *are* as accurate as the nature of the thing will bear: see that your general divisions and distributions *be* just and exact: see that your axioms *be* sufficiently evident: see that your principles *be* well drawn."—L. Part 4.

All these members are correct, except the first where the verb is put in the indicative mode instead of the *Subjunctive*. All the four have the same turn: they are all in the same mode, or manner: they should, therefore, all have had the verb in the *same form*. They all required the subjunctive form.

PARTICIPLES.

" Or, it is *the drawing* a conclusion, which was before either unknown, or dark."—L. Introduction.

It should be, " the drawing *of* a conclusion;" for, in this case, the active participle becomes a *noun*. " The *act* of drawing " is meant, and clearly understood; and we cannot say, " the *act drawing* a conclusion." When the article comes before, there must be the preposition after the participle. To omit the preposition in such cases is an error very common, and, therefore, I have noticed the error in this instance, in order to put you on your guard.

ADVERBS.

" For thoughts are *only* criminal, when they are first *chosen*, and then voluntarily *continued*."—R. No. 8.

The *station*, or *place*, of the adverb is a great matter. The Doctor does not mean here that which his words mean. He means that " thoughts are criminal, *only when* they are first chosen and then voluntarily continued." As the words stand, they mean, that " thoughts are *nothing else*, or *nothing more*, than criminal," in the case supposed. But, here are other words not very properly used. I should like to be informed *how* a thought *can* be *chosen*; how that is possible: and also, *how* we can *continue* a thought, or how we can *discontinue* a thought at our *will*. The science here is so very profound that we cannot see the bottom of it. Swift says, " whatever is *dark* is *deep*. Stir a puddle, and it is deeper than a well." Doctor Johnson deals too much in this kind of profundity.

" I have heard *how* some criticks have been pacified with claret and a supper, and others laid asleep with the soft notes of flattery."—R. No. 1.

How means the *manner in which*. As, " *how* do you do?" That is, " *in what manner* do you carry yourself on." But, the Doctor tells us here, in other words, the precise *manner in which* the Criticks were pacified. The *how*, therefore, should have been *that*.

" I hope *not much* to tire those whom I shall not happen to please."—R. No. 1.

He did not mean that he did not *much hope*, but that he hoped not to *tire much*. " I hope I shall not *much tire* those whom I may not happen to please." This was what he meant; but he does not say it.

" And it is a good judgment alone can dictate how *far* to proceed in it and *when* to stop."—L. Part 4.

Doctor Watts is speaking here of writing. In such a case an adverb, like how *far*, expressive of longitudinal space, introduces a *rhetorical figure*; for the plain meaning is, that judgment will dictate *how much to write on it*, and not *how far to proceed in it*. The figure, however, is very proper, and much better than the literal words.

But, when a figure is *begun* it should be carried on throughout, which is not the case here; for, the Doctor begins with a figure of longitudinal space, and ends with a figure of *time*. It should have been, " *where* to stop." Or, " How *long* to proceed in it and *when* to stop." To tell a man *how far* he is to go into the Western Countries of America, and *when* he is to stop, is a very different thing from telling him *how far* he is to go and *where* he is to stop. I have dwelt, thus, on this distinction, for the purpose of putting you on the watch, and guarding you against confounding figures. The less you use them the better, till you understand more about them.

" *In searching out* matters of *fact* in times past or in distant places, in which case moral *evidence* is sufficient, and moral *certainty* is the utmost that can be attained, *here* we derive a greater assurance of the *truth of it* by a number of persons, or multitude of circumstances concurring to bear *witness to it*."—L. Part 3.

The Adverb, *here*, is wholly unnecessary, and it does harm. But, what shall we say of the *of it* and the *to it*? What is the *antecedent* of the *it*? Is *matters of fact* the antecedent? Then *them*, and not *it*, should have been the pronoun. Is *evidence* the antecedent? Then we have circumstances bearing *witness* to *evidence*! Is *certainty* the antecedent? Then we have the *truth* of *certainty*! Mind, my dear James, this sentence is taken from a treatise on Logic! How necessary is it, then, for *you* to be careful in the use of this powerful little word, *it*!

PREPOSITIONS.

" And, as this practice is a commodious subject of raillery *to* the gay, and of declamation *to* the serious, it has been ridiculed . . . . . ."—R. No. 123.

With the gay; for, *to* the gay, means, that the raillery is *addressed* to the gay, which was not the author's meaning.

" When I was deliberating *to* what new qualifications I should aspire."—R. No. 123.

With regard to, it ought to have been; for, we cannot *deliberate a thing*, nor *to a thing*.

" If I am not commended *for* the beauty of my works, I may hope to be pardoned *for* their brevity."—R. No. 1.

We may commend him *for* the beauty of his works; and we may *pardon* him *for* their brevity, if we deem the brevity *a fault*; but, this is not what he means.   He means, that, at any rate, he shall have the *merit* of brevity; " If I am not commended for the beauty of my works, I may hope to be pardoned *on account of* their brevity."   This was what the Doctor meant; but this would have marred a little the *antithesis*: it would have unsettled a little the balance of that *see-saw*, in which Dr. Johnson so much delighted, and which, falling into the hands of novel-writers and of Members of Parliament, has, by moving unencumbered with any of the Doctor's reason or sense, lulled so many thousands asleep!   Doctor Johnson created a race of writers and speakers.   " Mr. Speaker, that the state of the nation is very critical, all men must allow; but, that it is wholly desperate, few men will believe."   When you hear, or see, a sentence like this, be sure that the person who speaks, or writes it, has been reading Doctor Johnson, or some of his imitators.   But, observe, these imitators go no further than the frame of the sentences.   They, in general, take special care not to imitate the Doctor in knowledge and reasoning.

I have now lying on the table before me forty-eight errors in the use, or omission, of Prepositions, by Doctor Watts.   I will notice but two of them; the first is an error of commission, the second, of omission.

" When we would prove the importance of any scriptural doctrine, or duty, the multitude of texts, wherein it is *repeated* and *inculcated upon* the reader, seems naturally to instruct us, that it is a matter of greater importance than other things which are but slightly or singly mentioned in the Bible."—L. Part 3.

The words *repeated* and *inculcated* both apply to *upon*; but we cannot *repeat* a thing *upon* a reader, and the words, here used, mean this.   When several verbs, or participles, are joined together by a copulative conjunction, care must be taken that the act described by each verb, or participle, be such as can be performed by the agent, and, performed, too, in the manner, or for the purpose, or on the object, designated by the other words of the sentence.

The other instance of error in the use of the *Preposition* occurs on the very *first sentence* in the treatise on Logic.

" Logic is the art of using reason well in our enquiries after truth, and the communication of it to others."—L. Introduction.

The meaning of the *words* is this: that " *Logic* is the art of using reason well in our enquiries after truth, and *is also* the communication of it to others." To be sure we do *understand* that it means, that " Logic is the art of using reason well in our enquiries after truth, and *in* the communication of it to others;" but, surely, in a case like this, no room for doubt or for hesitation ought to have been left. Nor is " using reason *well* " a well-chosen phrase. It *may* mean *treating* it *well*: not *ill-treating* it. " Using reason *properly*," or " *employing* reason well," would have been better. For, observe, Doctor Watts is here giving a *definition* of the thing of which he was about to treat; and he is speaking to persons unacquainted with that thing; for as to those acquainted with it no definition was wanted. Clearness, every where desirable, was here absolutely necessary.

CONJUNCTIONS.

" *As*, notwithstanding all that wit, or malice, or pride, or prudence will be able to suggest, men and women must, at last, pass their lives together, I have never, *therefore*, thought those writers friends to human happiness, who endeavour to excite in either sex a general contempt or suspicion of the other."—R. No. 149.

The *as* is unnecessary; or the *therefore* is unnecessary.

" But the happy historian has no *other* labour *than of gathering* what tradition pours down before him."—R. No. 122.

" Some have advanced without due attention to the consequences of this notion, that certain virtues have their correspondent faults, and *therefore*, *to exhibit* either apart is to deviate from probability."—R. No. 4.

" But, if the power of example is so great as to take possession of the memory by a kind of violence, care ought to be taken, *that*, when the choice is unrestrained, the best examples only should be exhibited; and *that which* is likely to operate so strongly, should not be mischievous or uncertain in its effects."—R. No. 4.

It should have been, in the first of these extracts, " than *that* of gathering:" in the second, " and *that* therefore:" in the third, " and that *that* which is likely." If the Doctor wished to avoid putting *two thats* close together, he should have chosen another form for his sentence. The *that which* is a *relative*, and the conjunction *that* was required to go before it.

" It is, therefore, an useful thing, when we have a fundamental truth, we *use* the synthetick method to explain it."—L. P. 4.

It should have been, *that* we use.

WRONG PLACING OF WORDS.

Of all the faults to be found in writing this is one of the most common, and, perhaps, it leads to the greatest number of misconceptions. All the words may be the proper words to be used upon the occasion; and yet, by a *misplacing* of a part of them, the meaning may be wholly destroyed; and, even made to be the contrary of what it ought to be.

" I asked the question with no other intention than to set the gentleman free from the necessity of silence, and give him an opportunity of mingling on equal terms with a polite assembly, from which, *however uneasy*, he could not then *escape, by a kind introduction* of the only subject on which I believed him to be able to speak with propriety."—R. No. 126.

This is a very bad sentence altogether. "*However uneasy*" applies to *assembly*, and not to *gentleman*. Only observe how easily this might have been avoided. " From which *he, however uneasy*, could not then escape." After this we have " *he* could not then *escape, by a kind introduction*." We know what is *meant*; but the Doctor, with all his *commas*, leaves the sentence confused. Let us see whether we cannot make it clear. " I asked the question with no other intention, than by a kind introduction of the only subject on which I believed him to be able to speak with propriety, to set the gentleman free from the necessity of silence, and to give him an opportunity of mingling on equal terms with a polite assembly, from which he, however uneasy, could not then escape."

" Reason is the glory of human nature, and one of the chief eminences whereby we are raised above our fellow-creatures, the brutes, *in this lower world*."—L. Introduction.

I before showed an error in the *first* sentence of Doctor Watts's work. This is the *second* sentence. The words, "*in this lower world*" are not words *misplaced* only: they are wholly *unnecessary*, and they do great harm; for, they do these two things; first, they imply, *that there are brutes in the higher world*; and, second, they excite a doubt, *whether we are raised above those brutes.*

I might, my dear James, greatly extend the number of my extracts from both these authors; but, here, I trust, are enough. I had noted down about two hundred errors in Doctor Johnson's Lives of the Poets; but, afterwards, perceiving that he had revised and corrected the RAMBLER with *extraordinary care*, I chose to make my extracts from that work rather than from the Lives of the Poets.

DOUBLE NEGATIVE AND ELLIPSIS.

Before I dismiss the Specimens of Bad Grammar, I will just take, from TULL, a sentence, which contains striking instances of the misapplication of *Negatives* and of the *Ellipsis*. In our language *two negatives*, applied to the *same verb*, or to the same words of any sort, amount to an *affirmative*: as "Do *not* give him *none* of your money." That is to say, "*give him some* of your money;" though the contrary is meant. It should be, "*do not* give him *any* of your money." Errors, as to this matter, occur most frequently, when the sentence is formed in such a manner as to lead the writer out of sight and out of sound of the first negative before he comes to the point where he thinks a second is required: as, "*Neither* Richard nor Peter, as I have been informed, and, indeed, as it has been proved to me, *never* gave James authority to write to me." You see, it ought to be *ever*. But, in this case, as in most others, there requires nothing more than a little *thought*. You see clearly, that two negatives, applied to the same verb, destroy the negative effect of each other. "I will *not never* write." This is the contrary of "I *will never* write."

The Ellipsis, of which I spoke in Letter XIX, paragraph 227, ought to be used with *great care*. Read that paragraph again; and then attend to the following sentence of Mr. TULL, which I select in order to show you, that very fine thoughts may be greatly marred by too free an use of the Ellipsis.

"It is strange, that *no* author should *never* have written fully of the fabrick of ploughs! Men of *greatest* learning have spent their time in contriving instruments to measure the immense distance of the stars, and in finding out the dimensions and *even weight* of the planets. They think it more eligible to study the art of ploughing the sea with ships, than of tilling the land with ploughs. They bestow the utmost of their skill, learnedly to pervert the natural use of all the elements *for destruction* of their own species by the bloody art of war; and some waste their whole lives in studying how to arm death with new engines of horror, *and inventing* an infinite variety of slaughter; but think it beneath men of learning (who only are capable of doing it) to employ their learned labours in the invention of new, or *even improving* the old, instruments *for increasing of bread.*"

You see the *never* ought to be *ever.* You see, that the *the* is left out before the word *greatest*, and again before *weight*, and, in this last-mentioned instance, the leaving of it out makes the words mean the " *even* weight;" that is to say, not the *odd* weight; instead of " *even the* weight," as the author meant. The conjunction *that* is left out before "*of tilling*;" before *destruction* the article *the* is again omitted: *in* is left out before *inventing* and also before *improving*; and, at the close, *the* is left out before *increasing.* To see so fine a sentence marred in this way is, I hope, quite enough to guard you against the frequent commission of similar errors.

━━━━

LETTER XXII.

ERRORS AND NONSENSE IN A KING'S SPEECH.

My Dear James,

In my first Letter I observed to you, that, to the functions of Statesmen and Legislators was due the highest respect which could be shown by man to any thing human; but I, at the same time, observed, that, as the degree and quality of our respect rose in proportion to the influence which the different branches of knowledge naturally had in the affairs and on the conditions of men; so, in cases of imperfection in knowledge, or of negligence in the application of it, or of its perversion to bad purposes, all the feelings opposite to that of respect, rose in the same proportion; and, to one of these cases I have now to direct your attention.

The Speeches of the King are read by him to the Parliament. They are composed by his Ministers, or select Councillors. They are documents of great importance, treating of none but weighty matters; they are always styled *Most Gracious*, and are heard and answered with the most profound respect.

The persons, who settle upon what shall be the topicks of these Speeches, and who draw the Speeches up, are a Lord High Chancellor, a First Lord of the Treasury, a Lord President of the Council, three Secretaries of State, a First Lord of the Admiralty, a Master General of the Ordnance, a Chancellor of the Exchequer, and, perhaps, one or two besides. These persons are called, when spoken of in a body, *the Ministry*. They are all Members of the King's constitutional Council, called the *Privy Council*, without whose assent the King can issue no Proclamation nor any Order affecting the people. This Council, Judge Blackstone, taking the words of Coke, calls " a *noble*, *honourable* and *reverend* assembly." So that, in the Ministry, who are *selected* from the persons who compose this assembly, the nation has a right to expect something very near to perfection in point of judgment and of practical talent.

How destitute of judgment and of practical talent these persons have been, in the capacity of Statesmen and of Legislators, the present miserable and perilous state of England amply demonstrates; and I am now about to show you, that they are equally destitute in the capacity of writers. There is some poet, who says;

> " Of all the arts, in which the learn'd excel,
> The first in rank is that of *writing well*."

And, though a man may possess great knowledge, as a Statesman and as a Legislator, without being able to perform what this poet would call *writing well*; yet, surely, we have a right to expect in *a Minister* the capacity of being able to write *grammatically*; the capacity of putting his own meaning clearly down upon paper. But, in the composing of a King's Speech, it is not *one* man, but *nine* men, whose judgment and practical talent are employed. A King's Speech is, too, a very *short* piece of writing. The topicks are all distinct. Very little is said upon each. There is no reasoning. It is all plain matter of fact, or of simple observation. The thing is done with all the advantages of abundant time for examination and re-examination. Each of the Ministers has a copy of the Speech to read, to examine, and to observe upon; and, when no one has any thing left to suggest in the way of alteration or improvement, the Speech is agreed to, and put into the mouth of the King.

Surely, therefore, if, in any human effort, perfection can be expected, we have a right to expect it in a King's Speech. You shall now see, then, what pretty stuff is put together, and delivered to the Parliament, under the name of King's Speeches.

The Speech, which I am about to examine, is, indeed, a Speech of the Regent; but, I might take any other of these Speeches. I choose this particular Speech, because the subjects of it are familiar in America as well as in England. It was spoken on the 8th of November, 1814. I shall take a sentence at a time, in order to avoid confusion.

"My Lords and Gentlemen, It is with *deep regret* that *I am again obliged* to announce the continuance of His Majesty's lamented indisposition."

Even in this short sentence there is something *equivocal*; for, it *may* be, that the Prince's regret arises from *his being obliged* to announce, and not from the thing announced. If he had said: " With deep regret I announce," or, " I announce with deep regret," there would have been nothing equivocal. And, in a composition like this, all ought to be as clear as the pebbled brook.

" It *would have given* me great satisfaction to *have been enabled* to *communicate* to you the *termination* of the war between this country and the United States of America."

The double compound times of the verbs, in the first part of the sentence, make the words mean, that it would, *before the Prince came to the House*, have given him great satisfaction *to be enabled* to communicate; whereas, he meant, " it would, *now*, have given me great satisfaction *to be enabled* to communicate." In the latter part of the sentence we have a little nonsense. What does *termination*

mean? It means, in this case, *end*, or *conclusion*; and, thus, the
Prince wished to *communicate an end* to the wise men, by whom he
was surrounded! To communicate is *to impart* to another any thing
that we have in our possession or within our power. And so, the
Prince wished to *impart* the *end* to the Noble Lords and Honourable
Gentlemen. He might wish to impart, or communicate, the *news*,
or the *intelligence*, of the *end*; but, he could not *communicate* the *end
itself*. What should we say, if some one were to tell us, that an
Officer had arrived, and *brought* home the termination of a battle
and *carried* it to Carlton House and *communicated* it to the Prince?
We should laugh at our informant's ignorance of grammar, though
we should understand what he meant. And, shall we, then, be so
partial and so unjust as to reverence in King's Councillors that
which we should laugh at in one of our neighbours? To act thus
would be, my dear Son, a base abandonment of our *reason*, which is,
to use the words of Doctor Watts, the common gift of God to man.

"*Although* this war originated in *the most* unprovoked aggression
on the part of *the Government* of the United States, and was
calculated to promote the designs of the common enemy of Europe
against the rights and independence of *all other nations*, I never have
ceased to entertain a sincere desire to bring it to a conclusion *on just
and honourable terms*."

The *the most* would lead us to suppose, that there had been *more
than one* aggression, and that the war originated in the most
unprovoked *of them*; whereas the Prince's meaning was, that the
aggression was *an* unprovoked one, unprovoked in the superlative
degree; and that, therefore, it was *a most* unprovoked aggression.
The words *all other nations*, may mean all nations *except England*; or,
all nations *out of Europe*; or, all nations *other than the United States*;
or, all nations *except the enemy's own nation*. Guess you which of
these is the meaning: I confess that I am wholly unable to
determine the question. But, what does the close of the sentence
mean, when taken into view with the *although* at the beginning?
Does the Prince mean, that he would be justified in wanting to
make peace on *unjust* and *dishonourable* terms *because* the enemy had
been the aggressor? He might, indeed, wish to make it on terms
dishonourable, and even disgraceful, to the enemy; but, could he

possibly wish to make it on *unjust* terms? Does he mean, that an aggression, however wicked and unprovoked, would give him *a right* to do *injustice*? Yet if he do not mean this, what does he mean? Perhaps (for there is no certainty) he may mean, that he wishes to bring the war to a conclusion as soon as he can get *just and honourable terms from the enemy*: but, then, what is he to do with the *Although*? Let us try this. " I am ready," say you, " to make peace, *if you will give me just terms, although you are the aggressor*." To be sure you are, *whether I be the aggressor or not*! All that you can possibly have the face to ask of me is *justice*; and, therefore, why do you connect your wish for peace with this *although*? Either you mean, that my aggression gives you *a right* to demand of me *more than justice*, or you talk *nonsense*. Nor must we overlook the word " *Government*," which is introduced here. In the sentence before, the Prince wished to communicate the end of the war between " *this country* and the *United States*;" but, in this sentence we are at war with " the *Government* of the United States." This was a poor trick of sophistry, and as such we will let it pass with only observing, that such low trickery is not very becoming in men selected from " a *noble, honourable* and *reverend* assembly."

" I am *still* engaged in negociations for this purpose."

That is the purpose of bringing the war to a conclusion. A very good purpose; but, why *still*? He had not told his nobles and his boroughmen that he *had been* engaged in negociations. Even this short, simple sentence could not be made without fault.

" The success of them must, however, depend on my *disposition* being met *with* corresponding *sentiments* on the part of the enemy."

Now, suppose I were to say, " my waggon was met *with* Mr. Tredwell's coach." Would you not think, that somebody had met the waggon and coach both going together the same way? To be sure you would. But, if I were to say, my waggon was met *by* Mr. Tredwell's coach, you would think, that they had approached each other from different spots. And, therefore, the Prince should have said, " met *by*." This sentence, however, short as it happily is, is too long to be content with one error. *Disposition*, in this sense of the word, means, *state*, or *bent*, or *temper*, *of mind*; and the word *sentiments* means, *thoughts*, or *opinions*. So, here we have a *temper of mind* met by *thoughts*. Thoughts may correspond, or agree with, a temper of mind; but, how are they *to meet it?* If the Prince had said, " my disposition being met *by* a corresponding disposition on the part of the enemy," he would have uttered plain and dignified language.

" The operations of his Majesty's forces by *sea and land in the* Chesapeake, in the course of the present year, have been attended with the most brilliant and successful results."

Were there only the *bad placing* of the different members of this sentence, the fault would be sufficient. But, we do not know, whether the Prince means *operations by sea and land*, or *forces by sea and land.*

" The flotilla of *the enemy* in the Patuxent has been destroyed. The signal defeat of *their* land forces enabled a detachment of his Majesty's army to take possession of the city of Washington; and the spirit of enterprise, which has characterized all the movements in that quarter, has produced on the inhabitants a *deep* and *sensible* impression of the calamities of a war in which they have been so wantonly involved."

Enemy is not a noun of multitude, like *gang*, or *House of Commons*, or *den of thieves*; and, therefore, when used in the singular, must have singular pronouns and verbs to agree with it. *Their*, in the second of these sentences, should have been *his*. A *sensible* impression is an impression *felt*; a *deep* impression is one *more felt*. Therefore, it was " a *sensible* and *deep* impression." But, indeed, *sensible* had no business there; for, an impression that is deep *must be* sensible. What would you think of a man who should say: " I have not only been *stabbed*, but my *skin has been cut*"? Why, you would think, to be sure, that he must be a man selected from the noble, honourable, and reverend assembly at Whitehall.

" The expedition directed from Halifax to the Northern coast of the United States, has terminated in a manner *not less satisfactory.*"

Than *what?* The Prince has told us, before this, of nothing that has terminated satisfactorily. He has talked of a brilliant result, and of an impression made on the inhabitants; but of *no termination* has he talked; nor has he said a word about *satisfaction*. We must always take care how we use, in one sentence, words which refer to any thing said in former sentences.

" The successful *course* of this operation *has been followed* by the *immediate* submission of the extensive and important district east of the Ponobscot *river to his Majesty's arms*."

This sentence is a disgrace even to a Ministry with a JENKINSON at its head. What do they mean by *a course* being *followed* by a *submission*? And then, " *has been* followed by the *immediate* submission." One would think, that some French emigrant priest was employed to write this speech. He, indeed, would say, " *a été* suivie par la soumission immédiate." But, when we make use of any word, like *immediate*, which carries us back to the time and scene of action, we must use the *past time* of the verb, and say, " *was* followed by the *immediate* submission." That is to say, *was then* followed by the *then* immediate; and not, has *now* been followed by the *then* immediate submission. The close of this sentence exhibits a fine instance of want of skill in *the placing* of the parts of a sentence. Could these noble and reverend persons find no place but the *end* for " *to his Majesty's arms?*" There was, but they could not see it, a place made on purpose, after the word *submission*.

It is unnecessary, my dear James, for me to proceed further with an exposure of the bad grammar and the nonsense of this speech. There is not, in the whole speech, one single sentence that is free from error. Nor, will you be at all surprised at this, if ever you should hear these persons uttering their *own* speeches in those places, which, when you were a naughty little boy, you used to call " the *Thieves' Houses*." If you should ever hear them there, stammering and repeating and putting forth their nonsense, your wonder will be, not that they wrote a King's Speech so badly, but that they contrived to put upon paper sentences sufficiently grammatical to enable us to guess at the meaning.

LETTER XXIII.

ON PUTTING SENTENCES TOGETHER, AND ON FIGURATIVE LANGUAGE.

My Dear James,

I have now done with the subject of grammar, which, as you know, teaches us to use *words* in a proper manner. But, though you now, I hope, understand how to avoid error in the forming of sentences, I think it right not to conclude my instructions without saying a few words upon the subject of *adding sentence to sentence*, and on the subject of *figurative language*.

Language is made use of for one of three purposes; namely, to *inform*, to *convince*, or to *persuade*. The first, requiring merely the talent of telling what we know, is a matter of little difficulty. The second demands *reasoning*. The third, besides reasoning, demands all the aid that we can obtain from the use of figures of speech, or, as they are sometimes called, *figures of rhetorick*, which last word means, the power of persuasion.

Whatever may be the purpose, for which we use language, it seldom can happen that we do not stand in need of more than one sentence; and, therefore, others must be added. There is no precise *rule*; there can be no precise rule, with regard to the manner of doing this. When we have said one thing, we must add another; and so on, until we have said all that we have to say. But, we ought to take care, and great care, that, if any words in a sentence relate, in any way, to words that have *gone before*, we make these words correspond grammatically with those foregoing words; an instance of the want of which care you have seen in paragraph 178.

The *order* of the matter will be, in almost all cases, that of your thoughts. Sit down *to write what you have thought*, and not *to think what you shall write*. Use the first words that occur to you, and never attempt to *alter a thought*; for, that which has come of itself into your mind is likely to pass into that of another more readily and with more effect than any thing which you can, by reflection, invent.

Never stop to *make choice of words*. Put down your thought in words just as they come.   Follow the order which your thought will point out; and it will push you on to get it upon the paper as quickly and as clearly as possible.

Thoughts come much faster than we can put them upon paper. They produce one another; and, this order of their coming is, in almost every case, the best possible order that they can have on paper: yet, if you have several in your mind, rising above each other in point of force, the most forcible will naturally come the last upon paper.

Mr. Lindley Murray gives *rules* about *long sentences* and *short sentences* and about *a due mixture* of long and short; and, he also gives rules about the *letters* that sentences should *begin* with and the *syllables* that they should *end* with.   Such rules might be very well if we were to *sing* our writing; but, when the use of writing is to *inform*, to *convince*, or to *persuade*, what can it have to do with such rules?

There are certain *connecting words*, which it is of importance to use properly: such as *therefore*, which means *for that cause, for that reason*.   We must take care, when we use such words, that there is *occasion for using them*.   We must take care, that when we use *but*, or *for*, or any other connecting word, the sense of our sentences requires such words to be used; for, if such words be improperly used, they throw all into confusion.   You have seen the shameful effect of an *although* in the King's Speech, which I noticed in my last Letter.   The adverbs *when, then, while, now, there*, and some others, are connecting words, and not used in their strictly literal sense.   For example: " Well, *then*, I will not do it."   *Then*, in its literal sense, means *at that time*, or *in that time*: as, " I was in America *then*."   But, " Well, *then*," means, " Well, *if that be so*," or " *let that be so*," or " *in that case*."   You have only to accustom yourself a little to reflect on the *meaning* of these words; for that will soon teach you never to employ them improperly.

A writing, or written discourse, is generally broken into *paragraphs*.   When a new paragraph should begin, the nature of your thoughts must tell you.   The propriety of it will be pointed out to you by the difference between the thoughts which are coming and those which have gone before.   It is impossible to frame rules for regulating such divisions.   When a man divides his work into Parts,

Books, Chapters, and Sections, he makes the divisions according to that which the matter has taken in his mind; and, when he comes to write, he has no other guide for the distribution of his matter into sentences and paragraphs.

Never write about any matter that you do not well understand. If you clearly understand all about your matter, you will never want thoughts, and thoughts instantly become words.

One of the greatest of all faults in writing and in speaking is this; the using of many words to *say little*. In order to guard yourself against this fault, inquire what is the *substance*, or *amount*, of what you have said. Take a long speech of some talking Lord, and put down upon paper what the *amount* of it is. You will mostly find, that the amount is very small: but, at any rate, when you get it, you will then be able to examine it, and to tell what it is worth. A very few examinations of this sort will so frighten you, that you will be for ever after upon your guard against *talking a great deal* and *saying little*.

Figurative language is very fine when properly employed; but, figures of rhetorick are edge tools and two-edge tools too. Take care how you touch them! They are called *figures*, because they represent other things than the words in their literal meaning stand for. For instance: " The tyrants oppress and starve the people. The people would live amidst abundance, if those *cormorants* did not devour the fruit of their labour." I shall only observe to you upon this subject, that, if you use figures of rhetoric, you ought to take care that they do not make nonsense of what you say; nor excite the ridicule of those to whom you write. Mr. Murray, in an address to his students, tells them, that he is about to offer them some advice with regard to " their future *walks* in the *paths* of literature." Now, though a man may *take a walk* along *a path*, a walk means also *the ground* laid out in a certain shape, and such a walk *is wider than a path*. He, in another part of this address, tells them, that they are in "the *morning* of life, and that that is the *season* for exertion." The morning, my dear James, is *not a season*. The *year*, indeed, has seasons, but the *day* has none. If he had said the *spring* of life, then he might have added the *season* of exertion. I told you they were *edge-tools*. Beware of them.

I am now, my dear son, arrived at the last paragraph of my treatise, and I hope, that when you arrive at it, you will understand grammar sufficiently to enable you to write without committing frequent and glaring errors. I shall now leave you, for about four months, to read and write English: to practise what you have now been taught. At the end of those four months, I shall have prepared a Grammar to teach you the *French Language*, which language I hope to hear you speak, and to see you write, well, at the end of one year from this time. With English and French on your tongue and in your pen, you have a resource, not only greatly valuable in itself, but a resource that you can be deprived of by none of those changes and chances which deprive men of pecuniary possessions, and which, in some cases, make the purse-proud man of yesterday a crawling sycophant to-day. Health, without which life is not worth having, you will hardly fail to secure by early rising, exercise, sobriety, and abstemiousness as to food. Happiness, or misery, is in the *mind*. It is the mind that lives; and the length of life ought to be measured by the number and importance of our ideas; and not by the number of our days. Never, therefore, esteem men merely on account of their riches or their station. Respect goodness, find it where you may. Honour talent wherever you behold it unassociated with vice; but, honour it most when accompanied with exertion, and especially when exerted in the cause of truth and justice; and, above all things, hold it in honour, when it steps forward to protect defenceless innocence against the attacks of powerful guilt.

[*Cobbett's edition of 1819 ended here.   The Six Lessons that follow were added for the first time in the edition of 1823.*]

LETTER XXIV.

SIX LESSONS, INTENDED TO PREVENT STATESMEN FROM USING FALSE GRAMMAR, AND FROM WRITING IN AN AWKWARD MANNER.

———

Harpenden, Hertfordshire, 23 *June*, 1822.

My Dear James,

In my first Letter I observed, that it was of the greatest importance that *Statesmen*, above all others, should be able to *write well*. It happens, however, but too frequently, that that which should be, in this case as well as in others, is not; sufficient proof of which you will find in the remarks which I am now about to make. The *Letter to Tierney*, a thing which I foresaw would become of great and lasting importance; a thing to which I knew I should frequently have to recur with satisfaction, I wrote on the anniversary of the day, on which, in the year 1810, I was sentenced to be imprisoned for two years, to pay a fine of a thousand pounds, and to be held in bonds of five thousand pounds for seven years, for having, publicly and in print, expressed my indignation at the flogging of English Local-Militia men in the town of *Ely*, under a guard of German soldiers. I thought of this at a time when I saw those events approaching which I was certain would, by fulfilling my predictions, bring me a compensation for the unmerited sufferings and insults heaped upon me with so unsparing a hand. For writing the present little work, I select the anniversary of a day which your excellent conduct makes me regard as amongst the most blessed in the calendar. Who but myself can imagine what I felt, when I left you behind me at New York! Let this tell my persecutors, that *you* have made me more than amends for all the losses, all the fatigues, all the dangers, and all the anxieties attending that *exile* of which their baseness and injustice were the cause.

The bad writing, on which I am about to remark, I do not pretend to look on as the *cause* of the present public calamities, or of any part of them; but, it is a proof of a *deficiency in that sort of talent*, which appears to me to be necessary in men intrusted with great affairs. He who writes badly thinks badly. Confusedness in words can proceed from nothing but confusedness in the thoughts which give rise to them. These things may be of trifling importance when the actors move in private life; but, when the happiness of millions of men is at stake, they are of importance not easily to be described.

The pieces of writing that I am about to comment on I deem *bad writing*, and, as you will see, the writing may be bad, though there may be no *grammatical* error in it. The best writing is that which is best calculated to secure the object of the writer; and the worst, that which is the least likely to effect that purpose. But, it is not in this extended sense of the words that I am now going to consider any writing. I am merely about to give specimens of badly-written papers, as a warning to the Statesmen of the present day; and as proofs, in addition to those which you have already seen, that we ought not to conclude that a man has great abilities, merely because he receives great sums of the public money.

The specimens that I shall give consist of papers that relate to measures and events of the very first importance. The first is the Speech of the Speaker of the House of Commons to the Regent, at the close of the first Session of 1819, during which Mr. Peel's, or the Cash-Payment Bill had been passed: the second is the Answer of the Regent to that Speech: the first is the work of the House; the second that of the Ministry.

In Letter XII I gave the reasons why we had a right to expect perfection in writings of this description. I there described the persons to whom the business of writing king's speeches belongs. The Speaker of the House of Commons is to be taken as the man of the greatest talent in that House. He is called the " First Commoner of England." Figure to yourself, then, the King on his throne, in the House of Lords; the Lords standing in their robes; the Commons coming to the bar, with their Speaker at their head, gorgeously attired, with the mace held beside him; figure this scene to yourself, and you will almost think it sedition and blasphemy to suppose it possible, that the Speech made to the King, or that his Majesty's Answer, both prepared and written down long before-hand, should be any thing short of perfection. Follow me, then, my dear Son, through this Letter; and you will see, that we are not to judge of men's talents by the dresses they wear, by the offices they fill, or by the power they possess.

After these two Papers I shall take some Papers written by *Lord Castlereagh*, by the *Duke of Wellington*, and by the *Marquis Wellesley*. These are three of those persons who have, of late years, made the greatest figure in our affairs with foreign nations. The transactions, which have been committed to their management, have been such as were hardly ever exceeded in point of magnitude, whether we look at the transactions themselves or at their natural consequences. How much more fit than other men they were to be thus confided in; how much more fit to have the interest and honour of a great nation committed to their hands, you will be able to judge when you shall have read my remarks on those of their Papers to which I have here alluded.

In the making of my comments, I shall insert the several papers, a paragraph, or two, or more, at a time; and I shall *number* the paragraphs for the purpose of more easy reference.

LESSON I.

Remarks on the Speech of the Speaker of the House of Commons to the Prince Regent, which Speech was made at the close of the first Session of 1819, *during which Session Peel's Bill was passed.*

" May it please your Royal Highness,

1. We, his Majesty's faithful Commons of the United Kingdom of Great Britain and Ireland in Parliament assembled, attend your Royal Highness with our concluding Bill of Supply.

2. The subjects which have occupied our attention have been more numerous, more *various* and more important *than are* usually submitted to the consideration of Parliament in *the same* Session."

It is difficult to say what is meant, in Paragraph No. 2, by the word *various*. The Speaker had already said, that the *subjects* were more *numerous* which was quite enough; for they necessarily *differed* from each other, or they were one and the same; and, therefore, the word *various* can, in this place, have no meaning at all, unless it mean, that the subjects were *variegated* in themselves, which would be only one degree above sheer nonsense.

Next come the " *than are* " without a nominative case. Chambermaids, indeed, write in this way, and, in such a case, " the dear unintelligible scrawl " is, as the young rake says in the play, " ten thousand times more *charming* " than correct writing; but, from a Speaker in his robes, we might have expected " than *those which* are usually submitted."

And, what does the Speaker mean by " in *the same* Session "? He *may* mean " in *one and* the same Session;" but, what business had the word *same* there at all? Could he not have said, " during *one* Session, or during a *single* Session?"

3. " Upon many of these subjects we have been engaged in long and unwearied *examinations*; but such *has* been the pressure of other business, and particularly of that which ordinarily belongs to a first Session of Parliament—and such the *magnitude* and *intricacy* of many of *those inquiries*, that the limits of the present Session have not allowed of bringing them to a close."

There is bad taste, at least, in using the word *examinations* in one part of the sentence, and the word *inquiries* in the other part, especially as the pronoun *those* was used in the latter case. The verb " *has* " agrees in number with the noun " *pressure*;" but the Speaker, notwithstanding the aid of his wig, was not able to perceive, that the same verb did not agree in number with the nouns " magnitude *and* intricacy." " Such *has* been the pressure, and such *have* been the magnitude *and* intricacy."

4. " But, Sir, of those measures which we have completed, the most *prominent*, the most important, and, as we trust, in their consequences, the most *beneficial* to the public, are the measures which have grown out of the *consideration* of the present *state of the country*—*both in its* currency and *its* finances."

There is not here any positive error in grammar; but, there is something a great deal worse; namely, unintelligible words. The epithet " *prominent* " was wholly unnecessary, and only served to inflate the sentence. It would have been prudent not to anticipate, in so marked a manner, *beneficial consequences* from Peel's Bill; but, what are we to understand from the latter part of the sentence? Here are measures *growing out* of *the* consideration of *the state* of the

country, *in* its currency and finances. What! *The state* of the
country *in its* currency? Or, is it *the consideration* in its currency?
And, what had the word *both* to do there at all? The Speaker
meaned, that the measures had grown out of, or, which would have
been much more dignified, had been the result of *a* consideration of
the present state of the country, with regard to its currency as well
as with regard to its finances.

5. " Early, Sir, in the present Session, we *instituted* an inquiry *into* the
effects produced *on the* exchanges with foreign countries, *and the* state of
the circulating medium, by the restriction on payments in cash *by* the Bank.
This inquiry was *most anxiously* and *most deliberately* conducted, and *in its
result* led to the *conclusion*, that it was most desirable, quickly, but with due
precautions, to return to our ancient and *healthful* state of currency:—*That*,
whatever *might* have been the expediency of the Acts for the suspension of
payments of cash at the different periods at which they were enacted, (and
doubtless they *were expedient*), whilst the country was involved in the most
expensive contest that ever weighed down the finances of any country—still
that, the necessity for the continuance of these Acts having *ceased*, it became
us with *as little delay as possible* (avoiding carefully the *convulsion* of *too rapid a
transition*) to return to our ancient system; and that, if at any period, and
under any circumstances, this return could be effected without national
inconvenience, it was *at the present*, when this mighty nation, with a proud
retrospect of the past, *after having* made the greatest efforts, and achieved
the noblest objects, was *now reposing* in a confident, and, as we *fondly* hope,
a well-founded expectation of a *sound* and *lasting* peace."

Here, at the beginning of this long and most confused paragraph,
are two sentences, perfect rivals in all respects: each has 37 words
in it; each has 3 blunders; and the one is just as obscure as the
other. To " *institute* " is to *settle*, to *fix*, to *erect*, to *establish*; and not
to *set about* or *undertake*, which was what was done here. If I were to
tell you, that I have *instituted* an inquiry into the qualities of the
Speaker's speech, you would, though I am your father, be almost
warranted in calling me an egregious coxcomb. But, what are we to
make of the " *and the* " further on? Does the Speaker mean, that
they instituted (since he will have it so) an inquiry *into the state* of the
circulating medium, or into the *effects produced on the* circulating
medium by the cash suspension? I defy any man living to say which

of the two is meaned by his *words*. And, then we come to, " *by* the Bank;" and here the only possible meaning of the words is, that the *restriction* was *imposed by the Bank*; whereas the Speaker means, the restriction on payments made *at* the Bank. If *at*, instead of *by*, had happened to drop out of the wig, this part of the sentence would have been free from error.

As to the second sentence in this paragraph, No. 5, I may first observe on the incongruity of the Speaker's two superlative adverbs. *Anxiously* means *with inquietude*, and *deliberately* means *coolly, slowly, warily*, and the like. The first implies a *disturbed*, the latter a *tranquil*, state of the mind; and a mixture of these it was, it appears, that produced Peel's Bill; this mixture it was, which, " *in its result*, LED to the *conclusion*;" that is to say, the result *led* to the *result*; result being conclusion, and conclusion being result. But, *tautology* is, you see, a favourite with this son of the Archbishop of Canterbury, more proofs of which you have yet to witness. And, why must the king be compelled to hear the phrase " *healthful* state of currency," threadbare as it had long before been worn by HORNER and all his tribe of coxcombs of the Edinburgh Review? Would not " *our ancient currency* " have answered every purpose? And would it not have better become the lips of a person in the high station of Speaker of the House of Commons?

The remaining part of this paragraph is such a mass of confusion, that one hardly knows where, or how to begin upon it. The " *That* " after the *colon* and the *dash*, seems to connect it with what has gone before; and yet, what connection is there? Immediately after this " *That*," begins a *parenthetical phrase*, which is interrupted by *a parenthesis*, and then the parenthetical phrase goes on again till it comes to a *dash*, after which you come to the words that join themselves to the first " *That*." These words are, " still *that*." Then, on goes the parenthetical phrase again till you come to, " *it became us*." Then comes more parenthetical matter and another parenthesis; and, then comes, " *to return to our ancient system*." Take out all the parenthetical matter, and the paragraph will stand thus: " That it was desirable to return to our ancient and healthful state of currency:—*that*—still *that*, it became us to return to our ancient system."

But, only think of saying "whatever *might* have been the expediency of the acts," and then to make a parenthesis directly afterwards for the express purpose of positively asserting that they "*were expedient*"! Only think of the necessity for the continuance of the acts having *ceased*, and of its being becoming in the parliament to return to cash payments *as soon as possible*, and yet that a *convulsion was to* be apprehended from a *too rapid* transition; that is to say, from returning to cash payments *sooner* than *possible*!

After this comes a doubt whether the thing can be done at all; for, we are told, that the parliament, in its wisdom, concluded, that, if "*at any period* this return could be effected without *national inconvenience*, it *was* at the *present*." And then follows that piece of sublime nonsense about the nation's *reposing* in the *fond* (that is, *foolish*) hope of, not only a *lasting*, but also a *sound*, peace. A *lasting* peace would have been enough for a common man; but, the son of an Archbishop must have it *sound* as well as lasting, or else he would not give a farthing for it.

6. "In considering, Sir, the state of our finances, and in minutely comparing our income with our expenditure, it appeared to us, that the excess of our income was not *fairly adequate for the purposes* to which it was *applicable*—the gradual reduction of the national debt.

7. It appeared to us, that *a clear available surplus of* at least five millions ought to be set apart for that object.

8. This, Sir, has been effected by the *additional imposition* of three millions of taxes."

The word "*fairly*," in Paragraph No. 6, is a redundancy; it is mere *slang*. "Adequate *for*" ought to be "adequate *to*;" and "*applicable*" is *inapplicable* to the case; for the money was *applicable* to *any purpose*. It should have been, "the purpose (and not the *purposes*) for which it was *intended*;" or, "the purpose to which it was intended to be *applied*."

The 7th Paragraph is a heap of redundant Treasury-slang. Here we have *surplus*; that is to say, an *over*-quantity; but this is not enough for the Speaker, who must have it *clear* also; and not only clear, but *available*; and, then he must have it *set apart* into the bargain! Leave out all the words in *italicks*, and put *purpose* instead of *object*, at the end; and then you have something like common sense as to the words; but still foolish enough as to the political view of the matter.

Even the 8th Paragraph, a simple sentence of thirteen words, could not be free from fault. What does the Speaker mean by an " *additional* imposition"? Did he imagine, that the king would be fool enough to believe, that the parliament had *imposed* three millions of taxes without making an *addition* to former impositions? How was the imposition to be *other* than "additional"? Why, therefore, cram in this word?

9. " Sir, in adopting this course, his Majesty's faithful Commons did not *conceal from themselves*, that *they* were calling upon the nation for a great exertion; but well knowing that *honour*, and *character*, and *independence*, have at all times been the *first* and dearest objects of the hearts of Englishmen, *we felt assured*, that there was no difficulty that the country would not encounter, and no pressure to which she would not willingly and cheerfully submit, to enable her to maintain, *pure*, and *unimpaired*, that which *has* never yet been *shaken* or *sullied*—her public credit *and* her *national good*-faith."

This is a sentence which might challenge the world. Here is, in a small compass, almost every fault that writing can have. The phrase " *conceal from themselves* " is an importation from France, and from one of the worst manufactories, too. What is national " *honour* " but national " *character* "? In what do they differ? And what had " *independence* " to do in a case where the subject was the means of paying a debt? Here are *three* things named as the " *first* " objects of Englishmen's hearts. Which was the " *first* " of the three? Or were they the *first three*? To " *feel* assured " is another French phrase. In the former part of the sentence, the parliament are a *they*: in the latter part they are a *we*. But, it is the *figures of rhetorick*, which are the great beauties here. First it is *Englishmen*, who have such a high sense of *honour* and *character* and *independence*. Next it is the *country*. And next the country becomes a *she*; and, in her character of female, will submit to any " *pressure* " to enable her to "*maintain*" her *purity*; though scarcely any body but the sons of Archbishops ever talk about *maintaining* purity, most people thinking that, in such a case, *preserving* is better. Here, however, we have *pure* and *unimpaired*. Now, *pure* applies to things liable to receive *stains* and *adulterations*; *unimpaired*, to things liable to be *undermined*, *dilapidated*, *demolished*, or *worn out*. So the Speaker, in order to make sure of his mark, takes them *both*, and says, that the thing which he is about to name, " has never yet been *shaken* or *sullied*!" But, what is this fine thing after all? Gad! there are *two* things; namely, "Public Credit *and* National Good-Faith." So that, leaving the word *good* to go to the long account of redundancy, here is another instance of vulgarly false grammar; for the two nouns, joined by the conjunction, required the verb *have* instead of *has*.

10. " Thus, Sir, I have *endeavoured*, *shortly*, and I am aware *how imperfectly*, to *notice* the various duties which have devolved upon us, *in* one of the longest and most arduous Sessions *in the Records* of Parliament.

11. The Bill, Sir, which it is my duty to present to your Royal Highness, is entitled, 'An Act for applying certain *monies* therein mentioned for the Service of the year 1819, and for further appropriating the supplies granted in this Session of Parliament.' To which, with all humility, we pray his Majesty's Royal Assent."

Even here, in these common-place sentences, there must be something stupidly illiterate. The Speaker does not mean that his " *endeavour* " was " *shortly* " made, or made in a *short manner*; but, that his *notice* was made in a short manner; and, therefore, it ought to have been, " *to notice shortly*;" if *shortly* it must be; but, surely, phraseology less grovelling might have been used on such an occasion. " *In* the longest session," and " *in* the records of Parliament," are colloquial, low, and incorrect into the bargain; and, as for " *monies* " in the last paragraph, the very sound of the word sends the mind to Change Alley, and conjures up before it all the noisy herd of bulls and bears.

There is, indeed, one phrase in this whole speech (that in which the Speaker acknowledges the imperfectness of the manner in which he has performed his task) which would receive our approbation; but the tenor of the speech, the at once flippant and pompous tone of it, the self-conceit that is manifest from the beginning to the end, forbid us to give him credit for sincerity when he confesses his deficiencies, and tell us that the confession is one of those clumsy traps so often used with the hope of catching unmerited applause.

LESSON II.

Remarks on the Speech, which the Prince Regent made to the Parliament, on the occasion when the above Speech of the Speaker was made.

" MY LORDS AND GENTLEMEN,

12. It is with great regret that I *am again obliged to* announce to you the continuance of his Majesty's lamented indisposition.

13. I cannot close this Session of Parliament without expressing the satisfaction that I have derived from the zeal and assiduity with which you have applied yourselves to the several important objects which have come under your consideration.

14. Your patient and laborious *investigation* of the state of the *circulation and currency* of the kingdom demands my warmest acknowledgments; and I entertain a confident expectation that the measures *adopted*, as the result of *this inquiry*, will be productive of the most beneficial consequences."

The phrase pointed out by italicks, in the 12th Paragraph is *ambiguous*; and, as it is wholly superfluous, it has no business there. The 13th Paragraph (for a wonder!) is free from fault; but, in the 14th why does the king make *two* of the " *circulation* and *currency* "? He means, doubtless, to speak of the thing, or things, in use as *money*. This was the *currency*; and what, then, was the " *circulation* "? It is not only useless to employ words in this way: it is a great deal worse; for it creates a confusion of ideas in the mind of the reader.

" *Investigation* and *inquiry* " come nearly to each other in meaning; but, when the word " *this*," which had a direct application to what had gone before, was used, the word *investigation* ought to have followed it, and not the word *inquiry*; it being always a mark of great affectation and of false taste, when pains are taken to seek for synonymous words in order to avoid a repetition of sound. The device is *seen through*, and the littleness of mind exposed.

The *fine* word " *adopted* " is not nearly so good as the plain word *taken* would have been. The parliament did *not adopt* the measures in question: they were their *own*: of their own invention: and, if I were here writing remarks on the measures, instead of remarks on the language in which they were spoken of, we might have a hearty laugh at the "*confident expectation*," which the king entertained of the "*most beneficial consequences*" of those measures, which were certainly the most foolish and mischievous ever taken by any parliament, or by any legislative assembly in the world.

"Gentlemen of the House of Commons,

15. I thank you for the supplies which you have granted for the service of the present year.

16. I sincerely regret that the necessity should have existed of making any additions to the burdens of the people; but I anticipate the most important permanent advantages from the *effort* which you have thus made *for* meeting at once all the financial difficulties of the country; and I derive *much satisfaction* from the belief, that the means which you have devised for this purpose are calculated to press as lightly *as possible* on *all classes* of the community as could be expected when so great an effort was to be made."

Nobody, I presume, but kings say an "effort *for* meeting." Others say, that they make an effort *to* meet. And, nobody that I ever heard of before, except *bill-brokers*, talk about *meeting* money demands. One cannot help admiring the satisfaction, nay, the "*much satisfaction*," that the king derived from the belief, that the new taxes would press as *lightly as possible* on *all classes* of the community. I do not like to call this vulgar nonsense, because, though written by the Ministers, it is spoken by the king. But, *what is it?* The additional load *must fall upon somebody*; upon some *class or classes*: and, where, then, was the sense of expressing "*much satisfaction*" that they would fall lightly on all classes? The words, "*as possible*," which come after *lightly*, do nothing more than make an addition to the confusion of ideas.

" My Lords and Gentlemen,

17. I *continue* to receive from Foreign Powers *the strongest* assurances of their friendly disposition towards this country.

18. I have observed with great concern the attempts which have recently been made in some of the manufacturing districts, to take advantage of circumstances of local distress, to excite a spirit of disaffection to the institutions *and* Government of the Country. No object can be nearer my heart than to promote the *welfare* and *prosperity* of all classes of his Majesty's Subjects; but this cannot be effected without the maintenance of public order and tranquillity.

19. You may rely, therefore, upon my *firm* determination to employ, for

this purpose, the powers entrusted to me by law; and I have no doubt that, on your return to your several counties, you will use your utmost endeavours, in co-operating with the Magistracy, to defeat the machinations of those whose *projects*, if successful, could only aggravate the evils which *it professed* to remedy; and who, under the pretence of Reform, have *really* no *other* object *but* the subversion of our happy Constitution."

Weak minds, feeble writers and speakers, delight in *superlatives*. They have big sound in them, and give the appearance of *force*; but, they very often betray those who use them into absurdities. The king, as in Paragraph No. 17, might *continue* to receive *strong* assurances; but, how could he receive " *the strongest* " more than *once*?

In the 18th Paragraph we have " welfare *and* prosperity." I, for my part, shall be content with either (the two being the same thing), and, if I find, from the acts of the government, reason to believe that one is really sought for, I shall care little about the other.

I am, however, I must confess, not greatly encouraged to hope for this, when I immediately afterwards hear of a " *firm* determination " to employ " *powers*," the nature of which is but too well understood. " *Determination* " can, in grammar, receive no additional force from having " *firm* " placed before it; but, in political interpretation, the use of this word cannot fail to be looked upon as evincing a little more of *eagerness* than one could wish to see apparent in such a case.

In these speeches, nouns, verbs, adjectives, and adverbs generally go, like crows and ravens, in pairs. Hence we have, in the 18th Paragraph, "the *institutions* and *government*" of the country. Now, though there *may* be *institutions* of the country, which do not form a part of its *government*; the government is, at any rate, *amongst* the country's institutions. If every institution do not form a part of the government, the government certainly forms a part of the institutions. But, as the old woman said of her goose and gander, these words have been *a couple* for so many, many years, that it would be a sin to part them just at the last.

The gross grammatical errors in the latter part of the last Paragraph, where the singular pronoun, *it*, represents the plural noun *projects*, and the verb *profess* is in the *past* instead of the *present* time, one can account for only on the supposition, that the idea of *Reform* had scared all the powers of thought from the minds of the writers.   This unhappy absence of intellect seems to have continued to the end of the piece; for, here we have " no *other* object *but*," instead of no other object *than*; and, the word " *really*," put into the mouth of *a king*, and on such an occasion, is something so *very low* that we can hardly credit our eyes when we behold it.

INTRODUCTION

To the Four Lessons on the productions of Lord Castlereagh, the Duke of Wellington, the Marquis Wellesley, and the Bishop of Winchester.

FROM the literary productions of *Speakers* and *Ministries*, I come to those of *Ambassadors*, *Secretaries of State*, *Viceroys* and *Bishops*.   In these persons, even more fully, perhaps, than in the former, we are entitled to expect proofs of great capacity as writers.   I shall give you specimens from the writings of four persons of this description, and these four, men who have been intrusted with the management of affairs as important as any that the king of this country ever had to commit to the hands of his servants; I mean *Lord Castlereagh*, the *Duke of Wellington*, the *Marquis Wellesley*, and the *Bishop of Winchester*, the first of whom has been called the *greatest Statesman*, the second, the *greatest Captain*, the third, the *greatest Viceroy*, and the fourth, the *greatest Tutor*, of the age.

The passages which I shall first select from the writings of these persons, are contained in State Papers, relating to the *Museums at Paris*.

And here, in order that you may be better able to judge of the writings themselves, I ought to explain to you the nature of the matters to which they relate, and the circumstances under which they were written.   The *Museums at Paris* contained, in the year 1815, when the King of France was escorted back to that city by the armies of the Allies, a great many *Statues* and *Pictures*, which

Napoleon had, in his divers conquests and invasions, taken from the collections of other countries and carried to France. When, therefore, the Allies had, by their armies, possession of Paris, at the time just mentioned, they rifled these *Museums*, and took from them what had, or what they asserted had, belonged to the Allies respectively. The French contended, that this was unjust, and that it was an act of pillage. They said, that, in 1814, when the Allies were also in possession of the capital of France, they put forward no claim to the things in question, which were to all intents and purposes military booty, or prize; and that for the Allies to make this claim now was not only contrary to their own precedent of 1814, but that it was to assume the character of *enemies of France*, directly in the teeth of their own repeated declarations, in which they had called themselves friends and even *allies* of France; and in direct violation of their solemn promises to commit against the French nation no act of hostility, and to treat it, in all respects, as a friend. The Allies had now, however, the *power* in their hands; and the result was, the stripping of the Museums.

To characterize this act, committed by those who entered France under the name of *Allies* of the king and of the great body of his people, and who took possession of Paris in virtue of a convention which stipulated for the security of all *public property*; to characterize such an act is unnecessary; but we cannot help lamenting that the Ministers of England were open abettors if not original instigators in this memorable transaction, which, of all the transactions of that time, seems to have created the greatest portion of rancour in the minds of the people of France.

That the English Ministers were the instigators appears pretty clearly from the seizure (which was by *force of arms*) having been immediately preceded by a Paper (called a Note) delivered by Lord *Castlereagh*, in the name of the Prince Regent, to the Ambassadors of the Allies, which Paper was dated 11th September, 1815, and from which Paper I am now about to give you a specimen of the *writing* of this Secretary of State.

LESSON III.

Remarks on Lord Castlereagh's Note, of the 11th September, 1815, on the subject of the Museums at Paris.

THIS Note sets out by saying, that representations, on the subject of the Statues and Pictures, have been laid before the Ambassadors of the Allies, and that the writer has received the commands of the Prince Regent to submit, for the consideration of the Allies, that which follows. After some further matter, amongst which we find this "greatest Statesman" talking of "the *indulgencies*," (instead of *indulgences*) to which the French had a right " to *aspire*," (instead of *to hope for*); after saying that the purity of the friendship of the Allies had been " proved *beyond a question* " by their last year's conduct, and " *still more*," that is to say, *farther* than *beyond*, by their this year's conduct; after talking about the " *substantial integrity* " of France, and thereby meaning, that she was to be *despoiled of only a part* of her dominions; after talking about " *combining* " this " *integrity* with *such an adequate* system of temporary precaution as may *satisfy* what the Allies *owe to the security* of their own subjects;" after all this, and a great deal more of the same description, we come to the paragraphs that I am now going to remark on. Observe; I continue the *numbering* of the Paragraphs, as if the whole of the Papers, on which I am commenting, formed but one piece of writing.

20. " Upon what principle can France, at the close of such a war, expect to sit down with the same extent of possessions which she held before the Revolution, and desire, at the same time, to retain the ornamental spoils of all other countries? Is it, that there can exist a doubt of the issue of the contest or of the power of the Allies to effectuate what justice and policy require? If not, upon what principle deprive France of her late territorial acquisitions, and preserve to her the *spoliations appertaining to those territories, which* all modern conquerors have invariably *respected*, as inseparable from the country to which they belonged?

21. The Allied Sovereigns have perhaps something to atone for to Europe, in consequence of the course pursued by them, when at Paris, during the last year. It is true, they never did so far make themselves parties in the *criminality* of this *mass of plunder*, as to sanction *it* by any

stipulation in their Treaties; such a *recognition* has been on their part uniformly refused; but they certainly did use their influence to repress at that moment, any agitation of their claims, in the hope that France, not less subdued by their generosity than by their arms, might be disposed to preserve inviolate a peace which had been studiously framed to serve as a bond of reconciliation, between the Nation and the King. They had also reason to expect that His Majesty would be advised voluntarily to restore a considerable *proportion* at least of these spoils, to their lawful owners.

22. But the question is a very different one now, and to pursue the same course under circumstances so essentially altered, would be, in the judgment of the Prince Regent, *equally unwise towards France*, and *unjust towards our Allies*, who have a direct interest in this question.

23. His Royal Highness, in stating this opinion, feels it necessary to guard against the possibility of misrepresentation.

24. Whilst he deems it to be the duty of the Allied Sovereigns not only not to obstruct, but to facilitate, upon the present occasion, the *return of these objects* to the places *from whence* they were torn, it seems not less consistent with *their delicacy*, not to suffer the *position* of their armies in France, *or the removal* of *these works* from the Louvre, to become the means, either directly or indirectly, of bringing within *their* own dominions a *single article* which did not of right, at the period of *their conquest*, belong either to their respective family collections, or to the countries over which they now actually reign.

25. Whatever value the Prince Regent might attach to such exquisite specimens of the fine arts, if otherwise acquired, he has *no wish to become possessed* of them at the expense of France, or rather of the countries to which they of right belong, *more especially by following up a principle in war* which He considers as a reproach to the nation by which it has been adopted, and so far from wishing to *take advantage* of the occasion to *purchase* from the rightful owners *any articles* they might, from pecuniary considerations, be disposed *to part with*, His Royal Highness would on the contrary be disposed rather to afford the means of replacing them in those very temples and galleries, of which they were so long the ornaments.

26. *Were* it possible that His Royal Highness's sentiments towards the person and cause of Louis XVIII could be brought into doubt, or that the *position* of His Most Christian Majesty *was* likely to be *injured* in the *eyes* of His own people, the Prince Regent would not come to this conclusion without the most painful reluctance; but, *on the contrary*, His Royal Highness believes that His Majesty will rise in the love and respect of His own subjects, in proportion as He *separates* Himself from *these remembrances*

of revolutionary warfare. These spoils, which impede a moral reconciliation between France and the countries she has invaded, are not necessary
to record the exploits of her armies, which, notwithstanding the cause in
which they were achieved, must ever make the arms of the nation respected
abroad. But whilst these *objects* remain at Paris, constituting, as it were, the
title deeds of the countries which have been given up, the *sentiments of
reuniting* these countries again to France, will never be altogether extinct;
nor will the *genius* of the French *people* ever completely *associate itself* with
the more *limited existence* assigned to the *nation* under the Bourbons."

I shall say nothing of the *logic* of this passage; and I would fain
pass over the real and poorly disguised *motive* of the proceeding;
but this must strike every observer.

It is the mere *writing*, which, at present, is to be the principal
object of our attention. To be sure, the sentiments, the very
thoughts, in Paragraphs 24 and 25, which speak the soul, as they are
conveyed in the language, of the sedentary and circumspect keeper
of a huckster's stand, or the more sturdy perambulating bearer of a
miscellaneous pack, do, with voice almost imperious, demand a
portion of our notice; while, with equal force, a similar claim is
urged by the *suspicions* in the former of these paragraphs, and the
protestations in the latter, which present to the nations of Europe,
and especially to the French nation, such a captivating picture of
English *frankness* and *sincerity*!

But, let us come to the *writing*: and here, in Paragraph 20, we
have "*spoliations* appertaining to territories," though *spoliation*
means the *act of despoiling*, and never does, or can, mean the thing of
which one has been despoiled; and, next we have the word *which*,
relating to *spoliation*, and then the subsequent part of the sentence
tells us, that *spoliations* have invariably been *respected*.

In the 21st Paragraph, does the *it* relate to criminality or to mass
of plunder; and, what is meaned by a *sanction* given to either?
Could the writer suppose it possible that it was necessary to tell the
Allies themselves, that they had *not sanctioned* such things? And
here, if we may, for a moment, speak of the *logic* of our "greatest
Statesman," the Allies *did sanction*, not *criminality*, not a *mass of
plunder*, but the *quiet possession* of the specimens of art, by leaving, in
1814, that possession as they found it. At the close of this

paragraph we have *a proportion*, instead of *a part*, an error common enough with country fellows when they begin to *talk fine*; but one that, surely, ought to be absent from the most stately of the productions of a Secretary of State.

" Unwise *towards* France and unjust towards the Allies," and " *equally* " too, is as pretty a specimen of what is called *twattle*, as you shall find; while " the *return* " of these " *objects*," the not purloining of a " *single article*," the not wishing to " *take advantage*" and to "*purchase* any of the *articles* that the owners might wish to *part with*," form as fine an instance of the powers of the *plume de crasse*, or, *pen of mud*, as you will be able to hunt out of the history of a whole year's proceedings at the Police Offices.

But, in Paragraph 24, we have " *their* conquest." The conquest of *whom* or *what*? That of *the Allies*, that of *their dominions*, or that of *the* " *objects* "? It is impossible to answer, except by guess; but, it comes out, at any rate, that there was a *conquest*; and this " greatest Statesman " might have perceived, that this *one word* was a complete answer to all his assertions about plunder and spoliation; for, that which is *conquered* is held *of right*; and, the only want of right in the Allies forcibly to take these " articles," arose from their having entered France as *allies of the king of France*, and not as enemies and conquerors.

And what, in Paragraph 25, is meaned by " *following up a principle in war* "? The phrase, " follow up a principle," is low as the dirt: it is chit-chat, and very unfit to be used in a writing of this sort. But, as to the sense; how could the Regent, even if he had purchased the pictures, be said to *follow up* a principle " *in war* "? The meaning, doubtless, was, that the Regent had no wish to become possessed of these things at the expense of France, or, rather at the expense of the countries to which they belonged, especially as he could not thus gratify his taste for the arts without acting upon a principle, which *the French had acted on in war*. This meaning might, indeed, be supposed to be contained in the above phrase of Lord Castlereagh; but, in a writing of this kind, ought any thing to be left to *supposition*?

The 26th Paragraph is an assemblage of all that is incorrect, low and ludicrous. The " *was* " after Christian Majesty, ought to be *could be*; that is, " *were* it possible that his position *could be* likely to be injured;" and not " *were* it possible that his position *was* likely to be injured," which is downright nonsense. And, then only think of an *injured position*; and of the king's *position* being injured " *in the eyes* " of his people! " But, *on the contrary.*" On the contrary *of what*? Look back, and see if it be possible to answer this question. Next comes the intolerable fustian of the king " *separating himself* from *remembrances*;" and, from this flight, down the " *greatest Statesman* " pitches, *robs* the attorney's office, and calls the Statues and Pictures " *title deeds*, as it were;" and this " *as it were* " is, perhaps, the choicest phrase of the whole passage. But, in conclusion (for it is time to have done with it) what do you say to "the *sentiments of re-uniting* the countries to France"? And, what do you say, then, to the " *genius* " (that is, the *disposition*) of the French people " *associating itself* with the *limited existence* assigned to the *nation* under the Bourbons?" What do you say of the man, who could make use of these words, when his meaning was, "that, as long as these Statues and Pictures remained to remind the French people of the late extent of the dominions of France, their minds would not be completely reconciled to those more narrow limits, which had now been prescribed to her"? What do you say of the man, who, having this plain proposition to state, could talk of the *genius* of the *people* associating itself with the more limited *existence* of the *nation*, the *nation* being *the people*, and, therefore, his meaning, if there be any sense in the words, being, that the people, as a nation, had, under the Bourbons, had their *existence*, or length of life, abridged? What do you say, what can you say, of such a man, but that nature might have made him for a valet, for a strolling player, and possibly for an auctioneer; but never for a Secretary of State. Yet this man was *educated* at the *University of Cambridge*!*

---

* This LESSON was written, in June, 1822. On the 12th of August, 1822, this same Lord Castlereagh (being still Secretary of State) killed himself, at North Cray, in Kent, by cutting his throat. A Coroner's Jury pronounced him to have been *insane*; and, which is very curious, a Letter from the *Duke of Wellington* was produced, to prove that the deceased *had been insane for some time*!

LESSON IV.

Remarks on a Dispatch of the Duke of Wellington (*called the greatest Captain of the age*) *relative to the Museums at Paris.*

HAVING, as far as relates to the *Museums*, taken a sufficient view of the writing of the "*greatest Statesman*" of the age, I now come to that of " the *greatest Captain.*" The writing that I am now about to notice relates to the same subject. The Captain was one of the *Commanders* at Paris, at the time above spoken of; and, it is in that capacity that he writes. But, we ought to observe here, that he is not only a great Captain, but a great *Ambassador* also; that he was Ambassador at the Congress of Vienna just before the time we are speaking of; and, that he was formerly *Secretary of State* for Ireland.

The paper, from which I am about to make a quotation, is a " *dispatch* " from the " greatest Captain " to *Lord Castlereagh*, dated at Paris, 23rd September, 1815, soon after the Museums had been rifled. I shall not take up much of your time with the performance of this gentleman: a short specimen will suffice; and that shall consist of the three first paragraphs of his " *dispatch.*"

" MY DEAR LORD,

27. There has been a *good deal of discussion* here lately respecting the measures which I have been under the necessity of adopting, in order *to get for* the King of the Netherlands his Pictures, &c. from the Museums; and lest *these reports* should reach the Prince Regent, I *wish to trouble* you, for His Royal Highness's *information*, with the following statement of what has passed.

28. Shortly after the arrival of the Sovereigns at Paris, the Minister of the King of the Netherlands *claimed* the Pictures, &c. belonging to his Sovereign, *equally* with those of *other Powers*; *and*, as far as I could learn, *never could get* any satisfactory *reply* from the French Government. After several conversations with me, he *addressed* your Lordship *an official* Note, which was laid before the Ministers of the Allied Sovereigns, assembled in conference; *and* the subject was taken into consideration repeatedly, with a view to discover a mode of doing justice to the Claimants of the specimens of the arts in the Museums, without injuring the feelings of the King of France. In the mean time, the Prussians had obtained from His Majesty not only all the really Prussian Pictures, but those belonging to the Prussian territories on the left of the Rhine, and the Pictures, &c. belonging to all the

allies of His Prussian Majesty; *and* the subject pressed for an early decision; *and* your Lordship wrote *your* Note of the 11th inst. in which it was fully discussed.

29. The Ministers of the King of the Netherlands, still having no satisfactory *answer* from the French Government, appealed to me as the General in Chief of the army of the King of the Netherlands, to know *whether I had any objection* to employ His Majesty's Troops to obtain possession of what was His *undoubted property*. I referred this application again to the Ministers of the Allied Courts, and *no objection having been stated*, I considered it *my duty* to take the necessary measures to obtain *what was his right*."

The great characteristic of this writing (if writing it ought to be called) is the thorough-paced *vulgarity* of it. There is a meanness of manner as well as of expression, and, indeed, a suitableness to the subject much too natural, in all its appearances, to have been the effect of art.

The writer, though addressing a Minister of state, and writing matter to be laid before a Sovereign, begins exactly in the manner of a quidnunc talking to another that he has just met in the street. " There has been a *good deal of discussion* " (that is to say, *talk*) " *here*;" that is to say, at Paris, Castlereagh being, at the time, in London. The phrase " to *get for* " is so very dignified, that it could have come only from a great man, and could have been inspired by nothing short of the consciousness of being " *the Ally of all the nations of Europe*," as the writer calls himself in another part of this famous " *dispatch*."

But, *what* are " these *reports*," of which the great Captain speaks in the latter part of this paragraph? He had spoken of no *reports* before. He had mentioned " *discussion*," and a " *good deal* " of it; but, had said not a word about *reports*; and *these* reports pop out upon us like " *these* six men in buckram," in Falstaff's narrative to the Prince.

The Captain's " wishing to *trouble* " Lord Castlereagh, " for the Regent's *information*," closes this paragraph in a very suitable manner, and prepares the mind for the next, where the Regent would find *trouble* enough, if he were compelled to find out the English of it. The Dutch Minister " *claimed* the Pictures belonging to his sovereign, *equally* with those of *other powers*." What! did this Dutchman claim *the whole*; those belonging to the Dutch sovereign and those belonging to all the other powers besides! This, to be sure, would have been in the true Dutch style; but, this could hardly be the fact. If it were, no wonder that the Duke had learned, that the Minister " *never could get* any *satisfactory* reply;" for, it must have been a deal indeed that would have satisfied him.

The phrase, " he *addressed your Lordship* an official Note " is in the *counting-house* style; and then to say to Lord Castlereagh, " your Lordship wrote *your* Note of the 11th of September," was so necessary, lest the latter should imagine, that *somebody else* had written the Note! Nor are the four *ands* in this paragraph to be overlooked; for never was this poor conjunction so worked before, except, perhaps, in some narrative of a little girl to her mother.

The narrative is, in the last quoted paragraph, continued with unrelaxed spirit. The Dutch Minister can still obtain no satisfactory answer; he asks the Duke whether he have *any objection* to use force, and asserts, at the same time, that the *goods* in question are his master's " *undoubted property*." Upon this the Duke applies to the other Ministers, and, " *no objection having been stated*," he considers it *his duty* to obtain " *what was his right*;" that is to say, the Dutch king's right.

Never was there surely a parcel of words before put together by any body in so clumsy a manner. In a subsequent part of the " *dispatch*," we have this: " I added, that I had no instructions regarding the Museum, *nor no* grounds on which to form a judgment." In another place we have " the King of the *Netherlands'* Pictures." In another place we have, " that the *property* should be returned to *their* rightful owners."

But, to bestow criticism on such a shocking abuse of letters is to disgrace it; and nothing can apologize for what I have done but the existence of a general knowledge of the fact, that the miserable stuff that I have quoted, and on which I have been remarking, proceeded from the pen of a man, who has, on many occasions, had some of the most important of the nation's affairs committed to his management. There is, in the nonsense of Castlereagh, a frivolity and a foppery that give it a sort of liveliness, and that now-and-then elicit a smile; but, in the productions of his correspondent, there is nothing to relieve: all is vulgar, all clumsy, all dull, all torpid inanity.

LESSON V.

Remarks on a Note presented by Lord Castlereagh to the Ambassadors of the Allies, at Paris, in July, 1815, relative to the Slave Trade.

30. " VISCOUNT Castlereagh, his Britanick Majesty's Principal Secretary of State, &c., in reference to the communication he has made to the conference, of the orders addressed to the Admiralty to suspend all hostilities against the coast of France, observes, that there is *reason* to *foresee* that French ship-owners *might* be induced to renew the Slave Trade, under the supposition of the *peremptory* and *total* abolition decreed by Napoleon Bonaparte, having *ceased* with his power; that, *nevertheless*, great and powerful *considerations*, arising from *motives* of humanity and even of regard for the king's authority, require, that no time should be lost *to maintain in France*, the entire and *immediate Abolition* of the Traffic in Slaves; that if, at the time of the Treaty of Paris, the King's administration *could wish* a final but gradual stop *should be put* to this Trade, in the space of five years, for the purpose of affording the King the gratification *of having* consulted, as much as possible, the interests of the French Proprietors in the Colonies, now, that the absolute *prohibition* has been ordained, the question *assumes entirely* a different shape, *for* if the King were to revoke the said prohibition, he would *give Himself the disadvantage* of *authorizing*, in the interior of France, *the reproach* which more than once has been thrown out against his former Government, of countenancing re-actions, and, at the same time, *justifying, out of France*, and particularly in England, the belief of a systematic *opposition* to *liberal ideas*; that *accordingly* the *time seems to have arrived* when the Allies cannot hesitate formally to *give weight in France* to the immediate and entire *prohibition* of the Slave Trade, a prohibition, the necessity of which has been acknowledged, in principle, in the transactions of the Congress at Vienna."

Now, I put this question to you: *do you understand what this great Statesman means?* Read the Note three times over; and then say, whether you *understand what he wants.* You may *guess*; but you can go little further. Here is a whole mass of grammatical errors; but, it is the obscurity, the unintelligibleness, of the Note, that I think constitutes its greatest fault. One way of proving the badness of this writing, is, to express the meaning of the writer in a clear manner; thus:

" Lord Castlereagh observes, that there is reason to apprehend that the French ship-owners may be induced to renew the slave trade, from a supposition that the total abolition, recently decreed by Napoleon, has been nullified by the cessation of his authority; that motives of humanity as well as a desire to promote the establishment of the king's authority, suggest that no time should be lost in taking efficient measures to maintain the decree of abolition; that, at the time of the treaty of Paris, the king's ministers wished to abolish this trade, but, in order that the king might, as much as possible, consult the interests of the colonial proprietors, those ministers wished the object to be accomplished by degrees during the space of five years; that now, however, when the abolition has been actually decreed, the matter assumes an entirely different shape, seeing that it is not now an abolition, but the refraining from revoking an abolition, that is proposed to be suggested to the king; that, if the king were to do this, he would warrant, amongst his own people, the injurious imputation, more than once brought against his former government, of countenancing the work of undoing and overturning, and would, at the same time, confirm foreign nations, and particularly the English, in the belief, that he had adopted a systematic opposition to liberal principles and views; that, therefore, the interests of the king not less than those of humanity seem to call upon the Allies to give, formally, and without delay, the weight of their influence in favour, as far as relates to France, of an entire and immediate abolition of the Slave Trade, an abolition, the necessity of which has, in principle, at least, been acknowledged in the transactions of the Congress of Vienna."

Now, as to the several faulty expressions in the Note of Castlereagh, though I have made great use of *italicks*, I have not pointed out one half of the faults. Who ever before heard of a *reason* to *foresee* a thing? He meaned reason to *believe* that the thing would take place, and, as it was a thing to be wished not to take place, to *apprehend* was the word; because to apprehend means to think of with some degree of fear. Wishing to-morrow to be a fine day, what would you think of me, if I were to say, that I had *reason* to *foresee* that it would rain? The *might* is clearly wrong. If the abolition were *total* what had *peremptory* to do there? Could it be *more* than *total*? The *nevertheless* had no business there. He was about to give reasons why the abolition-decree ought to be confirmed; but, he had stated no reasons, given by any body, why it *should not*. To lose no time *to maintain*; and then the *in France*, and then the *immediate*; altogether here is such a mess of confusion that one cannot describe it. " To maintain *in France*," would lead one to suppose that there was, or had been, a *slave trade in France*. The next part, beginning with "*that if*," sets all criticism at defiance. Look at the verbs, *could wish*, and *should be*! Look at *of having*. Then comes *prohibition* for *abolition*, two very different things. To *assume entirely a* different shape is very different from to assume *an entirely different* shape. The latter is meaned and the former is said. Then what does the *for* do there? What *consequence* is he coming to? How was he going to show that the *shape* was different? He attempts to show no such thing; but, falls to work to fortel the evils which will fall on the king of France if he revoke Napoleon's decree. And, here, Goddess of Grub-street, do hear him talking of the king of France *giving himself the disadvantage of authorizing reproaches*! If the king's conduct would *justify* people in believing ill of him, why should it justify the English *in particular*? They might, indeed, be *more ready* to believe ill of him; but, it could not be *more just* in them than in others. An *opposition to ideas* is a pretty *idea* enough; and so is the *giving of weight in France* to an immediate prohibition!

Never was there, surely, such a piece of writing seen before! Fifty years hence no man, who should read it, would be able to ascertain its meaning. I am able to pick it out, because, and only because, I am acquainted with the history of the matter treated of. And yet, most momentous transactions, transactions involving the fate of millions of human beings, have been committed to the hands of this man!

It is not unnecessary for me to observe, that, though I have stated the meaning of this Note in a way for it to be understood, I by no means think, that, even in the words in which I have expressed it, it was a proper Note for the occasion. It was false in professions; and it was, as towards the king of France, insolent in a high degree. Even if it had been just to compel the king to abolish the Slave Trade, the matter might have been expressed in a less offensive manner; and, at any rate, he might have been spared the brutal taunt that we meet with towards the close of this matchless specimen of diplomatic stupidity.

Hoping that this book will outlive the recollection of the transactions treated of by the Papers on which I have been remarking, it seems no more than justice to the parties to say, that the abolition, which was thus extorted, had effect but for a very short time; that the French nation never acknowledged it as binding; that, at this moment (*June* 1822) complaints are made in the House of Commons of the breach of agreement on the part of the French; that the French have revived and do carry on the traffic in African slaves; that our Ministers promise to make remonstrances; but that, they dare not talk of war; and that, without declaring their readiness for war, their remonstrances can have no effect.

LESSON VI.

Remarks on passages in Dispatches, from the MARQUIS WELLESLEY, *Lord Lieutenant of Ireland, to Viscount Sidmouth and to Mr. Peel, Secretaries of State, dated Dublin Castle, from 3d. Jan. to 12th June, 1822; and also on the Charge of the* BISHOP OF WINCHESTER, *delivered in July, 1822.*

31. " CONCLUDING that your Lordship *had been* apprized, *before* my arrival in Dublin, of every important circumstance respecting the unhappy disturbances *which have* prevailed in this country, I proceed to *submit to you*, for his *Majesty's consideration*, such information as I have received on that subject during the few days which have passed since my *succession* to this Government.

32. I propose to *arrange* this information *with reference* to *each* county *respectively*, for the purpose of facilitating *a comparison with* such statements as may already be in your Lordship's possession, *and* of enabling you to form a judgment of the *relative* state *of each* particular district *at the different periods of time* specified in *each document*."

The Marquis's style is not, in general, *low* and *clumsy*: it has the opposite faults, *affectation* and *foppishness*; and, where the meaning of the writer is obscure, it is not so much because he has not a clear head, as because he cannot condescend to talk in the language and manner of common mortals.

" *Had been* apprized *before* of disturbances *which have* prevailed " presents great confusion as to times. We can hardly come at the precise meaning. It should have been: " concluding, that, before my arrival, your Lordship *were* apprized of every important circumstance respecting the unhappy disturbances, *prevailing* in this country." For, the prevalence was *still in existence*. To *submit* is to place at the *disposal of*, to *put under the power of*; and, therefore, *transmit*, or *send*, was the proper word; for, it is *the king* to whom the information is *submitted*. The Marquis *sent* the information to Lord Sidmouth that he might *submit* it to the king.

" *Succession* to this *government* " is a strangely pompous phrase at best. But, it is not correct; for, his *succession* (if it were one) took place at his *appointment*; and he is about to speak of what he has learned since his *arrival* in Dublin; and, why not say *arrival*?

The 32nd Paragraph is, perhaps, as complete a specimen of smoothness in words and of obscurity in meaning as ever found its way upon paper; and yet this was an occasion for being particularly clear, seeing that the Marquis was here *explaining the plan* of his dispatch. *With reference to* means *in relation to*, *as appertaining to*, *having a view towards*. The first is the best for the Marquis; and that is little short of nonsense; for, what is *arranging* information *in relation to* each county? What does it mean? Not what the Marquis thought he was saying, which was, that he proposed to speak of the state of all the counties, and that the *information relating to each county he meaned to place under a separate head*. This was what he meaned; but, this he does not say.

And then, again, what does *respectively* do here after *each*? *Respectively* means *particularly*, or *relatively*; and, as he had before said, or meaned to say, that he proposed to place the information relating to *each* county under the head of that county, what need was there of the addition of this long and noisy adverb?

To be sure, to place the information under separate heads, each head confining itself to the information relating to one county, was a very good way of facilitating a comparison *of this information* with that which was already in Lord Sidmouth's possession; but, it was not enough to say " *facilitating a comparison with such statements*;" and, there appears, besides, to be no reason to conclude, that the information before possessed was arranged according to counties:

on the contrary, the Marquis's laying down of his *plan* would induce us to suppose that the arrangement of his matter was new.

The latter part of the sentence is all confusion. The Marquis means, that, by placing his information as before described, he shall enable Lord Sidmouth to form a judgment of the state of each district *now*, compared with the state in which it was at the date of the *former information*. The "*relative state* of *each* particular district" may mean, its state at *one period compared with its state at another period*; but, "at *different periods* of time" by no means gives us this idea. And, even if it did, what are we to do with the "*each document*" at the close? *Each* means *one of two, one of more than one.* So that here we have the *relative state* of a district at the *different periods of time* specified in *one document*; and the main point that the Marquis was driving at was, to show Lord Sidmouth the manner in which he was going to enable him to compare the contents of the present document with those of the documents already held in his possession.

I have taken, here, the first two sentences of the dispatch. They are a fair specimen of the Marquis's style, the great characteristic of which is, *obscurity* arising from *affectation*. What he meaned was this: "I propose to place the information relating to each county under a distinct head, for the purpose of facilitating a comparison of this information with that which your Lordship may already possess, and also for the purpose of enabling you to form a judgment of the present state of each county, compared with the state in which it was at the date of former dispatches." And, would it not have been better to write thus than to put upon paper a parcel of words, the meaning of which, even if you read them a hundred times over, must still remain a matter of uncertainty?

But, there is another fault here; and that is, all the latter part of the sentence is a mere *redundancy*; for *of what* was Lord Sidmouth to "form *a judgment*"? A judgment of the *comparative state* of the country at the two periods? What could this be *more* than *the making of* the comparison? *Judgment*, in this case, means *opinion*: and, if the Marquis had said, that his object was to enable Lord Sidmouth to form a judgment as to *what ought to be done*, for instance, in consequence of the change in the state of the country, there would have been some sense in it; but, to enable him to *see the change* was all that the Marquis was talking about; and the very act of making the comparison was to *discern*, or *judge* of, the change.

It is not my intention to swell out these remarks, or, with this Dispatch before me, I could go on to a great extent indeed. Some few passages I cannot, however, refrain from just pointing out to you.

33. " The Commanding Officer at Bantry *reports a daring attack* made a few nights previously, on several very respectable houses in the immediate vicinity of that town, by a numerous banditti, who succeeded in obtaining arms from many: and the Officer stationed at Skibbereen *states his opinion*, that the spirit of disaffection, which *had been* confined to the northern Baronies of the country, *had spread* in an alarming measure *through* the whole of West Carbery; that nightly meetings *are* held at various places on the coast, and that bands of offenders *assemble*, consisting of not less than three hundred in each band.

34. It further appears, from various communications, that the greater part of the population of the northern part of the county of Cork *had* assembled in the mountains, and that they *have* in some places made demonstrations of attack, and in others, *have* committed outrages by day, with increased forces and boldness."

" *Reports* an attack " is of the *slang military*, and should not have forced its way into this Dispatch. " *States* his opinion, that " is little better. But, it is to the strange confusion in the *times of the verbs* that I here wish to direct your attention. This is a fault the Marquis very frequently commits.

35. " The Magistrates resident at Dunmanaway report, *that* illegal oaths *have for a long time been* administered in that neighbourhood; *that* nocturnal meetings have frequently been held; *that* in the adjoining parishes, notices of an inflammatory description have been posted; *and in one* parish, arms have been taken from the peaceable inhabitants.

36. The *Rector of* ———— reports, on the 10th, that six houses of his parishioners had been attacked on the preceding night, and some arms obtained from them, *and then* an attempt had been made to *assassinate* Captain Bernard, an active yeomanry Officer, when only a short distance behind his corps, but that owing to the pistol presented at him missing fire, he escaped, and his brother shot the assailant."

We do not know, from the words, " *have for a long time been* administered," whether the oaths were administered a *long time ago*, or are now, and long have been, *administering*. The *that* should have been repeated between the *and* and the *in* towards the close of Paragraph 35; for, the want of it takes the last fact *out of the report* of the Magistrates, and makes it an assertion of the Marquis. The same remark applies to the 36th Paragraph, where, for the want of the *that* between the *and* and the *then*, it is the Marquis and not the Rector, who asserts the fact of an attempt to *assassinate* the Captain. An odd sort of an attempt to *assassinate*, by-the-bye, seeing that it was made by a *pistol openly presented at him*, and that, too, when his troop was just on before, and when his brother was so near at hand as to be able to *shoot the assailant*! But *assassinate* is become a fashionable word in such cases.

37. " On the evening of the same day a detachment of the 11th regiment was attacked, on its march from Macroom to Bandon, by a party of 60 men, who followed *it* for three miles, and took advantage of the inclosures to fire, and to retard the march of the *King's troops.*"

The meaning is, that the party of 60 men followed *it* [the Regiment], took advantage of the inclosures to fire on *it*, and to retard *its* march; but, the Marquis, from a desire to write *fine*, leaves us in *doubt*, whether the *Regiment* and the *King's troops* be the *same* body of men; and this doubt is, indeed, countenanced by the almost incredible circumstance, that a *regular regiment* should be *followed* for three miles and actually have its march retarded by *sixty men*!

38. " A countryman's house is also stated to have been attacked by forty men, well mounted and armed, who severely beat and wounded him and took his horse. ———— *reports an attack* on the house of Mr. Sweet, near Macroom, who, having received previous intimation of the attack, and having prepared for defence, succeeded in repulsing the assailants, about two hundred in number, with *a loss* of *two killed*, who were *carried off by their associates*, although their horses were secured."

Here we have *reports an attack* again; but, your attention is called to the latter part of the paragraph, where it would appear that *Mr. Sweet* sustained *a loss of two killed*; and yet these two dead men were *carried off by the assailants*. If the Marquis had stopped at the word *killed*, it would have been impossible not to understand him to mean, that Mr. Sweet had two of his men killed.

39. "A Magistrate communicates, that information had been received by him of several intended attacks upon houses in that neighbourhood, but that they had been prevented by *the* judicious *employment of the police*, stationed at Sallans, under the Peace Preservation Act."

By *employing the Police in a judicious manner* the Marquis means; but, says quite another thing.

40. "The Police Magistrate of Westmeath reports *the setting fire* to a farmer's outhouses, which, together with the cattle in them, WAS consumed."

It should be "the setting *of* fire;" and, it should be *were*, and not *was*; for, the deuce is in it, if *outhouses*, *together with* the cattle in *them*, do not make up a *plural*.

41. "The *result of the facts* stated in this dispatch, *and its* inclosures, seems to *justify an opinion*, that although no material change has occurred in any other part of Ireland, the disturbances in the vicinity of Macroom *have assumed a more decided aspect of general disorder*, and accordingly I have resorted to additional measures of precaution and military operations."

There should be an *in* between the *and* and the *its*. But, it is not the *result* of the *facts* that seem to justify the opinion: it is the *facts themselves* that justify the opinion, and the *opinion is the result*. *Measures of military operation*, too, is an odd sort of phrase. This paragraph is all bad, from beginning to end; but I am merely pointing out prominent and gross errors.

42. "Another Magistrate reports several *robberies of arms* in the Parishes of Skull and Kilmoe, and the burning of a corn store at Crookhaven; and another, in representing the alarming state of the county, adds, that the *object* of the insurgents, in one district at least, has not been *confined* to the lowering *of rents and tithes*, but *extended* to the *refusal also* of the *Priest's dues*."

To *rob* applies to the person or thing *from* whom or which something is violently and unlawfully taken. Men rob a man *of* his money, or a house *of* its goods; but, it is not the *money* and *goods* that are *robbed*. Yet this is a very common phrase with the Marquis, who, in other places talks of "*plundering* arms *from* people," and who, by saying, " *six hundred and seventy-six fire arms*," and the like, leaves us clearly to understand, that *he* is at liberty to use this noun in the *singular*, and, of course, to say *a fire arm* whenever he may choose; a liberty, however, which I would, my dear James, earnestly recommend to you never to think of taking.

To *confine* and *extend* an *object* does not seem to be very clear sense; and, at any rate, to say, that the object of *lowering* rents and tithes has been extended to the *refusal also* of the Priest's dues makes sad work indeed. Without the *also*, the thing might pass; but, that word makes this part of the sentence downright nonsense.

43. " No additional military force, no improvement nor augmentation of the police, would now be effectual without the aid of the Insurrection Act; with that aid, it appears to be rational to expect that tranquillity may be maintained, confirmed, and extended throughout Ireland. It is therefore my duty, in every view, to request the renewal of the law, *of which the operation forms the subject of this dispatch.*"

Did any man, in any writing of any sort, ever before meet with any thing like this? Suppose I were to say, " *the writings of which the inaccuracies* form the subject of these remarks," what would the world think and say of me? This is indeed "prose *run mad.*"

44. " With respect to Westmeath, the Chief Magistrate of Police has *stated* the *revival* of those *party feuds* and *personal conflicts* in the neighbourhood of Mullingar, which are considered in this country to be indications of *the* return of public tranquillity, and from which the Magistrate expects *the detection of past offences* against the State."

One loses sight of all about language here, in contemplating the shocking, the horrible fact! For, what is so horrible as the fact here officially stated, that *party feuds* and *personal conflicts* are deemed indications *favourable to the government*, and that they are expected by the magistrate to lead *to the detection of past offences* against the state! As to the grammar: to " *state the revival* " is just as good English as it would be to say, that the magistrate has *stated the fine weather*. The "*the return*" ought to be "*a return.*"

45. " The early expiration of the Act would, at least, *hazard the revival* of that tyranny; the restraints imposed on violence have not yet been of

sufficient duration to form any solid foundation of a better and more disciplined disposition in the minds of the people. Even now it is believed that arms are retained in *the hope of the expiration* of the law on the 1st of August; and although a more auspicious sentiment may exist in the hearts of some, even of the guilty, it would be contrary to all *prudent policy and provident wisdom*, by a premature relaxation of the law, to afford facility to the accomplishment of the worst designs, and to weaken the protections and safeguards, which now secure the lives and properties of the loyal and obedient, before the spirit of outrage had been effectually extinguished."

" To *hazard the revival* " is not correct. To *hazard* is to *expose to danger*; and certainly the Marquis did not mean, that the *revival of the tyranny* was a thing that ought not to be *put in danger*. The word *hazard* had no business there. Another mode of expression ought to have been used; such as, " exposed *the country* to the danger of a revival of the tyranny."

The *semi-colon*, after tyranny, ought to have been a *full point*. "In the hope *of the expiration* " is bad enough; but, it is the *arrangement* of this sentence; the *placing of the several parts of it*, which is most worthy of your attention, and which ought to be a warning to every one who takes pen in hand. " *Prudent* policy and *provident* wisdom " would seem to say, that there are such things as *imprudent* policy and *improvident* wisdom; but, still, all the rest is inferior, in point of importance, to the *confusion* which follows, and which leaves you wholly in doubt as to the meaning of the writer. Now, observe with what facility this mass of confusion is reduced to order, and, that, too, without adding to, or taking from the Marquis one single word. I begin after the word *wisdom*: "to afford, by a premature relaxation of the law, facility to the accomplishment of the worst designs, and to weaken, before the spirit of outrage had been effectually extinguished, the safeguards which now secure the lives and properties of the loyal and obedient."

How clear is this! And, how much more harmonious and more elegant, too, than the sentence of the Marquis; and, yet the words are all the same identical words! Towards the close of Letter XXI, I gave you, from Dr. JOHNSON and Dr. WATTS, some striking instances of the *wrong placing* of words in sentences; and, lest these should be insufficient to keep so great a man as the Marquis in countenance, I will here show that *a Bishop* can commit errors of the same sort, and greater in degree.

I have before me " *a Charge delivered to the Clergy of the Diocese of Winchester, at a primary visitation of that diocese, by* GEORGE TOM-LINE, *D.D. F.R.S. Lord Bishop of Winchester, Prelate of the Most Noble Order of the Garter.*" We will not stop here to inquire what a "*prelate's*" office may require of him relative to an *Order* which history tells us arose out of a *favourite lady* dropping *her garter* at a dance; but, I must *observe*, that, as the titles here stand, it would appear, that the *last* is deemed the *most honourable*, and of *most importance to the Clergy*! This Bishop, whose name *was* Prettyman, was the *tutor* of that *William Pitt*, who was called the *heaven-born* Minister, and a history of whose life has been written by this Bishop. So that, we have here, a *Doctor of Divinity*, a *Fellow of the Royal Society*, a *Prelate of the Most Noble Order of the Garter*, and a *Bishop of one of the richest sees in the whole world*, who, besides, is an *Historian*, and was *Tutor to a heaven-born Minister*. Let us, then, see what sort of *writing* comes from such a source. I could take an incorrect sentence, I could even take a specimen of downright nonsense, from almost any page of the *Charge*. But, I shall content myself with the *very first sentence of it*.

46. " My Reverend Brethren, being called to preside over this distin-guished Diocese at a late period of life, I have thought it incumbent upon me not to delay the opportunity of becoming personally acquainted with my Clergy longer than circumstances rendered absolutely necessary."

There are *two* double meanings in this short sentence. Was he called, at some former time, to preside over the diocese *when he should become old*? or, was he, *when he had become old*, called to preside over the diocese? But what follows is still worse. Does he mean, that he thought it incumbent on him to become acquainted with his Clergy *as soon as possible*, or, *as short a time as possible*? To *delay* an *opportunity* is not very good; and, that which is of a man's own appointment and which proceeds purely from his own will, cannot strictly be called an *opportunity*. But, it is the double meaning, occasioned by the *wrong-placing* of the words, that I wish you to attend to.

Now, see how easily the sentence might, with the same words, have been made unequivocal, clear and elegant:—" My Reverend Brethren, being called, at a late period of life, to preside over this distinguished Diocese, I have thought it incumbent on me not to delay, longer than circumstances rendered absolutely necessary, the opportunity of becoming personally acquainted with my Clergy."

How easy it was to write thus! And yet this Bishop did not know how to do it. I dare say, that he corrected and re-corrected every sentence of this Charge. And yet, what *bungling* work it is, after all! And, these are your *college* and *university* bred men! These are the men who are called *Doctors* on account of their literary acquirements, *doctus* being the Latin word for *learned*! Thus it is that the mass of mankind have been imposed upon by *big-sounding names*, which, however, have seldom failed to ensure, to those who have assumed them, power, ease, luxury and splendour at the expense of those who have been foolish or base enough to acquiesce, or to seem to acquiesce, in the fitness of the assumption.

Such acquiescence is not, however, so general now-a-days as it formerly was; and the chagrin which the " *Doctors* " feel at the change is not more evident than it is amusing. In the very Charge, which I have just quoted, the Tutor of the heaven-born Minister says, " A spirit is still manifest amongst us, producing an impatience of controul, *a reluctance to acknowledge superiority*, and an eagerness to *call in question the expediency of established forms and customs.*" What! is it, then, a *sin*; is it *an offence against God*, to be reluctant to " *acknowledge superiority* " in a Bishop who cannot write so well as ourselves? Oh, no! We are not to be censured, because we doubt of the *expediency* of those establishments, those Colleges and Universities, which cause immense revenues, arising from public property, to be expended on the education of men, who, after all, can produce, in the literary way, nothing better than writings such as those on which we have now been remarking.

END.

COTTAGE ECONOMY

WILLIAM COBBETT

Preface by G. K. Chesterton

'I view the tea drinking as a destroyer of health, an enfeebler of the frame, an engenderer of effeminacy and laziness, a debaucher of youth and a maker of misery for old age.' First published in 1822, Cobbett's classic handbook for smallholders was many times revised and enlarged, and is now reissued in its latest edition (1850). Cobbett tells us, among much else, how to brew beer, make bread, keep cows, pigs, bees, ewes, goats, poultry, and rabbits. And the book is full of splendid passages of social and political invective, making it a manifesto for Cobbett's philosophy of self-sufficiency. 'A couple of flitches of bacon are worth fifty thousand Methodist sermons and religious tracts.'

'a masterpiece of English dottiness' *The Times*

ADVICE TO YOUNG MEN

WILLIAM COBBETT

Preface by George Spater

Cobbett's accounts in this book of learning grammar in an army barracks, selecting a girl to marry (and nearly betraying his chosen bride), warding off barking dogs on a hot night in Philadelphia, and many other equally diverse activities, display to the full the talents which brought him the widest readership of any journalist of his day on either side of the Atlantic. The six 'Letters' that make up *Advice to Young Men* are his prescription for those who wish to be happy, addressed to a Youth, a Bachelor, a Lover, a Husband, a Father, and a Citizen.

'Even when he's talking nonsense about the bad effect of the reading of "romances" . . . or of "the punning and smutty Shakespeare", he writes with a sturdy vividness that must give pleasure to anyone with an ear.' *Times Educational Supplement*

THE ENGLISH GARDENER

WILLIAM COBBETT

Introduction by Anthony Huxley

'It is a most satisfying read on early gardening, much of Cobbett's advice being as relevant today as it was when he wrote it.' *Yorkshire Evening Post*

'I was surprised and soon delighted at finding *The English Gardener* in paperback . . . [Cobbett's] early writing is a reminder that much about the past has still to be rediscovered.' *Country Life*

'A masterpiece of general gardening' *Observer*

THE KING'S ENGLISH

THIRD EDITION

H. W. Fowler and F. G. Fowler

Generations of students, scholars, and professional writers have gone to *The King's English* for answers to problems of grammar or style. The Fowler brothers were particularly concerned to clarify the more problematic and obscure rules and principles inherent in English vocabulary and composition, and also to illustrate with examples the most common blunders and traps. They wrote with characteristic good sense and liveliness, and this book has become a classic reference work.

A DICTIONARY OF
MODERN ENGLISH USAGE

H. W. FOWLER

Revised by Sir Ernest Gowers

Fowler is a household word; for over fifty years in successive editions *Modern English Usage* has been the standard work on the correct but easy and natural use of English, in speech or writing.

Modern English Usage deals with points of grammer, syntax, style, and the choice of words; with inflexions; with pronunciation; and with punctuation and typography. But its great popularity is based not only on its usefulness, but also on its iconoclasm and wit. Fowler is at his most readable and funny on such unpromising subjects as split infinitives or 'the false first-personal ONE', and when debunking affectation. Well-thumbed copies of *Modern English Usage* will today fall open naturally at the indispensable entries on *disinterested, due to, jargon, sociologese,* or *which, that, who.*

'Let me beg readers as well as writers to keep the revised Fowler at their elbows. It brims with useful information'
Raymond Mortimer, *Sunday Times*

SYDNEY SMITH
A BIOGRAPHY

ALAN BELL

'Madam, I have been looking for a person who disliked gravy all my life; let us swear eternal friendship.' Food features frequently in the effortless wit of the Revd Sydney Smith (1771–1845), a wit that above all else has secured his fame. But he made his reputation also as a Whig divine, preacher, and polemical journalist (the *Edinburgh Review* was his idea: 'I never read a book before reviewing it; it prejudices a man so').

Throughout his life as a parson in Yorkshire and Somerset, and later as a canon of St Paul's ('I am just going to pray for you at St Paul's, but with no very lively hope of success'), Sydney Smith was lionized by great families for his conversation. He was also a tireless letter-writer. One thousand of his letters were published in 1953, but Alan Bell has discovered 2,000 more (he has a new edition of the letters in preparation). In this vigorous and sprightly biography he has distilled the essence of the new material and given us an unforgettable portrait of an extraordinary man.

'a model biography' Philip Toynbee, *Observer*

'richly enjoyable' J. W. Lambert, *Sunday Times*

'worthy of its enchanting subject' Karl Miller, *London Review of Books*

SELECTED LETTERS OF SYDNEY SMITH

EDITED BY NOWELL C. SMITH

Introduction by Auberon Waugh

The wit and charm of Sydney Smith run throughout his letters as he comments on the people and events of his day with an eye for both the tiny detail at home and more general affairs. Himself a clergyman, he was ever ready to poke fun at the Church, in the nicest possible way. Those who took themselves too seriously were also subjects for his scorn.

But he was not merely amusing—his outspokenness on literary, political, and religious affairs betrayed a rare moral courage, which went alongside the warmth and generosity he showed in his daily life.

Much of his wit had a basic good-sense quality, which many found endearing. This blend of wit and wisdom can be seen in his profound remark: 'I am convinced digestion is the great secret of life.'

The World's Classics